MW01088494

# RIP IT UP

# RIP IT UP

## THE BLACK EXPERIENCE
## IN ROCK 'N' ROLL

EDITED BY

KANDIA CRAZY HORSE

palgrave
macmillan

First published 2004 by
PALGRAVE MACMILLAN™
175 Fifth Avenue, New York, N.Y. 10010 and
Houndmills, Basingstoke, Hampshire, England RG21 6XS.
Companies and representatives throughout the world.

PALGRAVE MACMILLAN is the global academic imprint of the Palgrave
Macmillan division of St. Martin's Press, LLC and of Palgrave Macmillan
Ltd. Macmillan® is a registered trademark in the United States, United
Kingdom and other countries. Palgrave is a registered trademark in the
European Union and other countries.

ISBN 1–4039–6243-X

Library of Congress Cataloging-in-Publication Data
Rip it up : the Black experience in rock 'n' roll / edited by Kandia Crazy
Horse.
      p.   cm.
   Includes index.
   ISBN 1–4039–6243-X
   1. Rock music—History and criticism.   2. African American rock
musicians.   I. Crazy Horse, Kandia.

ML3534.R54   2003

                                                                2003055377

A catalogue record for this book is available from the British Library.

Design by Letra Libre, Inc.

First edition: January 2004
10  9  8  7  6  5  4  3  2  1

Printed in the United States of America

**FOR MY TWIN:**

Dr. Camara Dia Holloway

**FOR MY BLACK ROCK QUEENS:**

Mama Louise (Hudson)
Margaret Ann Holloway
Claudia Lennear
Cynthia Robinson
Devon Wilson
Betty Davis
and
Madame Efua Theodora Sutherland

**AND**
**FOR MY RED HOT MAMA:**

The Honorable Anne M. Forrester Ph.D.

# CONTENTS

Foreword     ix
   *Greg S. Tate*

"Live at Philmore": Introduction     xiii
   *Kandia Crazy Horse*


Ten Questions for Little Richard     1
   *Andy Gill*

The Ike and Tina Turner Revue:
Streatham Locarno, London     5
   *Bill Millar*

Paint Me White:
Bad Days, Black Rock, and Arthur Lee's Love Story     9
   *Barney Hoskyns*

Bold as Love? Jimi's Afrocyberdelia and
the Challenge of the Not-Yet     25
   *Paul Gilroy*

A.K.A. Sly Stone:
The Rise and Fall of Sylvester Stewart     39
   *Dalton Anthony*

Blues for Betty Davis's Smile:
The Betty Davis Lacuna     53
   *Vivien Goldman*

Interview with Venetta Fields     59
   *Kandia Crazy Horse*

Hardcore Jollies in the Himalayas,
Staring at the Cosmic Slop: The Mothership
Connection between Triple and Quadruple Consciousness     71
   *Michael C. Ladd*

Lorraine O'Grady Q & A     85
   *Jennifer Rice*

Play Like a White Boy:
Hard Dancing in the City of Chocolate      91
     *Darryl A. Jenifer*

How the Bad Brains Inspired Two Garden-Variety
Black Dots from Queens to Be as Rock 'n' Roll
as They Wanna Be (and Probably You Too)      97
     *Sacha Jenkins*

The White Noise Supremacists      103
     *Lester Bangs*

Prince Leads Black Pop Through the Back Door      115
     *Barry Walters*

The Birth of New Blackness:
The Family Stand's *Moon In Scorpio*      121
     *Mark Anthony Neal*

Interview with Vernon Reid      129
     *Harry Allen*

Rock, Racism, and Retailing 101:
A Blueprint for Cultural Theft      145
     *Darrell M. McNeill*

Interview with Lenny Kravitz      165
     *Knox Robinson*

"Ain't Nothin' Like Real Ghetto Music":
Pharrell Williams, Mos Def, and Andre 3000
Form a Rap-Rock Poetics      175
     *Jon Caramanica*

The Last Maverick:
Me'Shell NdegeOcello and the Burden of Vision      185
     *Amy Linden*

if I can get into it, it's commercial enough for me      189
     *Knox Robinson*

Interview with Slash (Saul Hudson)      195
     *Jessica Willis*

*Black Rock Glossary*      203
*About the Contributors*      215
*Permissions*      217
*Index*      219

# GREG S. TATE

# FOREWORD

**B**lack rock has been known to make some folk hostile. Some of these folk even happen to be black. Some I might even describe as rock-headed, but why be nasty? The very term is thought by some to be not only oxymoronic but also moronic and insulting. Rock, they declare, is already black, so why does it need a color-coding modifier? *Au contraire,* I reply. Indeed, rock and roll is black in origin—and when Alan Freed stamped the sex slang–derived term as a marketing brand on the race music/youth music of the 1950s, the music of Bill Haley, Little Richard, and The Platters were included in the catchall. "Rock" though tells a different set of stories, describes another time, pertains to a later place, a later generation of people, and another set of historical conditions and paradoxes. Rock's leading esthetician, Greil Marcus, once defined rock as black music played by white people—largely the way a lot of people hear it, though whether he thought Jimi Hendrix's and Arthur Lee's rock was black or some off-brand of honorary white remains in question. Wynton Marsalis has declared that any form of music that uses that African American invention known as backbeat becomes black by default no matter if the singer is crooning in pidgin Korean. The riddle in all this conflamma isn't musical though, but social—which in America means racial. (The important thing in Marcus's definition is the white people part and not black music, which is where a lot of black folk tend to get tripped up, imagining equality where none exists.)

All forms of music are social and cultural in origin, or as Ornette Coleman once put it, all music is folk music, as he hadn't heard any music made by kangaroos. Many of the world musics and most of the musics contained in the global catchall known as world music are largely defined by the ethnicity and geographic coordinates of the cultures from which they originate. By this reasoning all the musics we consider black—ragtime, early jazz, swing, Delta blues, classic blues, bebop, doo-wop, boogie woogie, rhythm and blues, zydeco, soul, funk, calypso, disco, house, techno, electro, salsa, reggae, Afrobeat, zouk, meringue—

should be called American or Afro-Caribbean or African. But given slavery, segregation, civil rights, Black Power and post-soul culture, and given that we Americans define ourselves to ourselves by race before nationality, only those musics whose cultural base is also a land base get described as Nigerian, Dominican, Trinidadian, and Cuban rather than black. In the United States, black qualifies as its own country, its own private Idaho. In the absence of a nation or a land base we can comfortably, exclusively, and multigenerationally call our own, African Americans are left to define themselves apart from their pinker brethren and sistren by our history of multigenerational political struggle against racism or white supremacy and by the cultural acts we engage in in majority-black settings. To cut to the chase: Attending concerts featuring performances by young white men playing their version of black music has not tended to be one of those cultural acts where googobs of black people can be found rolling mob deep. Rock concerts are, however, a place where one can generally be guaranteed to find large numbers of whitefolk amassed in marauding hordes. It is, then, a tribal, cultural act, this rock (even when black artists like Ben Harper or Lenny Kravitz perform it for mass-white audiences), one supported by radio stations that call themselves rock and brag about their "no nigger music" or, excuse me, "no-rap" policy. If it were simply a matter of musical form, of genre, of amped-up Hendrixesque guitar playing, then an entire generation of black bands with badass guitar players would not have been absent from rock radio in the 1970s. Bands like those of Funkadelic, The Isley Brothers, Mandrill, War, Rufus, Curtis Mayfield, Mother's Finest, Maxayn, Edwin Birdsong, and the like.

By the fall of 1985, when Vernon Reid pulled a motley crew of like-minded thinkers together in a gallery called JAM in Soho owned by an African American woman named Linda Bryant who had already established that conceptual art was not something only white men could do, rock was firmly established in the public imagination as a white, tribal affair, and anyone black who chose to play it was designated either an Oreo, a fool, or a freak.

What the Black Rock Coalition sought to establish was that black and rock could mix without large numbers of white people being there to validate us. Large numbers did turn up for Living Colour concerts after they broke on MTV, but by then Living Colour was known for selling out CBGB's to majority-black crowds at Coalition-organized gigs.

Choosing to call the organization the Black Rock Coalition was perceived by many of us then as a vestigial militant act, and in fact our first BRC orchestra event was called the Apartheid Concert, preceded only months before by our first dance party, our Drop the Bomb festival, the poster for which featured Little Richard's face plastered over the Japanese symbol of the rising sun.

Many have subsequently thought that black rock is a sound defined by Living Colour, though as we stated in our first manifesto, it meant black artists could count on as much support as white artists from major labels in performing whatever form of black music they choose, as we saw occurring with, say, Sting's adventures into the jazzesque. Those were the days, and naive days they were indeed when it was still rather novel to see black faces on MTV.

These were the days before hip-hop became the cultural act white youth rallied around as a tribe, though not a day when black people who played loud, guitar-oriented rock weren't still considered something of an aberration at home and abroad.

The varied tales in *Rip It Up* tell of life inside this crazed, accursed corner of the music purgatory world we like to call the world of the black rocker. Having lived among its slings and arrows and outrageous fortunes and egregious misfortunes for over thirty years, I remain amazed that as simple an act as a young black man or woman deciding not to sing straight-up reggae, blues, or hip-hop can still get people's panties in a knot. God bless 'em all, past, present, and future.

# KANDIA CRAZY HORSE

# "LIVE AT PHILMORE": INTRODUCTION

A t the tail end of the 1980s—a decade viewed almost universally by younger American music fans as the twentieth century's pop cultural nadir—I moved to Manhattan and, as a wide-eyed and naive eighteen year-old, fumbled my way uptown to attend the Black Rock Coalition's meetings at the Frank Silvera Theater Workshop in Harlem. Throughout my previous boarding school years, I had somehow managed to read cultural critic Greg Tate's work in the *Village Voice*. Tate being a friend of the family, I figured inchoately that it was time to eschew the cloud cuckooland of Dead and Phish concerts and that whole neo-hippie scene to get alert to what he and fellow BRC cofounder Vernon Reid were espousing: the right for blacks to play their own music, the music they invented—i.e., rock 'n' roll. Mostly I lurked in the back of the room up those musty stairs, trying to think up clever things to say to honcho Don Eversley after the meetings (awed not merely by being the youngest present but inevitably one of very few "chicks"). And I appeared as an extra outside Central Park's iron-gated Quiet Zone one morning before film class, simulating a black musician unwelcome at Graceland for Living Colour's "Elvis Is Dead" video. Blink and you miss me. Such are my "black rock" bona fides.

I say black rock between quotes because, fourteen years later, I still have no idea what it is, and many folks would not recognize it as a genre. Eventually I became a rock critic—Tate calls me the last of them—and even sometimes write for the *Voice,* although my own is primarily in service of the Redneck Underground. In essence, my ears and soul only process music as The Sublime or pure shit, occasionally interrupted by question marks that soon achieve resolution. Perhaps Brother Reid and Gregory have some Rosetta Stone stashed away, to be revealed in future as prophecy in a format akin to Earth, Wind & Fire's classic late 1970s "kemetic" album covers or genius illustrator Pedro Bell's kozmic work for

Funkadelic. Those most militant supporters of black folks' right to rock would probably echo Gregg Allman's one-time quote about "southern rock" in debating the term: "That's like saying rock rock."

Oxymorons, lifelong vinyl fetishes, the digestion of Jimi Hendrix's and Ishmael Reed's entire oeuvres, many P-Funk ticket stubs, and the fate of following in Tate's fleet footsteps as a rock critic (in a parallel to Sidney and Denzel. Not that I'm Denzel, mind) have precisely brought me to this point where we, my colleagues and I, have attempted to provide a brief collection of essays and interviews on the subject of black musicians' postwar experiences in the musical genre of rock 'n' roll. This starter collection, *Rip It Up,* certainly seems timely and necessary in a period when mass-circulation music magazines are painting the umpteenth "Return of Rock" with an exclusively white male face (consider the White Stripes' Meg White a token for our purposes. And correctly so). Nowhere in the year 2002's trumpeting of Great White Hypes and their predominantly retro sounds was there much if any room for the current crop of rock star hopefuls on the black-hand side: Tamar-Kali, Kregg Ajamu, Santi White & Stiffed, Cherry, Cody ChesnuTT, Joi, Martin Luther, Martha Redbone, Jerome Jordan, Mascara, and even Cee-Lo (ex–Goodie Mob), who worked with some interesting hybrids on his solo debut and often sings The Doors in concert.

Sadly, I probably have to inform a considerable number of you that the book's title was chosen in honor of Little Richard, the self-claimed and legendary "Architect of Rock 'n' Roll." Richard Penniman, the Georgia Peach from Macon, and his contemporaries such as Chuck Berry with ace boon pianist Johnnie Johnson, Bo Diddley, the late Otis Blackwell, and others blazed a trail across America and the rest of the world with their galvanic sound derived from longtime minstrel traditions, childhood years of carney infatuation, tent revivals, electric blues, assists from country and western, and the speeded-up life of the postwar years. Other perennially sought music tomes speak more precisely to the influence of Thomas Dorsey's gospel, swing jazz, Louis Jordan's jump boogie, and other subgenres on the emergence of rock 'n' roll.

I could be flippant and advise you to go buy Funkadelic's 1973 masterpiece *America Eats Its Young* (if you don't already own it), saying therein you'd find an answer. However, I am serious. Some critics condemn *AEIY* as too scattershot in its exploration of varied styles and inconsistent in terms of songwriting, but I disagree; if you have to make such value judgments, consider this double album as the across-the-tracks version of the Rolling Stones' *Exile On Main Street,* equally provocative in evoking the aftermath of the 1960s, dread about the Vietnam War and a society in chaos (especially the black American world within a world), the joys of balling, the horrific stasis of drug addiction, and the two-headed beast of hedonism and racism in the rock business. At any rate, *America Eats Its Young* is worth any cost for the glories of "Balance" alone.

The hope for this book is that its spotlight on the importance of such obscure classics as *America Eats Its Young* will serve as a primer on *some* of the key figures who have made not just rock history but pancultural history. More schooled rock fans born in the 1940s and 1950s tend to be aware of the ways in which guitarist Keith Richards of the Rolling Stones is indebted to Chuck Berry. That would suggest that every time one hears the Stones' well-known catalog the seed of Berry's power is also present. Nevertheless, thirty-odd years after the death of Jimi Hendrix, perhaps the greatest ever guitar revolutionary this planet will see, the notion of a "black" guitar hero is still inconceivable to many—or at least to record executives and other power players in the rock biz. This despite the mainstream success of Lenny Kravitz (again a token). These days ghetto gals in hip-hop videos and on the streets of urban USA even dress like redneck girls at a Lynyrd Skynyrd show circa 1975, yet for the most part neither they nor their ex-frat white counterparts on the other side of the country's Great Racial Divide readily embrace "black rockers" or otherwise eccentric artists in the vein of the provocative Chocolate Genius who aren't afraid to play with an exposed electric cord and a bathtub full of water aesthetically. The more palatable and cunning construct of a sassy, poetry-spouting sistagurl in a *gelee*—which is not quite so progressive as it appears—is far more comforting than the angry, snarling glory of Tamar-Kali all the way live, wielding her ax like the forked tongue of the Indian deity that is her predecessor, calling warmongers and trifling lovers out of their names.

Yes, yes, rock 'n' roll is about Sex and Death (and fast cars and pissing off your parents), not politics (Curtis Mayfield and Bono being the exceptions to this rule). However, it's not me nor this book's contributors making the music a "racial" thing; it has been ever since the first song-catching and cross-racial borrowing of musical styles began between Africans brought to the Americas and their Scotch Irish brethren in indenture and outlaw culture. Certainly specific points can be traced to Daniel Emmett Rice's supposed authoring of "Dixie" and incessant rip-off schemes against artists established back in the early twentieth century when the race records industry flourished. If Keith Richards is considered the Great Spirit of rock 'n' roll—and to whites he invariably is—one of the best things he ever did was allowing Little Richard, Bo Diddley, and Chuck Berry to speak incredibly openly about the ways they had been stolen from by hitmen during a segment of Richards's cinematic tribute to Berry (*Hail! Hail! Rock 'n' Roll*).

Indeed, if any band ought to be called the Greatest Rock 'n' Roll Band on Earth, it's Ohio's Isley Brothers, not merely winners of a high-profile lawsuit against Michael Bolton for sonic infringement nor glaringly bankrupt whereas Sir Mick Jagger keeps his Stones rolling in ducats with a iron fist. For the achievement of being the sole act to chart in all of rock's five decades alone, we all must bow down. Still, the Isleys' greatness is not bound to little feats such as these but rather to the sublime heights of their back catalog, especially what may perhaps be their masterpiece, trumping even *3 + 3*, 1971's (*"It was a very good year"*) *Givin' It Back* (on their own T-Neck label). It's telling that Robert Greenfield's account of the Rolling Stones' 1972 tour of America describes an episode wherein the band sought to catch the Isleys live in Oakland and the bulk of the entourage scrambled to follow. By successfully employing "crazy Dada Negro" Jimi Hendrix and taking him in as kin instead of seeing him as a threat like his erstwhile boss Little Richard did, the Isleys somehow sealed their pact with the cosmos, ensuring longevity and eternal relevance. Although unable to picture the divine Ron Isley (or even his babe bruh Ernie) sleeping with the guitar he posed with on *Givin' It Back's* iconic sepiatone cover, he, like Mos Def, is Rock 'n' Roll for the sheer uncanny diversity of his voice and his perfectly absorbed ability to mimic lost brother Hendrix's guitar as on the chief one of the album's suite of astonishing covers: "Ohio/Machine Gun." As displayed on this record's highs, such as James Taylor's "Fire and Rain" and Stephen Stills's "Love the One You're With," Ron Isley's gift of interpretation, superior even to onetime collaborator Rod Stewart's in the arena of rock, both spotlights the fascinating period when the 1960s' foremost soul and edgier Motown stars raced to belatedly embrace the Love and Peace Movement via its more prominent composers (Lennon-McCartney, Dino Valenti, Dylan, etc.) and expanded their sonic vocabulary across the Afro-Celt continuum to arrive at later genius like the Isleys' "Summer Breeze," "The Highways of My Life," "Live It Up," "Hello It's Me," "Midnight Sky (Parts 1 & 2)," and their own reprised "That Lady" (a sin and a shame the original was a flop). This reverse crossover, funkdafying the Beatlesque and so forth, is a tale rarely told and a dynamic not wholly explored.

And so I am involved with this project with the sincere hope that the next generation will be so versant in the experiences, meaningful traditions, and important aesthetic ideas of rock musicians who happen to be black that there need not be the sense of having to reinvent the wheel with each decade in the wake of Hendrix. Eddie Hazel, Richie Havens, Shuggie Otis, and Phil Lynott in the 1970s, Prince and Vernon Reid in the 1980s, Kravitz in the 1990s, perhaps ChesnuTT and Jerome Jordan for the aughties have all maintained his legacy against considerable odds.

Now it's time for my generation of "Soul Baby" (a term coined by contributor Mark Anthony Neal) scholars and cultural critics, mostly born amid the civil rights era, to succeed the previous generation's revolutionary project by applying the skills of our particular fields to enlighten you, dear readers, via this book, which we believe is the first of its kind dealing with this topic.

The moment is auspicious, what with *New York Times* features heralding ChesnuTT's arrival, the underground rediscovery of black rock doyenne Betty Mabry (Davis) who managed to rein in not only members of Sly Stone's and Janis Joplin's bands for recording but Sylvester, too, and the innovations of several hip-hop outfits garnering acclaim at the other end of the spectrum, such as production duo the Neptunes, OutKast, and the X-ecutioners. Mos Def, platinum-selling New York–based rapper and sometime thespian, recently launched a rock 'n' roll band named Black Jack Johnson, suggesting that his outfit would wield power akin to what was once the mightiest (and most controversial) fist. Johnson was the first black world heavyweight boxing champion, a man who has been described as "fighting not only for his own dignity but also to knock white America off its haughty perch." With the name choice Mos Def echoed sentiments felt by many—that rock and roll is black music, a genre that has been bastardized since its inception by white hucksters. Mos Def also vaingloriously announced that his band would spearhead a "black rock revival." Perhaps a revival including the onetime collaboration of white death metal band Anthrax and black revolutionary rap gurus Public Enemy? Rock music, that quintessentially American phenomenon is, like so many things American, mired in racial ambiguity and contradictions. The existence of "black rock" directly contradicts the definition of rock held dear by some of the industry's most lauded critics and commentators: that rock is black music played by white people. Or Mexicans, too, since many black rockers' great hero and influence Carlos Santana affirms that everything he plays is "African music."

Lest you think *Rip It Up* is just a settling of old scores (I never had to tangle with the Chess Brothers, for instance, over song royalties but surely have parents once involved in the Movement who have groaned at my generation's apathy through the years, accusing us of not giving back to The People after their struggle), its purpose is moreover to celebrate the joys of the music and share the stories of artists both known and overlooked in the sporadically recognized yet always tenacious black rock movement. There is something heady about shopping for vinyl and thereafter spending countless hours beside your turntable tripping into other worlds. Encountering the personal philosophies and badass attitude (and sartorial splendor) of litanies of artists is a vital rite of passage from youth unto adolescence. Nothing much rivals the thrill and rush of the Rock 'n' Roll Show. Through the arduous process of editing this volume, those illusory boons remained present in mind. Even if I and my collaborators have not arrived at satisfactory responses to "What is black rock?" or "Is rock race neutral or constantly plagued by mummery and racial subjectivity?" or, as the immortal Funkadelic mob best put it, "Who says a funk band can't play rock?!" *Rip It Up* digs into the essence of black Americana to praise rock's pioneering heroes and latter-day road warriors. May your loose booties shake and your heads bang on the One.

I wish to thank the following: James Spooner, for insisting that a history of black rock should be written, Miriam Jiménez Román y Juan Flores, Eva Klapalová, Bernie and Judie Worrell, Jaimoe, Joshua Taylor and all the numerous music nerds who contributed to the Glossary, David Walker at Badazz Mofo, the Isley Brothers, Sly and the Family Stone, Funkadelic, Jenny Lee Rice, Jackie Gotthold, Venetta Fields, Sherlie Matthews, Charles Cobb Jr., Sala Patterson, Ahmad Larnes, Mike Ladd, Judy Richardson, Jason Isbell, Mildred Shaw Hayes, Walter Bgoya, Robert Cohen @ Finyl Vinyl (Gotham), Dennis W. Kennedy, Patty Smith, Mary Lee Grisanti, Mylène Falloux, Lorraine O'Grady, Kregg Ajamu, Kevin and gang at the Pink Teacup in Manhattan, Darrell McNeill and the Black Rock Coalition for the support of the project from the beginning, Michael Lydon, David Sandison, Karen Spellman, Greg Tate, Peter Folger, Kimberly Gamble Payne, and my fearless and exuberant colleague at Palgrave, Gabriella Pearce, without whom this book would not exist.

I am eternally grateful to Ms. Chuck Bartelt for achieving the impossible at the last minute & to Kenneth Benson too (my man!).

Very special thanks to: Anne Forrester, Camara Dia Holloway, Shirley Cooks, Sarah Childress "Gay" Reynolds (Harper), Andy Schwartz and Leslie Rondin, my "Unc" Stanley Booth, Doreen Boyd, Margaret Ann Holloway, and Madame Efua Theodora Sutherland (*in memoriam*).

—*Kandia M. Crazy Horse,*
*Manhattan, September 27, 2002*

# RIP IT UP

ANDY GILL

# TEN
# QUESTIONS FOR
# LITTLE RICHARD[1]

AG: When you started out, rock 'n' roll was primarily a regional thing, wasn't it?

LITTLE RICHARD: You got to remember, when it first started, it wasn't rock 'n' roll. It was your Elmore Jameses, your Sonny Boy Williamsons, your Howlin' Wolfs, your Little Walters, y'understand me? Rock 'n' roll came from Billy Ward and the Dominoes, they had a song called "60 Minute Man"—"I rock 'em, roll 'em all night long, I'm a 60 minute man, if you don't believe I'm all I say, come up and see your dad"— that's where the words *rock 'n' roll* came from. When I came out, there wasn't no one singing rock 'n' roll, there was country—like Bill Monroe and His Blue Grass Boys, with them fiddles?—and there was a bandleader called Swingin' Sammy Kaye, singing a song called "Pennies from Heaven," but they wasn't fallin' over in my neighborhood, so I had to get out and create somethin'. So I took rhythm and blues and boogie-woogie, put it together, and came up with rock 'n' roll. But I was only able to use my own singing style when I went to Specialty. I had that style all the time, but the other companies wouldn't accept it! They wanted me to sound like other people, to be a blues singer. I had this other thing, they'd never heard nothin' like it, so they was afraid of it. But when I went to Specialty with Awopbopaloobopalopbamboom! they said, "OK!"

AG: You used some of the same musicians as Fats Domino on your records, didn't you—the New Orleans crew from Dave Bartholomew's band?

LITTLE RICHARD: Me and Fats, we would record with the same band. He would record one week and then next week I would come in and record. That was with Earl Palmer, Lee Allen, Red Tyler, and all of those guys, they had a great recordin' band. But it was strange, each of us had a different style, and they would play our individual styles, they'd adapt to our personalities, y'know? I had some amazing musicians in my live band too. Jimi Hendrix was my guitarist, James Brown was my vocalist, Billy Preston was my organist at fourteen years old. I'm the Architect of rock 'n' roll, the originator, the Emancipator. Before me, there wasn't nothin' but a few pigs, and they didn't have no ham, y'know?

AG: What kind of technology were those early sides cut on?

LITTLE RICHARD: Just three tracks! That's the reason I had to scream for the sax solo, 'cause they didn't have but the one microphone, hangin' over the piano. I had to scream so the saxophone player, Lee Allen, would know it was time for him to blow. I'd go, "*Aaaaaaaaah!*" and Lee Allen would go, *Da-da-da-doo-da*. When I hollered, he knew it was time to get it! It was a little bitty room, Cosimo's, not much bigger than a toilet, but it was a funky little room! I would teach them the songs in the studio. If you ever heard my outtakes, I would hum them the solos they were going to make. The solo that Lee Allen was about to play, I would hum it for him, and he would duplicate it. The rhythms, I would do them on the piano, and they would duplicate them, too.

AG: Listening to the *Specialty Sessions* box, it's interesting that other tracks may develop over a dozen takes or so, but "Tutti Frutti" is right there from the start, first take. Where on earth did it come from?

LITTLE RICHARD: That's right. I had been sayin' "Awopbopaloobopalopbamboom!" for a long time, but I didn't know anything about writer's rights, 'cause some of the writer's rights they gave the girl [Dorothy LaBostrie], they should not have given her, because I already had "Tutti Frutti." I had Awopbopaloobopalopbamboom! in my hometown, it was word that I said. People'd say, "How you doin', Richard?" I'd say, "Awopbopaloobopalopbamboom!"

AG: It must have been annoying for you to see Pat Boone, of all people, getting bigger hits than you with your own material.

LITTLE RICHARD: It was. Both of us are out of the South—I'm from Georgia, he's from Tennessee—and they didn't like it 'cause the white girls was screamin' over me, and they put him out to block that. With way bigger promotion. That's the reason I started wearin' makeup, so that they wouldn't feel threatened when I was in clubs, around the white girls, 'cause they think you're comin' 'round to get them, when your mind ain't nowhere like that. Their mind is sex, y'know? Everybody thinkin' that you're comin' to get a piece when I didn't want nothin'. I took a piece of cake, but I didn't want nothin' else! My mind was on business, and on music, and I wasn't goin' out just for sex. I think anybody goin' out just for sex, they're not true entertainers. A true entertainer loves his craft, and wants to do the best for his music.

AG: Is there a difference between gospel and secular R&B? People talk about "the devil's music."

LITTLE RICHARD: There's a little difference. Some of it sounds like the blues, some it sounds like rock, according to the type of gospel song you're doin'. And what makes the difference is the lyric. There were some great gospel singers around then—the Clara Ward Singers, Sister Rosetta Tharpe, Marion Williams with the Ward Singers, Albertina Walker and Shirley Caesar with the Caravans, Brother Joe May—they used to call him the Thunderbolt of the Middle West, he was like a bolt of lightnin' comin' out of the sky!—and we had the Soul Stirrers, with Sam Cooke. I toured with Sam in London right before he died, about two weeks before he passed. Mahalia Jackson was a big idol of mine, too; but a lot of the effects and rhythms you hear on my songs, I got 'em from the trains that passed by my house. Like "Lucille" came from a train—Dadas-dada-dada-dada, I got that from the train.

AG: You took a break from music for a while. Was that for religious reasons?

LITTLE RICHARD: No, I went to school. I really needed to study business, I needed to learn how to take care of my financial means and needs, so that's what I did. It'd be good for all musicians to take a course in business, because you can't control no accountant that knows figures better than you do, and when you get ready to retire, you won't have nothin' to retire with. It's a cold cut business.

AG: Elvis apparently used three different types of hair pomade at the same time. What do you use to keep yours so spectacular?

LITTLE RICHARD: I spray mine. But you know, my hair is much harder than Elvis's, it's more coarse than his, and so it stands up anyway. Elvis and I was very good friends—people try to make out we was rivals, but it wasn't like that, we were real good friends; but later Colonel Parker wouldn't let him have no visitors. He was a nice, humble guy, and a great entertainer.

AG: Be honest—how many times have you slipped out to Hollywood Boulevard to check out your star?

LITTLE RICHARD: I haven't! I pass it all the time and forget to look over there. My son says, "Richard, it's your star," but I forget about it. It took so long to get it, y'understand? I wish my mother could have been alive to see it, but like everything I got, it took a long time to get. Because really and truthfully, they didn't want me to have it, y'know? I worked like a dog for what I got, 'cause they wasn't used to no person at the time bein' flamboyant like I was. Before Elton John and David Bowie, I was dressin' like that—although both Elton John and David Bowie are unbelievable entertainers, fantastic, I love both of them, they're sweet people.

AG: If you could pick one greatest achievement of your life, what would it be?

LITTLE RICHARD: To me, in my life, 'cause I came from a poor black family of twelve in a little country town [Macon, Georgia], my greatest achievement would have to be "Tutti Frutti." It took me out of the kitchen—I was a dishwasher at the Greyhound bus station, makin' ten dollars a week workin' twelve hours a day, and "Tutti Frutti" was a blessin' and a lesson. I thank God for "Tutti Frutti"!

## NOTE

1. The piece originally appeared in *Mojo* (December 1999). It appears courtesy of Andy Gill.

# BILL MILLAR

ABSOLUTELY THE BEST

IKE & TINA TURNER

# THE IKE AND TINA TURNER REVUE: STREATHAM LOCARNO, LONDON[1]

In September 1966, some 7,000 people saw the Rolling Stones and Ike and Tina Turner at the Royal Albert Hall and—judging by audience reaction—about ten came specifically to see the latter, so it was a welcome change to watch their performance where, billed as the star attraction, they undoubtedly attracted more of their own admirers.

The revue opened with the gray check-suited, eight-piece Kings of Rhythm pounding away at "I Was Made To Love Her" à la King Curtis, with mighty fine blowing from tenorist Gerald Gray. The full lineup contained Leon Blue (piano), Lee Miles (bass), Odell Stokes (guitar), Howell Portier (drums), and horn men Eddie Burks, Jimmy Reed, Gerald Gray, and David Kines. A brief jazzy instrumental led into "Our Day Will Come," for which the brass men doubled on maracas to provide an appropriate Latin tinge.

Ike stepped out, brilliantly clad in a green suit, and contributed a superbly executed King-Rush blues guitar solo. Superbly amplified, his skillful note-bending echoed round the hall. Jerking like a puppet, Ike performed a short but hugely exciting rocking blues, and with the tenor man playing fit to blow his reed out, it was music I would have preferred to hear more of, even to the omission of some subsequent vocals.

However, it was not to be. Jimmy Thomas, resplendent in white, took up the stand for "Knock on Wood" and "Respect." It is odd that Jimmy works as a little-known feature act on a revue of this kind. Someone has to fill the spot, but somehow, as with Prince Albert in 1966, Jimmy seemed to be as exciting and polished as many a more well-known soul artist. Not the greatest choice of material, but his shrill, wild voice was the equal of those heard on the definitive versions. More rock 'n' roll came with the surprising inclusion of "Nadine," on which Ike provided two admirable solos.

In the lull that followed, while Ike replaced a broken string, Odell Stokes played solo on "Soul Serenade." The Ikettes, utterly gorgeous in brightly colored minishifts, took command with a rousing version of "You Got Me Humming." Female groups are not everybody's favorite, but Ike chooses his girls well, and three of the team, although fairly new to the revue, proved to be more than adequate replacements. With Paulette in the lead, they swung into "Dancing in the Street" and followed with "So Fine" close harmony; hectic but exact dancing; great gospel-inclined lead vocals and bewitching looks—the four girls excelled at everything.

It was obvious, from her first number, that Tina Turner is the most exciting female performer in the rhythm and blues idiom today. Superlatives like "wild" or "primitive" cannot do her justice. With the Ikettes remaining on stage, Tina, in a figure-hugging red mini, opened with "Sweet Soul Music." Almost uninteresting now that everyone features it, but Tina and the Ikettes made it unmistakably theirs. How she manages to dance like she does one will never know. On "A Love Like Yours" the Ikettes wailed in authentic gospel style while the band ceased playing and Tina preached with an intensity that was embarrassing for some.

A noisy, jumping version of "A Fool in Love" preceded "River Deep Mountain High." From the point of view of bettering their reception, it might have been more appropriate to save the latter for the finale, but, nevertheless, it was received, not unnaturally, with more gusto than anything else and the strings were not missed at all. Tina, frantically screaming into the stand mike, her hips and hair swinging in unison, clearly equals James Brown for pure emotional raving. Magical Two more pulsating numbers with "Land of 1000 Dances" and "Respect" and the scene on stage became one of utter frenzy. Tina wailed as if in torment and the Ikettes danced and shook maracas as if it were their last public appearance!

"Tell The Truth" closed the show, and what a finale! A strobe light flickered over the gyrating Ikettes while Tina and Jimmy Thomas danced, Tina screaming and her hair flying in all directions. A really explosive performance and one to which an encore could only have been an anticlimax.

## NOTES

1. This piece originally appeared in *Soul Music Monthly* (April 25, 1968). It appears courtesy of Bill Millar.

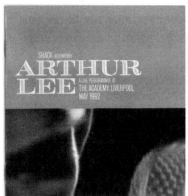

# PAINT ME WHITE: BAD DAYS, BLACK ROCK, AND ARTHUR LEE'S LOVE STORY

**H**igh up in Laurel Canyon, with all of Los Angeles spread out around him, Arthur Lee would sit and stare and contemplate death—"sitting on a hillside, watching all the people die," as he sang it in "The Red Telephone," the brilliantly creepy song that concluded side 1 of Love's *Forever Changes*.

It was 1967, and all the world was caught up in the joy of flowers and beads and drugs, swimming in the colors that swirled through the psychedelic haze. Down on the Sunset Strip, where for a year Love had reigned as the hippest band in town, hippies floated about in a state of cosmic bliss. But Arthur Lee wanted no part of it. He'd either seen too much or not seen enough; no one was too sure which.

"I don't think Arthur wanted to leave his space," reflects Bryan Maclean, the singer and guitarist who was Lee's foil in Love. "Every place he lived, he'd have gates you had to get through to his house. He would venture out to score whatever he needed, whether chemical or sexual, and that was it. He didn't hang out, he didn't show up at clubs."

"Arthur was so difficult to get along with," remembers David Anderle, then the chief A&R scout at Love's label, Elektra. "He was always afraid of something, and I could never figure out what it was. He was such an enigma. He wasn't a hang on the scene like a David Crosby. That's how I think of him, really, as one of the L.A. greats: Brian, Beefheart, Zappa, Neil Young, Arthur—all haunted, reclusive, baffling people."

"Arthur was, and perhaps still is, one of the smartest, most intelligent, and finest musicians I ever met in my entire career of making records," said Jac Holzman, founder of Elektra and now president of Discovery Records. "As large as his talent, however, was his penchant for isolation and not doing what was necessary to bring his music to his audience. Which was a shame, because he was one of the few geniuses I have met—in all of rock 'n' rolldom."

It is July 1993, and I'm sitting opposite Arthur Lee in a restaurant on Van Nuys Boulevard, on the other side of Laurel Canyon from Hollywood. Thirty years ago, Arthur probably could have looked down on this very spot from his gated eyrie atop Lookout Mountain. Now he lives here in the Valley with the mere mortals.

It's clear that Arthur is already a little tipsy, and he will down three or four more Bloody Marys during the course of our conversation—if "conversation" you can call a rambling interchange in which he dodges, and for the most part evades, my questions. He is still lean and handsome, it must be said, though still fond of a cheap and unsubtle hairpiece.

"I went on a big campaign for a year, telling everyone not to drink," Arthur grins at me. "But, well, you know . . ." His voice trails off into an indistinct sigh. The word is that Arthur actually achieved sobriety for the aforesaid year and was even engaged to a girl he'd met through AA. Whether this is the same girl to whose nearby apartment he later takes me, I choose not to ask. The girl in question seems fairly together if faintly exasperated by Arthur, who all but ignores her as he busies himself with making me a tape of Rosa Lee Brooks's "My Diary," a cracking little soul single he produced way back in 1964, featuring (so he claims) the first session ever played by his friend Jimi Hendrix.

A story about Hendrix is one of several disjointed anecdotes with which Arthur regales me in the restaurant in Van Nuys. In 1969, it seems, Jimi and Arthur were in San Diego together, and Hendrix brought a call girl up to Arthur's hotel room as a kind of present for his friend. According to Arthur, the guitarist then joined them in bed, but—get this—proceeded to come on to Arthur rather than to the girl. When I evince eye-bulging disbelief at this claim, Arthur gives me a nervous laugh, then protests, "I'm serious, man!"

Unsure exactly what to believe, I suspect there's a subtext at work here, and one that has much to do with Arthur's bitterness at the way Hendrix, Sly, and others appropriated his black-rock/psychedelic-soul style and then received all the kudos for it.

"I was the first black person wearing those clothes and doing that stuff," he later says. "And then the credit went to Jimi." Oh, the pain of being a forgotten pop pioneer—the one who never sold any records.

"We constantly referred to the fact that Arthur was black and I was white," Bryan Maclean is telling me. "I'm sure it crossed my mind that this was kinda cool—that this could work to our advantage—but we never thought we were gonna change the world."

I'm sitting beside Maclean in an open-topped red pickup, flying down Sunset Boulevard with a hot wind on my face. It is August 1996, exactly three years after my encounter with Arthur Lee.

Maclean is a surprise. I'd expected some born-again Brian Jones and what I get is a burly surfer guy, not unlike Gary Busey at the end of *Big Wednesday:* big and intense and slightly crazed, talking nineteen to the dozen as he bombs along Sunset toward the Pacific Ocean. So much for the Beverly Hills pretty boy who, at the age of eighteen, warbled "Softly to Me" in an artless folk-rock tenor.

Much of what Bryan Maclean says on a long drive to Venice and back is shot through with anger toward Arthur, albeit anger tempered by awe at the man's genius and the spell he seemed to cast over everybody during that heady mid-'60s period.

"Arthur had the dominant personality, so his songs got done," he says matter-of-factly. "I was writing prolifically all through those years, but when we went into the studio he'd say no to every song. Had I been tougher I'd have grabbed him by the collar and thrown him up against the wall."

"There was a slightly twisted, almost homoerotic relationship between Lee and Maclean," says David Anderle. "Let's just say Arthur made Bryan's life miserable."

When Lee and Maclean first met in the summer of 1965, Love had already been going for several months. Except that the band wasn't called Love, it was called the Grass Roots, and had evolved out of two bands—the LAGs and the American Four—that Lee had led before seeing the folk rock light at an early Byrds show.

Lee had been born not in Los Angeles but in Memphis, on March 7, 1945. "My mother was very light-skinned, she could pass for white," he told me. "She was a schoolteacher, and she came from a long line of schoolteachers."

Uprooted and brought to California at the age of five, Lee, in his own words, was "an only lonely child" whose sole solace seemed to lie in music. "I started giving him music lessons when he was about ten or eleven," his mother, Agnes, recalled on the phone before her death in the late 1990s. "His teacher told me that he could play better than she could and that he didn't need to take any more lessons."

What was Arthur like as a kid? "He was a spoiled brat, but he had a good heart."

"I would listen to Nat 'King' Cole, and I'd look at that purple Capitol Records logo on his records," Arthur said. "I was determined to get a record deal with Capitol, and I did, without the help of a fancy manager or anyone else."

Unfortunately, the LAGs' sole Capitol 45 rpm release, the sub–Booker T instrumental "Rumble-Still-Skins," was a woeful disappointment when it appeared in 1963. "It was terrible, really a disgrace," admitted Arthur.

Lee never graduated from Dorsey High, where he'd excelled at basketball and track sports. He was too busy plotting his musical career. While at Dorsey, he'd watched the R&B star Johnny "Guitar" Watson step out of a gold Cadillac wearing a gold suit and flashing gold teeth, and "knew then that I had to have a guitar." In fact, the lure of gold might have led him into another lifestyle entirely. According to Bryan Maclean, Lee was "known as the baddest guy on the West Side of L.A."

Lee's first real musical accomplice—and a man who would stick with him right through to *Forever Changes*—was guitarist Johnny Echols. When Lee formed the LAGs to play R&B covers at local parties, Echols was his first recruit. And when the LAGs turned into the American Four and recorded the "Twist and Shout"–style single "Luci Baines" for the Del-Fi label, Echols (like Lee himself a light-skinned black kid with processed hair) was still there at his side. Arthur said he and Echols were very influenced by the look of Bobby Womack and the Valentinos, who had "long hair and stuff I'd never seen in my life."

The left turn into white pop culture came when Lee got wind of a happening new scene up in Hollywood in the early spring of 1965. The Byrds were playing at Ciro's on the Strip, and Lee and Echols went to check them out. Lee was blown away by the new freedom of Beatles-influenced folk rock and by the chiming sound of twelve-string guitars. Just as much of a revelation was seeing Mick Jagger singing "Time Is on My Side" on *The Red Skelton Show* and catching the Rising Sons—the short-lived, blues-based band formed by Taj Mahal and Ry Cooder—at the Ash Grove on Melrose Avenue. "That's when I really knew something was happening," he said.

"Arthur was playing R&B," said Maclean, "and somewhere along the line he decided to take a ride up to the Strip. I don't think it was opportunistic. I don't think he thought, 'Oh, I wanna get in on this.' I think he sincerely liked the music and the scene."

Barely a month after seeing the Byrds, Lee had given his band a comprehensive makeover, junking the previously obligatory covers of "Shotgun" and "Louie Louie" and embracing the punkier, more British Invasion–style sound that would surface on Love's debut album. It was as though McGuinn and friends had somehow formed a sonic alliance with Messrs. Jagger and Richards.

Maclean had grown up in an environment very different from the one that spawned Lee. He was a golden child of privilege, a kid whose parents mingled with Hollywood celebrities, a boy whose first sweetheart was a pubescent Liza Minnelli. "She and I would do songs from *The Wizard of Oz*. My whole background was Rodgers and Hammerstein—as a kid I'd stand in front of the mirror and conduct, or I'd be Curly in *Oklahoma*. I created my own world."

One day Maclean swung by the Sandal Shop in Westwood and heard a group of people singing Appalachian ballads. The conversion to folk music and its culture was instant. Soon he too was singing and playing guitar in coffeehouses and clubs like the Balladeer and the Troubadour.

After befriending David Crosby, Maclean was hired as a roadie by the Byrds. "For a seventeen-year-old kid it was heaven," he told me. "Crosby and I got along perfectly. I didn't understand what everybody was complaining about, because he was just like me!" Maclean parted company with the Byrds shortly before their English tour in August '65, "and when I came back to L.A. there was a whole scene that the Byrds had created, but without them."

Maclean said he knew nothing about Lee prior to meeting him in 1965. When the two got talking, Lee told Maclean about his band and Maclean hipped Lee to his relationship with the Byrds. "He invited me to come and hear him at the Brave New World," said Bryan. "And that was the beginning of it.

"Arthur was smart to get me in the band. I think he let me join more for who I knew than for what I could do. I brought him the whole Byrds scene, first at the Brave New World, then at Bido Lito's, and ultimately at the Whisky a Go Go. And we became the king of the street bands in Hollywood."

Rodney Bingenheimer ("the Mayor of Sunset Strip") recalls that Love was one of the first bands he saw after moving down to L.A. from northern California. "He was this black guy, but he always seemed like part of the white scene," he told me. "He wasn't playing soul, he was playing this jangly guitar music. It was almost like he was like the black Roger McGuinn."

It's hard now to imagine what a dash the group must have cut when they first broke through at the end of 1965. On one level they were one of a number of L.A bands walking a thin line between folk rock and garage punk. But on another they were unique: a "two-tone" band playing an amazing hybrid of folk, soul, and psychedelic pop at a time when there were still strong racial and stylistic divides in the American music industry. And at the center of it all was Arthur, a black freak on the white scene, a ghetto punk in beads and pebble glasses.

"He cut quite an imposing figure," wrote Three Dog Night's Jimmy Greenspoon in his autobiography *One Is the Loneliest Number.* "Dark glasses, a scarf around his neck, Edwardian shirts and—what was to become his trademark—an old pair of army boots with one unlaced. The audience became followers of King Arthur Lee. He was a Pied Piper who would lead them down the road to a different form of consciousness."

When Lee snarled his venom-fueled version of "My Little Red Book"— a Bacharach and David song that Manfred Mann had recorded—it was clear that Los Angeles had found its very own Mick Jagger. Only this one was a black Mick Jagger, a guy that L.A. music biz veteran Denny Bruce described wryly as "a black American imitating a white Englishman imitating a black American."

The British influence was only too manifest in Lee originals like "Can't Explain," its title borrowed from The Who and its drum fill from the Stones' "Get Off My Cloud." But the mesh of guitars—Lee's, Echols', and Maclean's—was pure L.A., as were the Byrdsy "You I'll Be Following" and the mournful pangs of "Message to Pretty" and "Signed D.C.," the latter supposedly a stark first-person account of drummer Don Conka's heroin addiction.

From the outset a highlight of Love's live set was Maclean's frantic rendering of "Hey Joe," delivered without a vocal safety net at every show. "The way Crosby had done it, it almost had a Mose Allison type feel," Bryan remembered. "When we did it, it was like punk rock. I lost my voice every night singing it. It was completely new—folk rock with a punk edge—and it put us on the map."

It took Maclean's live version of "Hey Joe" at Bido Lito's to convince thirty-four-year-old New York record executive Jac Holzman that he'd "found the band I was looking for" in Love. Holzman's Elektra label had been a bastion of folk music on the East Coast, but Holzman could see the times they were a-changin' and—like Atlantic's Ahmet Ertegun with Buffalo Springfield, whom Holzman had originally wanted to sign— made up his mind to muscle in on the emerging West Coast action.

By late January 1966 the band, complete with new rhythm section Ken Forssi (bass) and Alban "Snoopy" Pfisterer (drums), was recording its first album at the Sunset Sound Recorders studio. The results were engaging if primitive. "What you hear on that first album is just an enervated, attenuated version of what we were like live," Bryan Maclean sighed. "It didn't have the distortion or the energy or the impact."

*Love* remains one of the better debuts of its time, a punky, exciting mix of rockers and ballads. "Little Red Book," which got to number 52 on the U.S. chart, sizzles, as do "Hey Joe" and the unashamedly "Hey Joe"–esque "My Flash on You." "Gazing" is like an acid age remake of The Crystals' "Then He Kissed Me"—L.A. teen symphonics mutating into jangled psychedelia.

With its cover portrait depicting the band as a gang of hip Sunset Strip hoods—the picture was shot in the grounds of Bela Lugosi's old estate in Laurel Canyon—*Love* trumpeted the presence of a major new musical force on the southern California scene. By the end of the year their influence would be felt strongly in the sound of bands like the Seeds, the Leaves, the Lollipop Shoppe, and the Music Machine.

When the album appeared in May '66, Love was the toast of the town's underground, playing sold-out residencies at Bido Lito's and at the Hullabaloo on Hollywood Boulevard. "We were the biggest group in L.A.," Arthur said. "The street where Bido Lito's was, that whole street from Selma Avenue to Hollywood Boulevard was packed with people. At the Hullabaloo we had people lined up all the way down to Sunset."

When Love played the still hipper Whisky a Go Go, farther west along Sunset, Lee claimed they "started the whole hippie thing" in tandem with an in-crowd of freaks led by aging beatnik sculptor Vito Paulekas.

Bryan remembered these days as ones of innocent mischief. "We were just having a ball. We didn't care about the implications of being a multiracial group or about civil rights. We'd be riding around, holding, and Johnny would say it looked suspicious—a white guy in a car with 'a spade and an Ethiopian'!"

Love were early masters of surly pop attitude, as reporters from teen magazines like *KRLA Beat* and *Hit Parader* quickly discovered: Far from epitomizing "the whole hippie thing," the band came on like Jones and Rotten a decade before their time. When *KRLA Beat's* Rochelle Reed interviewed them in June 1966 in the legendary "Castle"—the exotic mansion they were renting in the Los Feliz hills—they treated her abominably, psyching her out with mind games and telling her they'd met during a gang fight.

Any fears that such attention-seeking arrogance was premature were allayed that month when Love cut the mind-shattering "Seven and Seven Is" at Sunset Sound Recorders. To say that this is one of the great rock singles of the 1960s is a sorry understatement; it's an apocalyptic masterpiece, hurtling furiously along for two and a quarter minutes before climaxing in the sound of an atomic bomb.

Blasting away any folk rock preconceptions lingering from Love's debut, "Seven and Seven Is" spelled out the obvious, which was that the band had plunged headfirst into the oceanic realm of hallucinogenic drugs. "If I don't stop crying, it's because I have got no eyes," Lee yelped. "My bible's in the fireplace and my dog lies hypnotized!" The single became Love's biggest hit, reaching number 33 in America and paving the way for the group's second album.

*Da Capo,* recorded in September and October 1966 at the RCA-Victor studio in Hollywood where the Rolling Stones had cut "Satisfaction," was a giant step forward from *Love,* introducing a psychedelic and almost baroque edge to the band's garage folk sound. "I feel that I found myself, or planted a seed of who I am today, in *Da Capo,*" Arthur told Lenny Kaye in 1970. "I was born in *Da Capo.*"

*Da Capo* almost ranks alongside its successor, *Forever Changes,* as a summer-of-love classic. Certainly there are few more astounding sequences of music than "Stephanie Knows Who," "Orange Skies," "Que Vida!" "Seven and Seven Is," "The Castle," and "She Comes in Colours," six extraordinary songs that blend psychedelia and punk rock with Latin and Broadway influences.

"*Da Capo* was the ultimate of what I call show-tune rock," said Bryan. "What you have is a guy who grew up on Rodgers and Hammerstein and Aaron Copland, and who worshipped Burt Bacharach, and then a guy who grew up on the West Side of L.A.—in the Crenshaw-Adams district—on R&B. And it was that mixture that made it interesting and made it unique. The Love sound, if you want to be really honest, was Arthur copying *me.*"

Self-serving as this sounds, it may not be so far-fetched when one considers the radical changes in Lee's writing on songs like "Que Vida!" and "Stephanie Knows Who"—or, for that matter, the precipitous decline in the quality of Lee's music after parting ways with Maclean.

"My theory is that Arthur didn't write all the songs he's credited with," says John Tobler, the self-styled "Captain of the Fleet in the Quest for Arthur Lee," whose early to mid-1970s *Zigzag* interviews with Lee did so much to keep the Love cult alive. "I think Maclean may have had quite a bit more to do with them than we realize."

Yet it was Lee who steered Love away from the pumped-up angst of "Hey Joe" toward a new strain of psychedelic muzak that David Anderle termed "punk with strings." Underground rock gonzo Sandy Pearlman, a disciple of Richard (*Aesthetics of Rock*) Meltzer, wrote that *Forever Changes* "finishes what *Da Capo* began—Arthur Lee's insane mutation of Mick Jagger into Johnny Mathis!"

"Love started out with a kind of garagey folk rock, but once they got into their own style it wasn't like anybody else," says Bomp Records boss and psych-punk sage Greg Shaw. "It had a kind of orchestral sense to it which wasn't influenced by The Left Banke and didn't sound like Tim Buckley but which was really unique."

A key point about Love was how much closer they were to the L.A. pop tradition of Brian Wilson (and even The Association) than they were to the loose, faux-live sound of the new San Francisco bands. For the Grateful Dead or the Jefferson Airplane, it would have been anathema to use strings or flutes on a record. For Love, it was part and parcel of a Hollywood pop sensibility that led seamlessly on to the lushly orchestrated *Forever Changes*.

Tied in with this was Lee's distance from—or unwillingness to be part of—the new acid rock scene. "When we played up in San Francisco [Love made their Bay Area debut at the Avalon Ballroom on April 8, 1966, and played the Fillmore with the Dead, no less, on July 3], Arthur would just stay in his hotel room," remembered Bryan. "I had a whole life up in San Francisco, but he didn't know anybody there. I think he was actually afraid of people." Undoubtedly one of the factors that really handicapped Love was Lee's insularity, his lack of interest in life outside Los Angeles. Even their Elektra labelmate Jim Morrison was moved to comment that "I don't think [Love] were willing to travel and go through all the games and numbers that you have to."

"Arthur was always very aloof," says Harvey Kubernik, who saw Love in all its incarnations and later interviewed Lee in his capacity as West Coast correspondent for *Melody Maker*. "He didn't exactly lead the league in schmoozing, and he certainly never understood the concept of ingratiating yourself. Arthur blocked people off from getting to know him. The whole point about those sunglasses he wore was that you couldn't see into him."

"We didn't do the things we should've done," Arthur admitted to Lenny Kaye in 1970. "We were always on the trip of wanting to do the right thing at the right time, making sure everything was the right time for us. And we passed up a lot of things, man."

Bryan Maclean put things more tersely: "We broke covenant with our record company by not cooperating, not making it worth their while to distribute our music. I didn't know any better—I really was naive as far as business was concerned—but I think Arthur did."

For a long time there was a theory that Lee had taken umbrage at the supposed favoritism displayed by Elektra toward labelmates The Doors. The irony here is that it was Lee who urged Jac Holzman to see The Doors playing at the Whisky and who even persuaded the Elektra boss to check them out again after he—like many record executives in Hollywood at the time—was left unimpressed by Jim Morrison's heavy-handed stage act. For their part, too, The Doors signed to Elektra primarily because of Love, a group they worshipped. "Jim Morrison used to sit outside my door when I lived in Laurel Canyon," said Arthur. "He wanted to hang out with me, but I didn't wanna hang out with anybody."

"When I came to Elektra, it was Love-land," said David Anderle. "Very quickly it became Doors-land. It had nothing to do with The Doors being all white it was just that The Doors thing was so fast. Nor was Arthur apparently that desperate for the success The Doors had. He was the night creature! As was Jim, of course, but there was some big fear cloud with Arthur. Believe me, Holzman loved Arthur, but something happened to him, and I don't know if it was drugs, alcohol, or something biochemical."

Drugs certainly played their part in Love's seeming lack of ambition. Introduced to the band after the release of *Da Capo* by their road manager Neil Rappaport—a long-term junkie whose overdose death was later commemorated in Four Sail's "Your Friend and Mine"—heroin soon had Echols and Forssi in its vice-like grip.

Word of Love's heroin use spread quickly through the rock community, confirming their outsider status and making them personae non grata at the big flower-power party during that summer of love. Many people found the band not just surly but intimidating, profoundly at odds with the prevailing spirit of peace and well, love.

"I don't want to say that Arthur was demonic," said David Anderle, "but he was very manipulative and destructive. See, Arthur was not really a hippie, he was more of a punk than a hippie. There was almost a gangster thing going on there—rule by intimidation. But at the same time, he could be so sweet. It was totally schizoid, and maybe that did have something to do with being black in a white world."

If Love's members were hoods, they were psychedelic hoods: The tension between punk and flower power—between menace and beauty—lay at the heart of what made their songs so compelling. Nowhere is this more evident than on *Forever Changes,* the album the band began recording in June 1967, the very midsummer of love.

The circumstances of *Forever Changes'* creation hardly augured well. When engineer turned producer Bruce Botnick convened with the band in early June, it was immediately obvious to him that they were in no fit state to record. With Lee tripping round the clock, and Maclean not even bothering to show up for rehearsals, it looked as if Love were going to need help from session musicians. Botnick proceeded to book drummer Hal Blaine, guitarist Billy Strange, and pianist Don Randi for the first session of June 9.

Fortunately, the presence of Blaine and company had the effect of literally shocking Love into action. "The band sat there and listened to the musicians recording "Andmoreagain" and "The Daily Planet," and it sparked them," Botnick recalled. "They were sitting there crying, but they realized they'd blown it, got their act together, and recorded the rest of the album." By late September, when David Angel's horn and string parts were added, *Forever Changes* had been finished.

Here, on one record, was the sound of Los Angeles undergoing a sea-change from jingle-jangle, Cuban-heel innocence into strange-days, Manson-era weirdness—the same direction in which The Doors were headed. If Lee could celebrate the Sunset Strip spirit of carnival on the exhilarating "Maybe the People Would Be the Times, or Between Clark and Hilldale," on other tracks he took a far darker view of the hippie bacchanal. Despite a musical palette more heavily weighted toward strings and mariachi-style brass than toward acid rock guitars, *Forever Changes* had a fix on the surreal and disturbing flavor of the times that only The Doors (and possibly the Brian Wilson of *Smile*) matched. "Sometimes my life is so eerie," Lee sang on "The Red Telephone," "and if you think I'm happy, paint me white."

"Arthur had this big house right on top of Mulholland Drive," recalled Ken Forssi, "and we'd look down over the city from there. Arthur would sit up there staring out and wondering about all the ambulances." Lee himself has said that he had "a thing about dying" at the time and that *Forever Changes* was meant to be "my last words to this life . . . it's like death is in there."

The album is strewn with images of horror and mutilation—of guns and blood, and sirens and accidents, of things that don't necessarily make a lot of sense but that stick stubbornly in the mind once heard: the "water mixed with blood" in "A House Is Not a Motel," the "snot caked against my pants" in "Live And Let Live," the toys that "plastic Nancy" buys to keep her kids "in practice/waiting on the war" in "The Daily Planet," the evocation of the madhouse at the end of "The Red Telephone." On few other '60s albums is the Vietnam war hovering so obviously in the background.

With its intricately crafted arrangements, idiosyncratic time changes, and overlapping vocal tracks, *Forever Changes* fully merits its reputation as L.A.'s very own *Sgt. Pepper*. Curiously, it fared considerably better in Britain than it did in America. Released in November 1967, as the year of the summer of love was drawing to a close, it reached number 24 on the U.K. album chart. (In America it never rose any higher than number 152.)

It could certainly be argued that the British have been largely responsible for keeping the album's "classic" status alive over three decades, notwithstanding its standing with neo-psychedelic acts in America.

Among Love's most ardent admirers is Robert Plant, who gave Lee the red-carpet treatment after inviting him to a Led Zeppelin show at the Forum in L.A. in 1975. It's no coincidence that a host of bands, from The Teardrop Explodes to Teenage Fanclub, has invoked the genius of Arthur Lee or that Alan McGee flew him over to London for Creation's tenth-anniversary bash at the Albert Hall.

Masterpiece though it was, *Forever Changes* marked the beginning of the end for Love's original lineup. "I really wanted a Love band, a Love thing," Arthur told me. "I wanted to be the Beatles, the Stones, a real unit, but everybody had different behavior patterns. One guy was this way, another guy was that way, and I'm not Atlas, man, I can't hold up the world."

With Bryan wanting to go in a more soft rock, ballad-oriented direction, Echols and Forssi tending more to the power-trio sound of Cream and Hendrix, and Arthur too stoned and disillusioned to pull them back together, a split was inevitable. There was one last release from Love Mk. 1, the brilliant single "Your Mind and We Belong Together" backed with "Laughing Stock," recorded at the end of January 1968, possibly as part of a fourth album that was never completed.

Maclean was the first member to jump ship, in the summer of 1968: "I went up to see Mike Gruber, who was managing the band at the time, and gave him my notice. Arthur was, like, 'You can't quit, 'cause you're already fired!'"

After Echols, Forssi, and Michael Stuart quit the band, rumors began filtering out of L.A. as to the state that Lee himself was in. "I think Arthur got demoralized," said Bryan. "I think that happened to a lot of people in those days. We all thought we were on a rocket ship that was just going to continue to go straight up. I thought this was always going to be my life."

What saved Lee was strolling into a Valley dive called the Brass Ring one night and seeing a band led by an old friend called Noony Ricketts. Backed up by guitarist Gary Rowles, bassist Frank Fayad, and drummer George Suranovich—musicians Lee himself had played with occasionally in an early 1960s band called The V.I.P.s—Ricketts was blasting out hard rock songs that fired Arthur up and made him question the music he'd been making with Love.

"When I went out there, I had done this soft album and been influenced by what people told me to do," he told Lenny Kaye. "I'd even written my songs according to this trip of trying to get airplay and all this bullshit with the soft rock trip so that we could expand our group. And here this four-piece group was. They were as loud as fuck. They were out of sight. And, like, Jimi Hendrix had come out, and it really tripped me out that here's a cat who came out three years after I had seen The Byrds and freaked out and did his whole trip—he comes out and plays this loud music that I always wanted to do in the studio."

Lee wasted no time in luring Fayad and Suranovich away from Ricketts and in hiring lead guitarist Jay Donnellan. The new Love set about recording almost thirty new songs, ten of which made up *Four Sail,* a final album for Elektra, and the remainder of which comprised *Out There,* Love's double-album debut for its new label, Blue Thumb.

Both records appeared in late 1969, and both, frankly, were dreadful—not a patch on anything Lee had done with the original band. The sad truth is that nothing Lee has written since "Your Mind and We Belong Together" and "Laughing Stock" warrants comparison with even the most lightweight song on *Love.* Fayad and Suranovich may have been the best rhythm section he'd ever had, but the Lee of *Four Sail* and *Out There* just sounds burned out, bereft of inspiration. Even when he joined forces with Hendrix during Love's May 1970 tour of Britain and cut a bunch of glorified jam sessions in London's Olympic Studios, the tapes only yielded "The Everlasting First," the indifferent first track on the execrable *False Start* (1970).

The point, surely, was this: The prince of orchestral acid pop found it painfully hard to survive in the era of heavy electric rock. *Forever Changes* could stand alongside *Sgt. Pepper,* but *Four Sail* and *Out There* weren't fit to stand in the same room as *Led Zeppelin II.*

The solo *Vindicator* (1972) had slightly more going for it: It was punchier, closer to barroom glam rock than to the hopeless albums by Love Mk. 2. Guitarist Charlie Karp kept things tight and gritty, and Lee's lyrics were at least zany: Song titles included "You Can Save Up to 50% But You're Still a Long Ways from Home" and "Every Time I Look Up I'm Down," or "White Dog (I Don't Know What That Means)."

By 1976 Lee had all but quit the music business and was apparently working with his stepfather painting houses in South Central L.A. "When I left the band, nothing ever happened for Arthur again, and I think that just galls him," said Bryan. "He's probably more bitter and resentful over that than anything." Maclean glosses over the fact that nothing much has happened for him either, although he did write "Don't Toss Us Away" for the 1985 debut album by his half-sister Maria McKee's band Lone Justice and recently had a song covered by country star Patty Loveless. The 1970s saw him bottoming out on booze and turning to Christianity in an attempt to halt the unraveling of his life.

En passant, Bryan mentioned the ill-fated, swiftly forgotten "Love reunion" of 1978. "It was another case of Arthur spinning out and me going, 'Okay, I've already experienced this, I'll see you around,'" he said.

"It's like the blush of youth goes and then it's just sort of the bitterness that starts to surface, and the anger, and the resentment."

It is two days (July 1993) since I watched Arthur Lee and Love play the Palomino, a rundown roots rock dive in the Valley that's played host to hundreds of country renegades over the decades. Backed by Baby Lemonade, a young four-piece band whose enthusiasm almost made up for its curious insensitivity to songs like "Orange Skies" and "Signed D.C.," Arthur did his best before a roomful of fans brandishing album sleeves for autographs. Love's next gig would be a support to Doors tribute band Wild Child—and if you don't think that's ironic, paint me black.

As he sinks the dregs of another Bloody Mary, I ask Arthur what effect acid had on his music back in the mid-1960s. He fixes me with a leery glare. "I don't know anything about acid at all," he suddenly snaps. "I have nothing good to say about any drugs or alcohol for young people. I'm not going to elaborate on anything that would put a dent in a young person's mind. I've been out there, man. Now I just live in an apartment, don't worry about the butcher."

A little less than two years after my evening with him, Arthur Lee was arrested at his apartment in Sherman Oaks, not far from Van Nuys. Police had been called to the third-floor apartment on Kester Avenue by a neighbor who claimed that Arthur had fired a shot, then pointed a gun at him and threatened to "blow him away."

"It was total rubbish," said Doug Thomas, who not only was with Arthur that Saturday night in July 1995 but claims that the gun in question was fired, accidentally, by himself. A drummer who has played for thirty years in West Coast–influenced bands in his native New Zealand, Thomas was visiting Lee in L.A. to discuss the possibility of releasing some new Love songs. "We were planning to put out an album called *Forever Changes II*," he told me on the phone.

Thomas said that he and his wife were sitting around with Arthur and his girlfriend, Susan Levine, drinking a little wine and watching a video of *Three Amigos*. At some point, Lee asked Thomas to look through some old boxes for videos of recent Love shows in Europe. Upon opening one such box in a closet belonging to Lee's ex-girlfriend, Thomas found what turned out to be a .44 Magnum. "So I pulled it out, walked through to the patio, and said, 'Hey, Arthur! Arriba!' The second time I pulled the trigger it went off, making the biggest noise I've ever heard."

Lee and Levine immediately grabbed the gun, since both knew that—as a felon who'd been convicted on a couple of assault and drugs charges back in the 1980s—Arthur could land in serious trouble for possessing such a thing. Thomas maintains that Arthur had no idea the gun was in his ex-girlfriend's closet.

After a short while, about ten policemen arrived, handcuffed Lee and the others, and took Lee to the Van Nuys central police station. A few hours later, they searched the apartment in Sherman Oaks and found a box of 500 armor-piercing bullets.

When Lee left L.A. to tour Europe in the summer, various Love fans suggested he stay in France or Spain as an exile rather than risk imprisonment by returning home. "He said he wouldn't," said Doug Thomas. "He said he was going back to prove his innocence." Little did he know that when the case came to trial he would be up against a notorious D.A. known as "the Dragon Woman" and a jury bused in—like the jury that acquitted the LAPD officers in the Rodney King case—from Simi Valley.

The jury ignored Thomas's evidence and found Lee guilty on all charges. A year after O. J. Simpson was set free, the Love singer was sentenced to eight years' imprisonment, a victim of California's stringent "three strikes and you're out" ruling. He served six years, emerging in 2002 to tour once again as the leader of Love.


Was Arthur Lee one of the all-time rock greats, or was he just an opportunist who happened to seize a moment of pop incandescence? Was he, in the words of David Anderle, someone "with a bigger vision than just making dumb rock music," or did he just cannily exploit the spirit of the Sunset Strip? Was he a genius or a rogue?

Perhaps he was both—half intimidating hood, half sweet-natured Pied Piper. He himself hinted at a radical split in his personality when he described *Vindicator* as "a Dr. Hyde World-Wide Production"; others have suggested that he is a borderline schizophrenic. "Arthur is not of this world," Jac Holzman once remarked. "He lives in a world of his own creation."

"It's hard to say how deep the imbalance and lack of integrity go with Arthur," said the born-again Bryan Maclean, two and a half years before the heart attack that killed him. "He lacked repentance, always."

"I'm a very private person," Lee told me. "Chico Hamilton said the music is in the street, but for me, the music is in me. I *am* the music."

# PAUL GILROY

# BOLD AS LOVE? JIMI'S AFROCYBERDELIA AND THE CHALLENGE OF THE NOT-YET

I am of no particular race. I am of the human race, a man at large in the human world, preparing a new race. I am of no specific region. I am of earth.

—Jean Toomer

In the absolute, [] truly what is to be done is to set man free.

—Frantz Fanon

What exactly did Jimi do to *sound* that black and that blue? To create those immortal articulations of the slave sublime, transposed into futuristic genre-defying statements of human suffering, yearning, and hope? His short life reveals so many inspired transgressions of redundant musical and racial rules that it's hard to know where to begin. Seattle, New York, and swinging London all provide promising points of departure. Each of them accents his life in significant ways, but none of them is adequate to carry its full weight or represent that itinerant existence properly in its beautiful, liquid complexity. Counterpointing the gypsy life that he chose and moralized, the music itself requires any convincing critical engagement with him to be polycentric. We have to be as able as he was to accommodate the absorption of the very different disciplines that were required by the U.S. Army, the South, and the chitlin' circuit. The bad sign under which he was born must be recognized as a complex constellation. There are ethnocentric pressures to be resisted and a whole lot of well-intentioned but unhelpful mystification that belittles Jimi by making him superhuman—somebody who did not have to work or practice in order to achieve greatness. The sheer, patient labor involved alone makes this music something more than an intuitive or, worse yet, a wholly instinctive emanation of black being.

We should start with the blues because that's where he started, but not get trapped there, on the threshold of the red house they accommodate. We begin with that dwelling in order to better appreciate how Jimi playfully possessed the blues and amended its workings so that they would be adequate to the technological and moral challenges arising from the unsettled cultural environment of the decolonizing cold war world. We must also see how he managed to overcome tradition's constraints, twisting them into creative opportunities, electrifying them, blending and bending them into different registers of protest and affirmation. He was always prepared creatively to damage the superficial integrity of the musical traditions in which he located himself. That modernist desire to destroy and shock was pivotal, and it was not just confined to what he did in the act of performing.

Gypsy that he was, he had wanted to be buried in England, his adopted homeland. Yet his greatest moment as a live performer was the Woodstock Festival's systematically artful assault on the patriotic musical heart of the imperial nation in whose paratroops he had previously served with pride, then hell-bent on destroying the Vietcong with the same fervor that currently guides its impossible and interminable war on terror. Through that exemplary boldness—a quality he links with love—we can understand what was and still is at stake in the unfolding of a revolution that draws its poetry and its soundtrack from the future.

Hendrix's reaching for and conjuring up not just the future but a more philosophically coherent "not-yet" unsettled his contemporaries. I think that assertively utopian quality is what still enables his work to speak to us so powerfully. It was a product of his desire not, as the previous generation had done, to interact mournfully with the sunrise of the next day by serenading it, greeting every condemnation to prolonged suffering in the industrialized valley of the dry bones with resignation and defiance. Albert King, whose epochal "Blues at Sunrise"[1] could be taken as the limit of that exhilarating approach, was famed as a driver on construction sites. His legend says he could pick up a carpet delicately with his bulldozer. Jimi, no habitué of the killing floor, seems only ever to have been a soldier and a musician. His alienation and his sense of what work could be and where it stood in relation to the freedoms that were necessary in order to feel free, stone free, were utterly different. The primal scene of Jimi's existential encounter with the prospect of radical autonomy was still the dawn, the approved neotraditional staging, but unlike Albert, from whom he had drawn such compelling inspiration, Jimi aimed to articulate musical sound that could approximate the power of those first rays in reilluminating the world.

It is easy to miss the full significance of this stance by just saying that Hendrix was ahead of his time or that it has taken thirty or so years to catch up with him. It certainly took that long for the Brazilians to come up with "Afrocyberdelia," a workable proper name for his revolution. A similar period has been required to make his technical departures part of the standard repertoire of his instrument. Comments on his "avant garde" position reveal fragments of a larger truth, but the real issue is not that Hendrix was ahead of his time, but rather that he was able to pronounce another time: shifting and sculpting temporality itself so that his willing listeners were transported from one time to another.

This was not the chance result of his ascent coinciding with the appearance of an oppositional, questioning youth culture to which recreational drugs had become integral. The gloriously damaged sound of those first songs announced and then dramatically enacted the impact of a colorful counterculture that beat back the monochrome tones in which a gray, decaying—Jimi would probably have said "plastic"—world had been enveloped.

A massive gesture of refusal was distilled in the anthemic insubordinate chorus of "If Six Was Nine," but it was evident everywhere: in his dandyism, in his characteristic mixture of politeness and assertiveness, and in his appetite for theatrical, "autodestructive" performances. I remember the impact of those daring, wild, and dissonant opening notes of "Purple Haze," which hit the airwaves in England in the spring of 1967 just as I was starting to become interested in being a guitar player myself. The line "lately things just don't seem the same" coupled with the singer's apparent ease of access to the sky on which he would bestow his kiss all confirmed the same historic novelty. Things were suddenly and dramatically different. To my awestruck ears, the question "Are You Experienced?" gave thrilling voice to the same cataclysmic, intergenerational rupture. The blues was there, allright, but this was not a Lightnin' Hopkins record or the archaic, beautiful fruits of an ethnomusicological excursion down to Stovall's Plantation. Blues temporality seemed to have been transformed in an act of modernist daring that was also instrumental in commanding the attention of new transnational audiences. These were often remote dissenting listeners who knew that six could indeed become nine without touching the quality of their fragile existence on the proliferating margins of the overdeveloped world and its abbreviated consumer freedoms.

This approach to specifying the enduring value of Hendrix's art as a fiery, insistent pulse within a novel, dissident culture runs counter to all the sentimental approaches that strive to folksify his very twentieth-century legacy, to imprison it in the blues that was both its launch pad and its ballast, to confine it to the United States or make it all roots and no routes, all voodoo child and no highway child. Those interpretative habits can be resisted in the name of the global network that he helped to animate.

Toward that end, we should always remember that Hendrix was a soldier and think of him as an ex-paratrooper who became a hippie in an act of profound and complete treason that would make him an enemy of power until this day. I was thinking about the ongoing potency of that moral decision as I stood at Jimi's windswept grave on the outskirts of Seattle, accompanied only by a dignified young man in military uniform who told me that he passed his interminable days listening to Hendrix mp3s on the computer in the local army recruiting station where he worked. Jimi's bold choice of peace and love instead of war was coupled with implacable opposition to the absurd and destructive "ego scene" that official politics had become. His understanding of that historic blend made him a marked man and a new man.

Talking back to Frantz Fanon's theories of revolution at about the same time Jimi moved to England, Martin Luther King, Jr. had argued that the choice of love required a special strength and paid a special dividend. He continued, "Humanity is waiting for something other than blind imitation of the past. If we want to advance a step further, if we want to turn over a new leaf and really set a new man afoot, we must begin to turn mankind away from the long and desolate night of violence. May it not be that the new man the world needs is the nonviolent man? A dark, desperate, confused and sin-sick world waits for this new kind of man and this new kind of power."[2] There is the sound of the future being enlisted in the struggle against racism, which is also a conflict over the nature of masculinity. At that moment, tomorrow was on the side of those who wanted to enhance democracy. Inequality, callousness, and merciless economic exploitation were briefly but powerfully associated with the past. Their presence was experienced fleetingly as anachronistic. "Third Stone from the Sun" is only the most obvious example of how Jimi makes that revolutionary feeling audible and attractive. The urgent warning communicated by "House Burning Down" provides an intriguing example of how Hendrix's music could ask tough, demanding questions about the ethics of care in a segregated society and refer his listeners not only to the alternative possibilities of the not-yet but to what he imagined were higher and better ways of existing in harmony with themselves, their environments, and each other. The mythic staging of what sounds like a cry of perplexed and defeated rage against the violence of a pogrom elevates a deliberately obscure reading of America's domestic conflicts to global significance. A space boat lands with eerie grace to take away the bodies of the dead, and thus the message to love becomes a message to the universe. A planetary vision supplied Jimi's global mind-set with a suitably futuristic vehicle for its existential critique. This was not a routine result of a new age, occult impulse. These were properly historical moods, tied to a new iconic immediacy of the planet, that had been captured for the first time from outside earth's orbit by cameras on the Apollo spacecraft in 1968. This is a planetary rather than a cosmic consciousness, and it seems also to have been derived straightforwardly from Jimi's repudiation of the belligerent geopolitical mission that young men like himself were then routinely being given by Uncle Sam.

It's worth repeating that Hendrix joined and then left that army. He acquired a subtle antipathy toward the military mentality that was inverted and reworked as the target of all his hopes for a better world. His journey toward peace was all the more convincing because the conversion was gradual and because along the way he had discovered the pleasures of jumping out of airborne war machines and falling through the sky. Perhaps that ontological shaking and sustained proximity to death nudged him into a mythic language that not only fostered an update in the poetics of world citizenship but invited us to imagine taming the U.S. military industrial complex in the subversive act of traveling by dragonfly rather than warplane or helicopter. The myths are part of this worldliness, too. They are broader and brighter-hued than the safer, unconvincing cosmography of the worn-out christianities they aimed first to undo and then to supplant.

It was Hendrix's exit velocity from the military that enabled him to borrow those arrows of desire from William Blake's Muggletonian quiver and bravely put them to work opposing both colonial war and moribund politics. His unpatriotic decision to choose peace and espouse nonviolence was offset by the tense and difficult relationship he enjoyed with Michael Jeffrey, the mysterious and ruthless Geordie manager who sometimes boasted of his own military activities in the murkiest depths of the colonial warfare to which Britain's secret state had committed the ailing, no longer imperial country. Jeffrey could speak Russian, had been stationed in Egypt during the Suez crisis of 1956, and does seem to have worked for British Intelligence in some capacity.[3]

While bravely opposing the war in Indochina, Hendrix managed to confound and disappoint anybody who wanted him to adopt conventional or facile political views and to enrage anyone who found his elliptical, mythic pronouncements on ethics, history, and governmentality too much to stomach. What we identify as environmentalist or green themes in his work should be acknowledged here as an additional measure of the global scale of his anxieties about the fate of humankind. The prospect of the larger tragedy involved in species death looms over his explorations of the contingency, tragedy, and brevity of fragile human life. His repeated references to Native Americans are part of this countercosmology, but it remains a mood rather than a program and is all the more powerful for that. There is only a Cherokee mist, the lingering trace of an indigenous, non-European sensibility, veiled in musical fog, swirling wordlessly with a spiritual energy drawn from the dopplered, harmonically unstable notes that are flying out from the spinning speaker of the Leslie cabinet.

That trail of tears, the suffering in that genocide, and the tragedy of reservation containment must all stay wordless if they are to retain their power to inspire, humble, and shame. In the bared teeth of this unspeakable history, words come too cheaply. Jimi's transethnic turn is neither a willful drift away from blackness into exoticism nor a belated programmatic bid to set history straight by invoking some interplanetary Seminole genealogy. The tragic outcome—the castle made of sand— refers us to the enduring presence of alternative possibilities. Another world is possible. Jimi conjures up the prospect of it—a castle in the air— and says that the resources for building that utopia are, unexpectedly and magically, already at hand.[4] To forget America's internal tragedies and the genocide of its conquest and expansion would be to deny the uniqueness of its hybrid identity and, in so doing, to sustain the passivity and renunciation that corrupt and inauthentic power now relies on. Opposing the alienated submissiveness that has been engineered from above requires recognizing the catastrophe of American progress. That acceptance in turn becomes part of acquiring the machinery of liberation. The pursuit of an alternative future requires the cultivation of countermemory, and even time, as Herbert Marcuse put it, "loses its power when remembrance redeems the past."[5]

The significance of Hendrix's many creative transgressions has been multiplied not only by the brevity of his life, but also by a sense of its radical incompleteness. This has encouraged critics to project images of him burdened and trapped by their own preoccupations. Rather than place Hendrix inside somebody else's dubious fantasy of what his music ought to have been, it seems to make more sense to treat his own mythic projections of his work more seriously, to reconstruct them in their historical setting and see whether, like his calculated refusals of shallow and trivial political language, they might help to explain why his music would not die along with him. Accordingly, I have tried to take both Jimi's appetite for utopian and mythic themes and his tacit politics more seriously than is now conventional.

His strange immortality has made his media afterimage unusually plastic and mutable. It may be better to accept that final evaluations of his boldness are impossible and to argue that understanding his music and its enduring popularity involves a number of historical and cultural puzzles.

The art's life after Jimi's death is more than a narrowly aesthetic matter. It raises a number of delicate interpretative problems that have the power to detonate all oversimple models of African American culture and identity and redirects us to a number of neglected issues. Among the more important are the history and phenomenology of the electric guitar, a consideration of the pivotal point where music-making becomes a matter of sound, and the tale of how electronic innovations derived from military research found new peaceful uses in sound-processing technology. We are obliged to answer a host of difficult questions about the cold war's cultural dimensions, about the combined and uneven development of racialized and globalized markets for popular cultural products, and about the unanticipated commercial value of what we can call video immortality.

Before we can even pose questions of that order, we are also required to ask what version of black cultural history his gypsy life might be used to construct. The repeated affirmation of itinerancy cannot be erased. Jimi's poetry of transience presents life as a journey without an arrival. His romanticism is betrayed by the projection of a self that is "essentially a traveler—a questing, homeless self whose standards derive from, [and] whose citizenship is of, a place that does not exist at all or yet, or no longer exists; one consciously understood as an ideal, opposed to something real . . . the journey is unending and the destination, therefore, negotiable."[6] We need to understand where existing frameworks, which defer too readily to the boundaries of national states or are inclined to respect the disciplinary authority of those who claim to know the proper course of culture, might have to be amended in order to make sense of the fluctuations and detours that have surrounded and nurtured this itinerant art. We need also to grasp how Hendrix's music has not only retained its special power but grown in stature, acquiring a new significance that lets it speak to several quite different generations of listeners, especially the more recent and remote audiences for whom the blues is not a primary point of musical reference. They have found their way to Hendrix nonetheless, because of the way that his musical imagination saturates the scene even as the electric guitar moves out of the central position he won for it.

Blues is not usually thought of as a modernist form. Its electrification has not been very well understood, appearing more usually as a linear development of unyielding traditions that are predictable and knowable. The standard script runs like this: Blasted out from the plantations where it had been formed, the blues was dispatched northward into the accelerated, vertiginous, and abject modernity of America's segregated cities. That degrading urban environment had been memorably explored by Richard Wright alongside Edwin Rosskam's selection of photographs in their historic 1941 collaboration *Twelve Million Black Voices,* published just before Jimi was born. Wright, an autodidact, philosopher-sociologist, and renegade postal worker as well as a writer of fiction, was the first African American chronicler of this new metropolitan tragedy to reach for the concept of modernity in order to make sense of what he was seeing around him in the iconic kitchenettes and alleys of Chicago's South Side. That racialized geography, where Jimi was only ever a visitor, provided a crucible in which adaptations of the form would be forged. There the custodianship of black culture was reinvested in the newly arrived urban populations that never quite managed to stand in for their rural antecedents. While other aspects of black vernacular existence were in a terrible flux, the blues was somehow able to resist the turbulence. Critical orthodoxy says that from that historic point, the form itself did not really change. Perhaps its development had been arrested by the extreme shock of this racially stratified hypermodernity. Certainly just a few years after Hendrix's death and scratching at a Stratocaster to complete the detour that "Red House" had begun, the cryptically postmodern blues of Albert King could announce the absolute invariance of the music while slyly celebrating the very mutability that his words denied.[7] Answering the conservative inclinations of the orthodox voices that prize sedentary culture above the itinerant and feral forms with which it is often in conflict, this counterhistory of black identities and identifications says that Jimi came along and changed the game. His intervention showed where tradition was not a simple repetition but a reflexive practice of custom that inclined toward the liberationist possibilities of the not-yet by valorizing a combination of "flexibility in substance and formal adherence to precedent."[8]

Wright's account of Chicago life associated modernity with cultural and existential complexity and saw how the experiential discrepancy visible along America's racial fault line had to be made intelligible, not in the pattern of W. E. B. Du Bois's "double consciousness," which had been absorbed too easily, but as a temporal disjunction. This is how he put it: "More than even that of the American Indian, the consciousness of vast sections of our black women lies beyond the boundaries of the modern world, though they live and work in that world daily."[9] His acute and thoughtful analysis of this lack of synchronicity offered two other telling comments on the black world that was coming into being inside the ghetto walls. He confides, "There are times when we doubt our songs," and then, with the help of one of Rosskam's pictures to underscore the point, he adds wearily, "strange moods fill our children." That was the broken world in which Jimi was raised and to which his revolutionary art responds with the subversive aim of reenchantment.


From this oblique angle, Jimi might now reappear attractively as a prodigal heir to the comparable revolutionary cultural legacies of Robert Johnson and Charlie Christian, two other guitar geniuses that the wider world still pays attention to. Their combination of musical innovations triangulates our reconstituted, transblack tradition. Johnson provides one axis of Hendrix's world by marking the historic transition of everyday blues art into the altered tempos of the industrial age. That fatal crossroads is only one of a number of special sites where tradition and modernity intersected or, more accurately, where two discrepant modernities—one of the plantation and the other of the metropolis—came into exhilarating and troubling contact. Johnson's favored deity is the devil, not the vengeful Old Testament presence of afro-Baptist lore. The spirits that haunt his melancholy art inhabit a profaned world in which the order of racial terror remains dominant but has started to shift and crack in response to new demands for different varieties of freedom. Accordingly, God retreated to a new position, and theodicy assumed a different character. Negroes who had walked with Jesus had started to learn to drive. There was no crosstown traffic in Clarksdale, Mississippi, so Johnson likened the body of his lover to a Terraplane car. His chuckling audience understood what he meant when he announced that he wanted to check the oil and get under the hood. The railroad had yielded up its special poetic place to the speed and style of the private automobile. Henry Ford's automotive commodities become infused with libidinal energy, and downpressed people could embrace their alienation as the starting point for existential challenges premised on their understanding of themselves and their fates as "a mirror of all the manifold experiences of America."[10]

The elemental force of Johnson's life is a complicated thing even if we must reject the suggestion that Hendrix was conceived close to the moment of the older man's murder. We need to make some space for the mediating figure of Muddy Waters and be prepared to acknowledge his mainstreaming of the blues, but the other axis of Jimi's world is most usefully identified with the youthful figure of Christian, who did far more than merely reveal where the distinctive musical language of the electrified guitar might commence. Making a moving and insightful consideration of his classmate's revolutionary musical achievements in giving the instrument a jazz voice, Ralph Ellison described the emergence within and around jazz of a ritual space where a real, rehumanizing pleasure could be derived from elemental contests in which "each artist challenges all the rest; [and] each solo flight or improvisation, represents (like the canvases of a painter) a definition of his identity: as individual, as member of the collectivity and as a link in the chain of tradition."[11] Setting aside Jimi's doubts about whether his own music could or should be described as jazz, with those words in mind, we can consider whether he fits into that famous definition of the jazz-making process.

Like both of the imaginary guitarist ancestors I have given him, Jimi certainly subscribed to endless improvisation on and reconstruction of traditional materials. But like Ellison's proto-be-bopping Christian in particular, the man who liberated the guitar from the rhythm section, Hendrix was absolutely prepared to have to lose his identity even in the process of finding it. He can therefore be thought of as both victim and beneficiary of the conflict between his instrument's existing technical vocabulary and its adequacy as a means to represent "those sounds which form a musical definition of Negro American experience."[12]

Du Bois had used what he called "sorrow songs" to frame his idea of double consciousness, two warring souls, one Negro and one American, locked adversarily in a single dark body on the way toward synthesis as "a higher, better self." His linkage suggests that these "ethnic" sounds were already becoming hard to identify, distinguish, and isolate from the other contending soundscapes of modern America even at the dawn of the twentieth century. Since then the desire to make music into the medium of cultural rebirth and to hear in it the characteristic signature of racial genius became a recurrent feature of critical thinking about black culture. Naming and positioning black music in this way was, it seems, a significant element in bringing that very result about. For a while, music became the center of black culture in a new and distinctively modern way. Although black art gradually and painfully separated itself from black life, music remained a potent means to link understanding of the new era to important, identity-building reflections on the simpler un-freedoms that had preceded it. These historical observations generate an objection to Ralph Ellison's implicit complacency and rather narrow spec-ification of what officially counts as jazz. Once we appreciate the double character of African American music, we are delivered into a new inter-pretative territory equally distant from assimilationist schemes and all pu-tatively afrocentric musings about the relationship among trumpet mutes, plungers, and wah-wah pedals.

Jimi's musical visions demanded sonic and technological changes. They seized on the Leslie speaker and other related innovations like the development of the Univibe, which employed light to destabilize and alter the phasing of sounds. These and many other features of Jimi's sonic revolution deserve more attention than they get when they are miscon-ceived as simple, preprogrammed effects of the attenuated African sur-vivals with which they are in complex dialogue.

With one ear turned back toward Du Bois, Alain Locke had raised these problems as early as 1936, many years before Jimi climbed aboard that Eagle's wing. This is what he wrote: "Jazz in its most serious form has also become the characteristic musical speech of the modern age. It in-corporated the typical American restlessness and unconventionality, em-bodied its revolt against the drabness of commonplace life, put pagan force behind the revolt against Puritan restraint, and finally became the western world's life-saving flight from boredom and over-sophistication to the refuge of elemental emotion and primitive vigor."[13] Locke's insight identifies music with doubling of a different variety from the dialectical logic Du Bois had borrowed from Germany. The evolution of culture ceases to be comprehensible as a simple matter of approved conscious-ness being distributed evenly into the willing receptacles that even di-vided racial souls provide. This discomforting development presents the exponential doubling of untidily folded selves in a pleated culture. Here it affords us with a means to reframe the internality of racial identity with-out presupposing either essence or interiority: "Folds incorporate without totalizing, internalize without unifying, collect together discontinuously in the form of pleats making surfaces, spaces, flows and relations."[14] Doesn't the multitracked guitar onslaught on our senses that Jimi orches-trated for the opening sections of "Ezy Rider" take us past the place where the idea of the original ceases to be worthwhile? In the multiplicity of swirls and screams, the issue of which track was laid down first starts to be irrelevant. The effect of their overall combination becomes more important. The guitar howls and is multiplied, chorused into a dynamic sonic image of unprecedented plurality. Its constantly shifting screams betoken a new conception of irreducibly complex identity.

Ellison's argument about Charlie Christian is also relevant because it carefully positions the guitarist's inventiveness on his recently amplified instrument between the poles of entertainment and experience. We can map those options onto the split between Hendrix the minstrel showman and Hendrix the immobile, serious musician, the shamanic pastor of the partly hidden public world he called "the electric church." In explaining artistic choices that felt eccentric then but no longer do so, Hendrix spoke about it from time to time. It was a collective social body of musical celebrants that gathered periodically to engage the amplified modernist offshoots of the Mississippi delta and harness them in the causes of human creativity and liberation. Its ritual events had become loud, he told Dick Cavett on the latter's show in July 1969,[15] not only because the appalling state of the world meant that many people were in need of being woken up by the shock that only elevated volume could supply, but also because, if the wake-up call could be delivered on the correct frequency, it might, in turn, promote a direct encounter with the souls of the people involved. Here Du Bois's sense of where sorrowful, transcendent music augmented the power of words and writing supplies an active presence, though Hendrix's comment suggests a departure from the savant's more conventional, and by then rather outdated, understanding of the workings of the embattled black public sphere. Hendrix's career tells us that by now, black music could produce its own public world: a social corona that could nourish or host an alternative sensibility, a structure of feeling that might function to make wrongs and injustices more bearable in the short term but could also promote a sense of different possibilities, providing healing glimpses of an alternative moral, artistic, and political order.

The electric church was all around us then, it was inseparable from the wider revolutionary upsurge of that moment. The traditional celebrations of afro-baptism, secularized, profaned, and fragmented had been adapted to the larger task of community defense. Under the banners of black power and anticolonial solidarity, its irregular services began to alter the political mentality of black people worldwide and to transform and even synchronize understanding of our emergent place in postcolonial conditions. This could be done without a recognizably political word being spoken aloud. The church's fundamentally oppositional character was disguised by its intimate relationship with the music and dance with which Negroes reaffirmed their infrahuman nature.

The dualistic pairing of the showman and the serious musician might be used to reveal yet another take on the shifting dimensions of double consciousness. But I hope to have suggested that dualism is neither appropriate nor sufficient in this case. Jimi reinforces that verdict by moving our sensoria away from the basic stereophony of his first recordings towards the raging would-be three-dimensionality of the later work.

A larger mapping of where Hendrix might be made over in order to fit the topography of an expanded jazz tradition and a reconceptualized grasp of the electric guitar is urgently needed.[16] We can, for example, map him in relation to the neglected contributions of Grant Green, Sonny Sharrock, and Kenny Burrell as well as those of Albert King, Steve Cropper, and Curtis Mayfield. We can draw on the wisdom of B. B. King[17] to show where Jimi found the ball and on the contemporary commentaries of figures like Steve Vai and Alan Holdsworth to identify where he left it. But, as people turn away from the electric guitar in hordes, that sort of archaeological operation has its limits.

Hendrix was somebody who occasionally checked into his many hotel rooms under the name H. Bean. This should not be overlooked or inflated into a self-conscious bid for overdue recognition as human. It is just another small clue that can help us to comprehend what is at stake in the basic metaphysical question that reverberates unashamedly throughout his work. That question is: What does it take to be heard?

In judging him today in a video-saturated visual culture, we must remember that being heard is thankfully not the same thing as being seen. Though they can be connected, Jimi's orphic demand is not Fanon's humanist appeal for recognition, which, you may recall, had been shaped by the impact of seeing himself being seen by somebody whose attachment to race hierarchy meant that they could neither concede black humanity or realize their own. The shocking power of amplified sound solicits identification differently. We are dispatched or drawn to new bodily predicaments. We discover ourselves prosthetically. Whether that mode of being in the world is ultimately compatible with the order of race remains to be discovered. We have Jimi Hendrix's art to assist us with these urgent inquiries, and his compelling creative answer to that question was no.

## NOTES

1. Albert King, "Blues at Sunrise" from the Stax Records LP *Live Wire/Blues Power* StX-41 28 (undated).
2. Martin Luther King Jr., *Where Do We Go From Here, Chaos or Community?* (New York: Harper &Row, 1967), p. 66.

3. Eric Burdon with J. Marshall Craig, *Don't Let Me Be Misunderstood* (New York: Thunders Mouth Press, 2002).

4. See Ernst Bloch, "Better Castles in the Sky at the Country Fair and Circus, In Fairy Tales and Colportage," in *The Utopian Function of Art and Literature: Selected Essays,* trans. Jack Zipes and Frank Mecklenburg (Cambridge, MA: MIT press, 1988), pp. 167–185.

5. Herbert Marcuse, *Eros and Civilisation* (London: Abacus Books, 1969), p. 164.

6. Susan Sontag, "Model Destinations," *Time Literary Supplement* (London, June 22, 1984), pp. 699–700.

7. Albert King, "The Blues Don't Change," from the Stax Records LP *The Pinch.* STX-3001, 1977.

8. Eric Hobsbawm, "Inventing Traditions," in E. Hobsbawm and T. Ranger, eds., *The Invention of Tradition* (Cambridge, UK: Cambridge University Press, 1982), p. 2.

9. Richard Wright, *Twelve Million Black Voices* (London: Lindsay Drummond Ltd., 1947), p. 135.

10. Ibid., p. 146.

11. Ralph Ellison, "The Charlie Christian Story," in *Shadow and Act* (New York: Random House, 1964), p. 234.

12. Ibid., p. 239.

13. Alain Locke, *The Negro and His Music* (Washington, D.C.: The Associates In Negro Folk Education, 1936), p. 90.

14. Nikolas Rose, *Inventing Ourselves: Psychology, Power, and Personhood* (Cambridge, UK: Cambridge University Press), p. 37.

15. Jimi Hendrix, "The Dick Cavett Show," *Experience Hendrix* DVD, 2002.

16. See Keith Shadwick, "Running the Voodoo Child Down," in *Jazzwise 60* (December 2002/January 2003), pp. 22–29.

17. " . . . the single factor that drove me to practice was that sound I had heard from the Hawaiian or country-and-western steel peddle guitar. That cry sounded human to me. I wanted to sustain a note like a singer. I wanted to phrase a note, like a sax player. By bending the strings by trilling my hand—and I have big fat hands—I could achieve something that approximated a vocal vibrato; I could sustain a note. I wanted to connect my guitar to human emotions: by fooling with the feedback between amplifier and instrument, I started experimenting with sounds that expressed my feelings, whether happy or sad, bouncy or bluesy. I was looking for ways to let my guitar sing." B. B. King with David Ritz, *The Blues All Around Me: The Autobiography* (London: Hodder and Stoughton, 1996), p. 123.

# DALTON ANTHONY

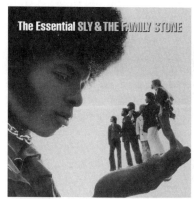

The Essential SLY & THE FAMILY STONE

# A.K.A.
## SLY STONE:
## THE RISE AND
# FALL OF
# SYLVESTER STEWART

Our hook-up with White radicals did not give us access to the White Community because they do not guide the White community. The Black community does not relate to them so we were left in a twilight zone where we could not enter the Black community with any real political education programs; yet we were not doing anything to mobilize Whites.

—Huey Newton, April 17, 1971[1]

"Ever catch a falling star? Ain't no stopping till it's in the ground"

—Sly Stone, 1970

I can still remember the first time I ever saw a picture of Sly. I must have been about ten years old and was sitting on my parents' living room floor looking at the inside jacket of the Family Stone's greatest hits LP. Surrounded by fellow band members (sister Rose and brother Freddie, Cynthia Robinson, Jerry Martini, Larry Graham, and Gregg Errico), Sly was radiating self-confidence and positive energy. Decked from head to toe in all-white clothes that were draped in multicolored beads, sequins, and fringes that nearly touched the ground, he had a rainbow choke collar wrapped around his neck, an Indian-feather dangling from a white-knit cap pulled down over his bulging afro, and legs covered in knee-high sheepskin boots. A mixed-race, mixed-gendered spectacle, for several heady years during the late sixties and early seventies Sly and the Family Stone put forward a style and sound that captured the nation's collective imagination. Rising to the top of the charts with a string of classic hits that were at once spiritually uplifting, hopeful, and *fun* (songs like "Dance to the Music," "Everyday People," and "Hot Fun in the Summertime"), their music, lyrics, and live performances championed the cause of integration and racial harmony at a time when the nation was torn by deep social divisions and radical activism. As America wrestled with its soul during the late sixties and early seventies—reeling from the war in Vietnam, the assassinations of John and Robert Kennedy, Malcolm X, Fred Hampton and Martin Luther King, torn apart by urban riots and political intrigue—Sly and the Family Stone became [were] the pied-pipers of the hippy generation. Their message seemed to point the way toward a cultural, if not a political, resolution to the country's crisis and millions on both sides of the racial divide became believers.

But there was another image from my parents' living room that left an impression on my young mind as profound as the picture of Sly and the Family Stone: it was a nearly life-sized poster of Huey Newton. In the photograph Huey is sitting in a wicker chair looking straight into the camera with a dead-serious, no bullshit, unflinching look. In one hand was an African spear; in the other was a rifle. Huey wasn't wearing white, glittery sequins or hippy feathers, that's for sure; he was wearing ebony, stone-cold black—and it was a far cry from the content, assimilationist image put forward by the Family Stone. The picture of Huey reminded us that no matter how good the groove, there was, indeed, a riot goin' on for the hearts, minds, and economic resources of the nation. Both Sly and Huey came bursting out of the San Francisco Bay Area in 1967. Together they were the carrot and stick of black liberation and any sense that there was a conflict of interest between the ideals of assimilation and militant direct-action was lost in my home at least.

Although on the surface their aesthetics and political program were diametrically opposed, Huey and Sly were united by their belief that they could effect meaningful, even revolutionary social change through their actions. After sending their flares into the sky in the late 60s, by the mid-70s, both visions for cultural and political uplift had crashed and burned in dramatic and oddly parallel fashions. Advocating direct action and local, grassroots political organization, Huey and the Panthers proved to be no match for the institutional authority of the American government, not to mention the ideology and practice of white supremacy that supported it. And when Newton was shot dead on an Oakland street corner in 1989, an alienated and disillusioned addict, his death came not at the hands of the feds, but from the gun of a local drug dealer in a crack deal gone bad. In the end he succumbed like so many others, to the collective demons that have haunted black communities in the wake of the political and cultural failures of the civil rights era.

It has been said that "dreams die hard," and although I didn't know it at the time, as I sat looking at the photograph of Sly, he already had one foot out the door. At the height of the Family Stone's "success," he turned his back on the utopian vision he had dedicated his life to creating. As he dug deeper into his own soul, laying it bare for the world to see, his life, like Huey's, descended into a personal hell of drug addiction and social disillusionment that mirrored the collapse of the heady ideals of the 1960's. For all his promise and obvious brilliance, the life of Sylvester Stewart is ultimately the story of a fall from grace. The only question is whether the fall was Sly's or ours.

# T FOR TEXAS, T FOR TENNESSEE

The story of Sly Stone begins in motion. California was the utopian state, the promised land of milk and honey where besieged southern blacks joined their white, dust-bowl cousins in migrating both during and after the Second World War. They came by the hundreds of thousands, a gritty people full of country funk, tired longing, and excess baggage. When KC and Alpha Stewart moved their family from Denton, Texas, to Vallejo, California, in the mid-1940s, they were following a trail already blazed by their extended family. It led them up the western coast to the church where Alpha's brother-in-law was pastor. Deeply religious, the Stewarts belonged to a musical tradition steeped in the homegrown gospel of the Church of Christ in God. One of the most fervent denominations of southern Baptists, to understand the Church of God is to delve into some of the deepest, darkest recesses of slavery, economic segregation, and cultural resistance. Founded in Memphis, Tennessee in the late nineteenth century, it quickly took hold in the cotton belt states of Arkansas and Mississippi. At the heart of their theological foundation was an emphasis on achieving direct access to the divine spirit through the communal and ecstatic production of *sound*. Using the holy scriptures as their guide, members of the church believed that the Holy Ghost first made its presence known to the disciples of Christ by way of the ear. As a result, creating sound became a libratory act, and they went about making noise as if not only their lives but also their very souls depended on it.

The future members of the Family Stone took from gospel an acute awareness that making music was a communal undertaking—one in which all of the members of an ensemble, whether a band, a family, or a nation, had the space, even the divine right, to express themselves openly and freely. Growing up in the Church of Christ, Sylvester, or "Syl" as he was then known, learned to approach sound as an extension of prayer. It was the affirmation of the here and now transcended; an active, tangible demonstration of faith and commitment that understood emancipation as an intensely personal, spiritual and, implicitly political enterprise. The production of sound was the holy communion and the living testament wrapped into one; and following this doctrine, the Stewarts made sound whenever they could, wherever they could, with whatever they could. The religion was full of endorphins and probed the boundaries of faith to its very edges. Idealistic and utopian, joyful, hurt and passionate, it was fiercely uncompromising when it came to the sins of this world. Instead of tolerating sin, adherents attempted to leap over and beyond the moral limitations of the flesh with an heroic, and at times even frightening, display of faith and devotion.

All of the Stewart children—Loretta, Sylvester, Rose, Freddie, and Vaetta—were surrounded by music from before the time they could speak, and by grade school, all of them could play some kind of instrument. When they weren't at home, the kids were either in school or playing straight-ahead gospel behind their uncle during services or at festivals and church functions from Berkeley and San Francisco to Stockton, Bakersfield, and even as far south as Texas. Their father, KC, who grew up listening to Roy Clark and the sounds of Tennessee's Grand Ole Opry, played the washboard and the washtub bass; their mother, Alpha, directed the church choir. Although they were all talented, it soon became clear that Syl, the Stewarts' second child, precocious and loud, was a prodigy when it came to making noise. By the time he was six, Syl and his brother and sisters had formed a group they called the Stewart Four. With Loretta, the eldest, at the helm, they made their first recordings, "On the Battlefield of the Lord," and "Walking in Jesus' Name," in 1952 when Syl was only eight. Although his first and most powerful instrument was his voice, by the age of eleven he had mastered the drums, bass, guitar and keyboards.

When the Stewarts arrived in California during the late forties, it was rapidly becoming home to what Dwight Eisenhower would dub "the military industrial complex." The jobs created by the Cold War and U.S. military expansionism in Southeast Asia, Latin America, and the Caribbean helped produce a new breed of middle-class blacks (the majority of them coming straight out of Texas), whose tastes were urbane and upwardly mobile. This new attitude called for a music with an edge, with an electric charge more raw and urgent than the acoustic country blues and organic gospel of the south. The new sound, called rhythm and blues, quickly became the front line of racial and economic integration. It was made by families like the Stewarts as well as dichotomies like Johnny Otis, the son of Greek immigrant parents who, although genetically white, was for all intents and purposes considered to be black by those around him. Born in Vallejo where the Stewarts moved after leaving Texas, Otis eventually married a black woman and became one of the premier producers of the new West Coast sound, helping launch the careers of such black rhythm and blues giants as Etta James, Esther Phillips, and Willie Mae "Big Mamma" Thornton, and popular doo-wop singing groups like the Coasters. These were the sounds that the young Sylvester Stewart began to assimilate with a passion after the family moved north.

Even as black musicians were secularizing gospel throughout the 1940s and 1950s, unrepentant southern Baptists were themselves beginning to stray beyond the sacred confines of the church to branch out into the secular, political domain of civil rights. With Martin Luther King, Jr. and the Southern Christian Leadership Conference at the helm, their rallying cry was constitutional reform and integration. Syl (ten years old when the supreme court ruled, in 1954, that school segregation was unconstitutional), Rose, and Freddie, belonged to the first generation of legally integrated blacks. Although KC and Alpha Stewart managed to nurture their children's spiritual development by immersing them in the church, they had little control over what happened when they left its domain and entered the mixed-race schools of Vallejo. Apartheid still reigned in the labor and housing markets, but in the entertainment business (on the performing end of the industry at least), within the school systems, and, increasingly, within the youth subcultures on the margins of society, the walls of racial division were beginning to show signs of wear and tear.

## BEHIND ENEMY LINES

By the late 50s record and movie companies were discovering the "young money" of the baby boom and in the process opening up new opportunities for black entertainers. With years of musical experience firmly under his belt, Sylvester Stewart quickly took Vallejo High School and the Bay Area by storm, managing to turn both his blackness (a commodity that was increasingly being consumed by "hip" white youth) and his musical genius into cultural and financial capital. With the money and independence he earned playing in a series of Top Forty doo-wop cover bands, he moved away from the moral restrictions of the church: He joined a small-time gang called the Cherrybusters, drove around in a car he nicknamed "Booty-green," and, by his sophomore year, was singing lead vocals with one of the Bay Area's most popular groups, the Viscaynes; an interracial sextet with a strong following on San Francisco's budding music scene. This is when Syl Stewart began to transform into Sly. Aside from Syl, the Viscaynes consisted of two clean-cut, middle-class white guys, a light-skinned Filipino, and two angelic-looking white girls. A prototype for the racial and gendered formula he would later use to assemble the Family Stone (the pieces of which were already coming together), their sound and image were as pure, clean-cut, and all-American as apple pie. Weaving clean, intricate vocal harmonies around standard Top-Forty classics, the boys dressed in immaculate white suits with black ties while the girls cooed in wide dresses that left everything to the imagination. In contrast to his later, flamboyant image, Cynthia Robinson, who first met Sly on the northern California church circuit, remembers the Sylvester Stewart of the late '50s and early '60s as being "observant, very quiet, mannerful and re-spectful." At any rate, his wholesome, unthreatening aura certainly helped allay any reservations his predominantly white audience might have had about his presence on stage with two young white girls in 1959. The Vis-caynes' relative success in the Bay Area taught Sly important lessons about the cultural and technical mechanics of the music business; in particular the potential cross-over market for integration.

When the group went into the studio to cut their first (and last) single, "Yellow Moon," they called in local session musician Jerry Martini, a white saxophonist whose main gig was playing with the rock and roll band Joey Piazza and the Continentals. Miles away from the gospel Sly was raised on, "Yellow Moon" was standard-fare, sentimental doo-wop. Openly commercial, it was aimed directly at the budding hormones of a pimply-faced, teenage, and primarily white audience. Although it never even came close to cracking the charts, it nevertheless displayed Sly's talent as an arranger, a skill he first learned interacting with the choir and other members of the Church of Christ. Using the song as a demo, Sly managed to work himself into the good graces of Tom Donahue and Bob Mitchell, two pioneers of free-form radio at San Francisco's number one Top Forty station KYA. Donahue and Mitchell were just beginning to promote live shows around the Bay Area, bringing in famous and semifamous acts like Chubby Checker and Bobby Freeman—a local star who had scored a national hit in 1957 with the song "Do You Want to Dance." More important to the evolution of Sly's career and future sound, however, was the fact that Donahue and Mitchell were opening up their own label: Autumn Records. Ignorant of the production process but impressed by his energy and creative talent, they took a leap of faith and hired Sly, then just eighteen years old, to be Autumn's in-house producer and A&R man.

From this point on, things began to move fast for Sly. Over the next two and a half years, Autumn Records became his personal playground, and he dedicated himself to producing commercial music designed almost exclusively to crack the *Billboard* charts. Autumn's target audience was the new generation of "liberated" white youth, and Sly formed his studio aesthetic working with mop-topped West Coast bands that attempted to express their increasing social discontent by mimicking the styles of the British Invasion that saturated commercial radio after the arrival of trans-Atlantic bands like the Beatles, Herman's Hermits, and Rolling Stones—all groups who were, themselves, trying their best to copy the musical culture Sly had been raised on since birth. In 1964 Sly struck gold by producing, cowriting, and playing various instruments on Bobby Freeman's comeback hit, "C'mon and Swim," a novelty track that made it to number 5 on the national charts, joining acts like Little Eva and the Isley Brothers in riding the teeny-bopper dance craze of the late fifties and early sixties. Sly followed up this success a year later by producing and arranging the more sophisticated Beau Brummels' hits "Laugh, Laugh" and "Just a Little." With these gold records under his belt, Sly became a certified local celebrity. In addition to producing for Autumn, he kept in the public eye as a quick-tongued MC for Donahue and Mitchell's live Bay Area shows. Despite his success, his own career as a performing artist and songwriter remained stalled. While Bobby Freeman was doing the "Swim" on the California coast surrounded by a small harem of young, blond, and bikini-clad white girls, Sly kept busy perfecting his own sound, using his access to the Autumn studios to cut a series of tracks with his sister Rose, brother Freddie, and talented young West Coast musicians like Billy Preston, a fellow Texan who shared the Stewarts' gospel roots. In these unsuccessful and often unfinished projects, Sly can be heard attempted to reconcile the untamed gospel of his youth with the more rigid commercial demands of surfer music, dance tunes, and doo-wop.

Despite Autumn's ability to hit the charts with Sly's help, by 1965, Donahue and Mitchell were losing both money and control of the studio. In a sign of the industry consolidation that was already transforming the music industry (and with it the creative options available to new artists), they sold the legal rights of Autumn Records to Warner Brothers—today the largest global media conglomerate in the world. In the restructuring that followed, Sly was forced from his position at Autumn and, now 21, he moved on to the microphones of San Francisco's KSOL (K-Soul), where he followed the footsteps of his mentors in expanding the cultural boundaries of commercial free-form radio. Changing the station's strict "race" format by mixing white acts like Bob Dylan, the Beatles, and Lord Buckley into his rotation, he effectively altered the Bay Area's aural, racial, and cultural landscape. A fast talker, with a quick wit and sharp sense of humor, the key to Sly's popularity rested on his ability to maneuver between the black and white communities. Throughout the early to mid-60s, when he wasn't in the recording studio or on the air of KSOL, Sly was saturating himself in the Bay Area's underground live music scene. Cruising between inner-city and suburban clubs until the late hours of the morning, hanging with friends like Hamp "Bubba" Banks (a motorcycle-riding pimp and ex-con who eventually married his sister Rose), Sly eventually crossed paths with Larry Graham and Gregg Errico with whom he formed a string of bands, such as The Stoners, that by 1967 had consolidated into what became known as Sly and the Family Stone. Ditching the conservative safety of his earlier teeny-bopper style, during this period he increasingly pushed the envelope of his public image, splitting the difference between the black inner-city and the white suburbs with a deft combination of tough-guy street smarts, hard, soulful music, and freaky, psychedelic clothes rummaged from local secondhand stores. This was the climate in which Sly and the Family Stone gelled their sound, and by the time David Kapralik, a self-described "middle-class Jewish Prince," came flying in from New York to sign them with Epic Records, they were busy tearing up the club scene at Oakland's Winchester Cathedral by reworking Wilson Pickett, James Brown, and Ray Charles covers with Sly's energetic and creative vocal and horn arrangements.

## IF YOU WANT ME TO STAY

1967 might have been the "summer of love" in Haight-Ashbury, but in Detroit, East Oakland, Newark, Atlanta, Cincinnati, and nearly 150 other cities and towns across the nation, there was literally blood in the streets. And it was no "simulacra," that's for sure. No mere impression, reproduction, or mirror of reality; it was the real thing, like Coke. In the summer of 1967 Motown was burning. It was the year of Black Power, Stokley Carmichael, H. Rap Brown and SNCC. It was the year that President Johnson declared his intention to deploy over half a million troops to Vietnam, and it was the year that Sly and the Family Stone dropped their first album, *Whole New Thing*. As visually captivating as they were culturally and musically diverse, they entered the national stage with all of the confidence, energy, and moral authority they could muster.

The album was, in truth, less a *whole* new thing than it was a deftly arranged panorama of the group's influences up to that point. It combined the psychedelic feel of San Francisco bands like the Jefferson Airplane with the smooth harmonic melodies of the Fifth Dimension and the clean, straight-ahead productions of Motown. The album threw in the raw, stripped-down proto-funk of James Brown, with the bluesy soul of Ray Charles, and the emotional intensity of Otis Redding and Stax. But on their first effort Sly and the Family Stone were, for the most part, still following the trends established by others. Jimi Hendrix was already making far more individual and creative headways into the white crossover audience that Sly coveted, and in the process creating a bold aesthetic that transformed not only how the guitar was understood, but also managed to challenge the very legacy of the blues, soul, R&B, and rock traditions. Similarly, the year that *Whole New Thing* was released, James Brown dropped his breakthrough "Cold Sweat," an album that pioneered the syncopated arrangements and chicken-scratch rhythm guitar work already being adopted by Sly's brother Freddie. Despite its lack of conceptual unity and lacking the synthesis of styles that would make Sly and the Family Stone a household name within a year, there were positive signs of things to come. Cynthia Robinson (with all of the attitude and cool sexuality of Pam Grier) and Jerry Martini (one of the hippest white boys in the Bay Area) were already in top shape, using their horns to create the Family Stone's trademark punchy rhythms and syncopated, contrapuntal textures; former guitar player Larry Graham's bass (whose thumb-slapping technique would help spark the low-end groove of psychedelic funk and inspire an entire generation of sweaty, recession-era dance music) was right where it should be, on time and driving the hooks; and although struggling on the faster tunes, drummer Gregg Errico managed to stray from his rock and roll roots long enough to hold his own with energy and a back beat with drive. Behind it all, of course, was Sly working as arranger, writer, and producer. Like all of the group's albums that would follow, *Whole New Thing* was his brain child. A grab-bag of diversity that defied easy classification, other than gaining the respect of a handful of musicians and producers, the album completely failed as a commercial venture.

When Sly and the Family Stone hit the scene in 1967, Motown and Stax (based in Memphis, Tennessee) were firmly in control of the charts. The yin and yang of black commercial radio, both labels had been setting the pace of the nation's airwaves for years with a formula that relied on a sound buffered around the edges and ultimately devoid of any explicit challenge to the stability of America's corporate order. The spectacle of the Detroit riots exploding on Motown's front doorstep—inflicting over $32 million in property damage over a six-day period and leaving forty-four people dead and hundreds more injured, a blow the city still hasn't recovered from—only reaffirmed the distance between their slick, upbeat product and the harsher realities of black daily life. Stax, meanwhile, whose artists were pushing the envelope of assertive blackness with a rawer and more sexually powered brand of soul than anything coming out of Motown, was embroiled in contract disputes with its parent company, Atlantic, and in December Otis Redding, the label's top-selling artist and most promising star, died in a plane crash while at the height of his career. The rich, understated breakthrough sound of Isaac Hayes's *Hot Buttered Soul* was still in the future. The turmoil of the summer of '67 posed a direct challenge to the musical establishment by accenting the growing limitations of music and popular culture more generally to effect, if not articulate, a meaningful antiestablishment politics that reflected the spirit of the majority of its (black) listeners. Both Motown and Stax had effectively regimented their sound and reduced the joyful spontaneity and depth of feeling of the black experience to a formulaic, if still enjoyable, racial showcase for popular consumption. The cornerstone of Sly's genius—a genius that was just beginning to be felt on *Whole New Thing* but that would slowly blossom over the band's next two albums, *Dance to the Music* and *Life* and peak with the 1969 classic *Stand!*—was his ability to organize the untamed elements that were seeping out as alternatives to these commercial sounds into a product that was commodifiable without losing its rugged honesty and emotional integrity.

Sly's tendency to portray social ostracism as an effect of personal lifestyle choices rather than racial oppression continued to be highlighted on the Family Stone's next three albums. Adapting to the commercial failure of *Whole New Thing,* Sly went back to work, simplifying both his message (which, although certainly subtle, had tentatively wandered into the realm of social commentary on the first album with songs like "Underdog" and "Run, Run, Run"). With this formula the Family Stone finally struck gold and captured the attention of a national audience with the anthemic title track of their next album *Dance to the Music.* They quickly followed up this success with the single "Everyday People," a song that finally took Sly and the Family Stone all the way to number one on the *Billboard* charts. Both tunes were perfect showcases for the band's gospel roots and phenomenal musical chemistry. With his first wave of albums and hit singles Sly didn't advocate much more than dancing, the importance of interracial harmony, and the power of the individual to persevere in the face of adversity. Even as the nation was being ripped apart by racial strife, he shied away from advocating any form of direct political action in his music. Instead, he focused his energy on consolidating the emotional impulses and structural unity of popular music and infused it with a passion and sincerity that, unlike the crossover formulas of his R&B and rock contemporaries, managed to *imply,* at least, a deeper political urgency.

Two songs from the Family Stone's first period, which began with *Whole New Thing,* lasted through 1969's *Stand!* and ended once and for all with the release of the breakthrough 1971 album *There's a Riot Goin' On,* revealed Sly's political sentiments toward black liberation and the racial upheavals of the time. The first was "Don't Burn Baby" from 1967's *Dance to the Music,* in which he cautioned inner-city blacks (and, indirectly satisfied the political anxieties of his white consumer base) not to ". . . burn, baby, burn/just learn, baby, learn/so you can earn, baby, earn." It was a naïve morality at the polar extreme of the equally naïve black nationalist call to armed insurrection. The message, though heartfelt, relied on a belief in social uplift through hard work (labor) and self-sacrifice that came straight out of the socially conservative (and ultimately Protestant based) lessons he had learned in the black church. Far from rocking any boats, the song was a homage to the unifying power of music, not direct political action, as an agent for social and personal change. Unlike the pop music coming out of Motown and Stax, and more akin to the work being produced by James Brown and Jimi Hendrix, whose hard-edged, metallic sounds Sly was beginning to adopt in order to evoke the personal demons that were increasingly haunting him, his songs managed to reach beyond the narrow confines of romance and, even if they didn't call for outright revolution, reflected and addressed the angst of larger social struggles.

Remaining on the charts for over two years and selling more than 2 million copies, the release of 1969's *Stand!,* along with the group's performance at the Woodstock festival that summer, where their 3:00 A.M. performance was considered by many to be the high point of the event, solidified the band's reputation. Sandwiched on the album between the more optimistic and celebratory songs "Stand!" and "I Want to Take You Higher," both of which earned heavy radio rotation, "Don't Call Me Nigger, Whitey/Don't Call Me Whitey, Nigger," attempted to express the anxiety Sly had experienced over the past decade living on the middle ground of social identity: a space that was becoming more untenable as American society was splitting into two armed and hostile camps. With the feel of a New Orleans funeral dirge, the song used Jerry and Cynthia's horns and Freddie's wah-wah pedal to create a dark effect, producing a hard-edge that marked Sly's growing isolation from both his own band and the world around him. It reflected the "twilight zone" of the middle ground that, ironically, Sly shared with his fellow Bay Area alumni Huey Newton. If songs from *Stand!* such as "Don't Call Me Whitey" and the esoteric, trippy, instrumental, and eclectic landmark funk song "Sex Machine" reflected the band's growing musical and philosophical maturity, it also presaged the profound disillusionment and alienation that would lead to their, and in particular Sly's, "fall." As it turned out, both *Stand!* and Woodstock were, quite literally, the Family Stone's "last stand" as a cohesive working unit. At the dawning of the Age of Aquarius, Huey Newton sat locked in a California state prison convicted of voluntary manslaughter in the death of an Oakland police officer and Sly, for his part, began to serve a self-imposed exile that marked a rapid retreat from the optimistic spirit of collectivity and family unity that had been the hallmark of his sound. Disenchanted activists from SNCC and the Black Panthers were expelling white members and calling for "a united black front" against the dominant, mainstream American culture, while Sly locked himself into an increasingly private zone of introspection and musical autonomy.

The trajectory of Sly's retreat can, perhaps, be heard best in the lines from *Stand!,* in which he poses the question, ostensibly to a weary underdog like himself, "Don't you know that you are free?" and answers his own question with the doubting reply, "Well at least in your mind, if you want to be." Saturated with the trappings of fame—money, cars, drugs, women, aggressive managers, and bureaucratic, corporate watchdogs— the journey toward spiritual fulfillment and rapture that had begun in the Church of Christ gradually retreated from the euphoria of ecstatic musical production to a far more tentative, if not "sober," internal search for meaning. After the release and success of *Stand!,* Sly's behavior became more eccentric. He regularly failed to appear for concerts and interviews, choosing instead the private domain of his Bel Air mansion. Filling himself with drugs and living, at one count, with twenty-eight dogs who roamed around the estate freely, attacked and menaced strangers, and left their shit scattered about on the floors, carpets and lawn, he lived in the dark, withdrew from the outside world and became increasingly violent and abusive toward those he had once nurtured as his "family"—including his still devoted crossover audience. Despite the band's gradual disintegration, however, they exited the sixties with a mainstream crossover audience that would keep their work, no matter how personal and antiestablishment, in the public eye for the next three years.

Sly had been getting high on one drug or another at least since his days at Autumn Records, but probably even before that. According to Jerry Martini and others, they were usually "harmless" drugs, like reefer or alcohol. But by the *Stand!* album he was already, like almost everyone else in the band including their manager and producer David Kapralik, heavily addicted to the demonic angel cocaine. In addition to the coke he was taking massive amounts of angel dust, speed, and a host of prescription drugs too numerous to mention. The end result was that Sly mortgaged away not only his own financial future, but that of the Family Stone as well. With Kapralik unable (or unwilling) to protect his interests, he signed front-loaded contracts that turned over the rights to his music, and eventually the group's master tapes to record companies and opportunistic managers. By 1973, Sly was broke.

For a while, it seemed that Sly's addiction only added fuel to his genius. We can hear his personal struggles on the single that is, arguably, Sly's most important, "Thank You (Falettinme Be Mice Elf Agin)." Although the song has been interpreted as everything from a recollection of his days in a small-time gang at Vallejo High School to an argument with a lover, it is, in truth, a brilliant musical and lyrical exposition of the effects of a free-base cocaine high mingled with the rising doubts and contradictions he was having about his mission as a cultural unifier and rock star. His struggle with the demons of drug addiction also provided the tension behind the eclectic, ethereal masterpiece *There's a Riot Going On,* in which Sly breaks every expectation his audience (and record company) might have had for his or anyone else's music from the time. Throwing the rule book out the window, he managed to harness the chaos of his fall to rewrite the palette of psychedelic funk, rock, and soul.

On *Riot,* Sly's genius takes a solipsistic and brooding turn. Instead of the upbeat, optimistic music the public had been used to from the Family Stone, he takes the listener on an inward voyage that explores the deepest pockets of his troubled psyche. Retreating from his earlier, controlled experiments in the studio, he began to record many of the tracks alone or by pulling random strangers off the street. Instead of the organic, live exchange that had marked the earlier albums, he began using drum machines and replacing members of the Family Stone (whom he had, by this time almost completely alienated) with musicians like Bobby Womack, whose guitar and arrangements help give *Riot* its hauntingly original sound. After making Epic wait two years for *Riot,* he made them wait another two years before following that success up with 1973's *Fresh. Fresh* produced Sly's last hit, "If You Want Me to Stay." Although it was a compelling album that showed off his genius and remains a classic to this day, it was a disappointment when measured against the creative breakthroughs he had achieved with *There's a Riot Goin On. Fresh* was the last of Sly's commercial successes. As the legacy of hard-edged funk made way for the more regimented commercial sounds of disco, Sly continued to struggle with his personal demons. In the seventies he released a series of truly mediocre albums and shuttled between the hardships of jail, debt, and mental illness. Whatever role drugs might have played in ending Sly's brilliant and all-too brief career, we cannot ignore the fact that his addiction was at least in part a response to his inability to resolve the bipolar schizophrenia not only of his own mind, but also of American society. In the end, Sly was a believer whose faith was shattered.

In 1970, Huey Newton was asked if he blamed Richard Nixon for his imprisonment and the persecution of the Black Panther Party. His answer was no. Instead, he said he placed blame directly on the 76 major corporations who were pulling the strings behind Nixon. In addition to a personal tragedy, the story of Sylvester Stewart must also be seen as mired in the contradictions of a corporate-sponsored declaration of independence; a paternalistic corporate liberty whose class lines continue to be distributed along racial lines. In the end, Sly fell victim to his own idealism and belief in the collective spectacle of music in which he had invested so much hope. Far from empowering him, the spectacle and promise of Sly and the Family Stone became a Gordian Knot that neither he, the band, nor his audience could untie or cut. His fall was, perhaps, the final gasp of America's dying dreams; one of the last hopes of a country that actually believed it could survive the drop cloth of commodification in order to enact meaningful and lasting social change—that it could actually harness the corporate musical culture to light the way toward freedom instead of slavery. If today we are still able to hear the legacy of Huey Newton and the Panthers in the calls to revolution of radical hip-hop groups like the Bay Area's Coup and New York's Dead Prez, it would be hard to imagine either's sound, or the politically nuanced southern psycho-funkadelic hip-hop of Outkast for that matter, without the musical legacy of Sly Stone.

As their dream of social justice and militant self-determination faded into the recession-plagued pessimism of the seventies, my parents settled into middle-class careers. I inherited their album collection. Choose your poison.

## NOTE

1. "On the Defection of Eldridge Cleaver from the Black Panther Party and the Defection of the Black Panther Party from the Black Community, April 17, 1971." Reprinted in *To Die For The People: The Writings of Huey P. Newton,* edited by Toni Morrison (New York: Writers and Readers Publishing, Inc, 1995).

 # BLUES FOR
## BETTY DAVIS'S
# SMILE:
## THE BETTY DAVIS
# LACUNA

The Pennsylvania woman who now has the last known telephone number of the 1970s futuristic, fire-spitting funkster Betty Davis returned my call from a hospital—an appropriately ominous locale, considering that no one in the general media/musical round seemed to know where Betty had vanished to. Registered letters were returned to sender. Word had it that the singer had reverted to her maiden name, Betty Mabry; but that moniker meant as little to the phone number's bemused inheritor as Betty's marital and stage name of Davis, relic of her short-lived, fiery marriage to jazz creator Miles Davis (1968–69; she was twenty-three, he forty-eight). La Davis's legend is marked by a particular composition on *They Say I'm Different* that was generally taken to refer to their complex relationship: "He was a big freak, I used to beat him with a turquoise chain."

Evidently Betty, the sizzling young model about town, was Miles's muse. Her beauty adorns the sleeve of Davis's *Les Filles du Kilimanjaro* and its haunting "Mademoiselle Mabry." She is saluted again on a later track, "Back Seat Betty," long after their split. Young enough to be his daughter, she had already scored a writing credit on the Chambers Brothers' *Uptown*. Betty wasn't in her native Pittsburgh anymore. A hip scene-maker, she plugged Pops into a new generation of her super-freak pals like Sly Stone and Jimi Hendrix, briskly vetted and edited his wardrobe of suits, and generally loosened up and remodeled the maestro. The result: Miles's watershed album, *Bitches Brew* (1970), wherein Miles internalizes the vibes of his trophy wife's crowd, all the young dudes like Jimi and Sly. Whether it was her extra-intimate rapport with Hendrix that caused the rift or not, it took just one year for Miles to decide, as he explained to his biographer Quincy Troupe, that "Betty was too young and wild for the things I expected of a woman. Betty was a free spirit, she was raunchy, all that kind of shit."

What manner of superwoman is this, to out-freak the notorious Master of Cool?

How deep is a footnote?

Only the most ardent funksters of the early twenty-first century recognize Betty Davis now, in the 2000s that she used to invent, way back in the 1970s. Thrashing dildo swingers in Williamsburg electroclash combos attempt to emulate (maybe without knowing it) her space princess clothes; few attempt her audio recipe of squealing, screeching, punky/funky vocalizing, riding that jazzy funk itching to be free, though Macy Gray's vocals can be said to swing like Betty's baton. Cognoscenti including Labelle's manager and co-creator, Vicki Wickham, thought Davis might be in Paris; writer Tom Terrell, who'd fantasized about her since he was a school kid in Washington, D.C.—always a hotbed of Betty fanaticism—wondered if her life had devolved into a long round of rehab. Or, it was said Betty Davis was dead. If so, does Betty Mabry still walk among us? There's no evidence for any of it, really; only Betty Davis was deemed wild enough for anything to be possible. Anything at all. But some way or other, somewhere, somehow, the general feeling seemed to be that surely Betty Davis had been tamed by now.

Or has she? Looking for Betty Davis was an almost uncomfortable process, because while people who'd never met her were wondering about her whereabouts and mental state, I was haunted by the question: What stopped Betty Davis's smile?

While waiting for feedback from various sources, the practical level of my quest ended when I came across and article by journalist James Maycock, who had actually tracked down the elusive Davis. "Poignantly, her career stalled when her fun, mischievous spirit was overcome by chronic depression following her father's death in the late 1970s," he wrote in the British newspaper the *Telegraph*. "Today one senses she lives a quieter life in Pennsylvania, although she's still passionate about music."

Still passionate. That was a relief. But her absence from the scene, with zero visibility for that smile, was still a loss that I felt. Unlike most of the others who'd been helping in my search, I actually knew Betty, briefly, back when her career was still careening to its destination. A surprisingly undiva-like presence, the sunny young singer's sweetness and dimples charmed the Island PR office where, fresh out of Warwick University in 1975, I was promoting the then-little-known Bob Marley, Burning Spear, Aswad, and *Nasty Gal*, Davis's third album. I remember Betty shrieking and panting, strutting and grinding, on the small stage of Ronnie Scott's jazz club; and her silver outfit, a curious amalgam of mid-twentieth-century futurism and eighteenth-century music hall "pantomime boys" (really, girls in drag). The business with the turquoise whip for her signature tune, "He Was a Big Freak," went down well. With each slash, Davis struck something deep in the British psyche; regular public school beatings of the junior elite were, after all, part of what made the British Empire great.

At the round table of the press office, there was much excitement about the audacious, charming Miss Davis. She graciously signed the shiny white jacket of a *Nasty Gal* test pressing for me, with a fat felt-tip; her signature was looped like a daisy with a butterfly for the dot on the "I." There were no press pictures, so I ordered a photo shoot and had her sassiest, sweetest, most juicy smile printed up as black-and-white eight-by-ten glossies. Her afro rippled round her dimples like a candy-floss halo. Proudly I pulled open the box for her manager. To all of our amazement, he dramatically ripped one up. "Destroy them," he urged. "Lose the negs." "B-b-ut look at that great smile," I stuttered. "That's the problem," he insisted. "She looks too nice. Betty has to look mean."

He watched me jettison the photos—though somewhere in a storage a couple of rogue pics may still lurk, obstinately chronicling her lethal blend of blithe innocence, carnality, and dark wit. It was offensive, his disbelief that a smiling young woman could shout and sweat hardcore funk to her bones. In a cocksure, muscular music, for Davis to be authentic and accepted, glowering was apparently compulsory. But after all, when Davis whipped Miles, if that was indeed the case, he'd no doubt asked for it. And by the sound of it, enjoyed the whole process.

I felt bleak as I systematically worked through two hundred eight-by-tens, like I was destroying the image of one of her most potent aspects as an artist—and as a female. Her smile was an invitation, and also a tool, and if necessary, a weapon in her defense. But that was all invisible to her manager, who reckoned she—we—couldn't smile and be wild. Playing the savage beast card had become part of Betty's M.O. by now; though really, she hadn't been all that animal or even outrageously wild. She just sang, vibrantly, what many a female feels on a Friday night, and done, exuberantly, what came naturally, her lust for life unrestrained by the girdle of anyone's expectations.

But there it was, her passion for being had to be characterized as angry and wild. She had to be *l'enfant sauvage*. Or she wasn't allowed to be free. Was her stirring of deep psychosexual fantasies less effective if she was smiling, not snarling? Personally it seemed to me that a slap would have no less stinging if delivered with Betty's sunny grin.

Those flying fragments of Betty's beaming photos fluttered into my mind some ten years later, as I rattled down fourteen floors in an elevator in an old building in Manhattan's Union Square, from the loft of singer Grace Jones's Svengali and husband, visual visionary Jean-Paul Goude. Wearing an electric blue lamé hot-pant one-piece, Jones huddled against the wall sobbing all the way down. Some months after doing Davis's P.R., I'd become a full-time writer, and I was now on assignment for London's *Harpers & Queen,* covering Jones's glamorous life with Goude. She, too, was a great man's muse. Goude's indelible, iconic interpretations of her lean, gleaming ebony torso summoned the panther in her, and the gazelle; the Giacometti and the Benin mask. Above all, she exuded the Amazon energy that would later serve her well as the deadly nemesis in action flicks. Given her impermeable image, I was slightly surprised by Jones's volcanic freak-out. Her lack of inhibition in front of an unknown writer was alarming, but also disarming.

Of course, Jones was the co-conspirator of her own image manipulation: ringing endless variations on Sheena the Jungle Woman. A champion national long-distance runner in her teenage years in Jamaica, Jones was as athletic as the big cats she channeled. Any warm-blooded mammal would have been partial to that snarl of hers.

But though Grace was able to work and cash in on that leopard-spotted persona for years to come, I never forgot her in that elevator, moaning between deep sobs, "He only wants me to be an animal!"

Meaning being that she just wanted, at least every now and then, to be wild—with a smile. Because it wasn't being mad, or bad, being wild. It just felt free.

Which brings us back to Betty.

As slender as her petite yet sturdy frame, Davis's recorded output consists of just four albums: *Betty Davis* (1973), *They Say I'm Different* (1974), *Nasty Gal* (1975), and *Crashin' From Passion/Hangin' Out In Hollywood* (1995/6; rec. 1979). The first two, in particular, are blazing entries from the psychological subtext of a free-spirited female, born in 1945, riding high out of the 1960s decade of the Pill and free love, into the infinite possibilities of the 1970s—before the actual costs had come in and been counted, with the shock of herpes, then AIDS, in the early 1980s. It was in that brief window—post-Pill, pre-AIDS—that girls generally began to claim the right to be as wild as the boys, to wo/manhandle love where they found it, at their own (in)discretion. "I start to wiggle my fanny . . . if I'm in luck I might just get picked up. . . . Take me home with you, say you will, say you will, baby. . . ." Though sensitive, these women were tough enough to handle rejection and choose solitude rather than half-arsed compromise: "Tonight I wish I had someone beside me but in the meantime I'll make do with what I have."

Davis represented a break from all the singers who came before her. She was no big, grieving blues Mama, like Bessie Smith, nor a tragic goddess like Billie Holiday. Equally, she wasn't an elegantly gowned church lady, like Aretha Franklin. Even her closest archetype, the rockin' Miss Tina Turner, that perennial hot chick, didn't dabble in Davis's outré extremism. Perhaps only Labelle, glittering in their own galactic silver, with their sexed-up songs like "Going Down (Makes Me Shiver)," matched her in voracious, untrameled life energy on their records; and there were three of them. Betty was solo. Perhaps too solo.

Says Labelle's Nona Hendryx, who still travels with Betty Davis music in her headphones, "We had a strong black following, from the Apollo; Labelle had a community. Betty didn't, because she came right out of the box, fully formed."

You can hear courage in the way Davis worked her vocal register—ratcheting her pretty alto into a drilling, grating vibrato and an off-the-meter soprano screech—suggesting a woman pushing herself to extremes, testing her mental and physical endurance, refusing to accept limits. "Game Is My Middle Name," she boldly announced; and Davis sure did know how to play with the big boys. In her prime, she was backed by musicians who were the architects of the full-blooded, grinding West Coast 1970s funk, a music unafraid of intensity and the surreal. The elite sidemen from Sly Stone's band, Gregg Errico and Larry Graham (the latter would later join forces with Davis' natural heir, Prince); Santana's Michael Carabello; the Pointer Sisters, and a sprinkling of Tower of Power members. They all supported Betty as she riffled through the deck of superwoman archetypes and added a few more bad cards: Swathed in gold, she was one sexy Egyptian mummy; poised for flight in silver, she was a space age huntress, Davis as the goddess Diana.

Davis's musical reputation is primarily based on her eponymous debut and its successor, *They Say I'm Different*. There she paraded the brutal realism of her take on love on tracks like "Anti Love Song": "'Cause I know you could possess my body . . . I know you could have me shaking. . . . That's why I don't want to love you . . . 'Cause you know I could possess your body too." But during the *Nasty Gal* period in which I threw away Betty Davis's smile, her songs began to be obsessed with stating and reasserting her position. It was as if she had succumbed and adopted tabloid values, agreeing that by virtue of being exuberant, sexual and con-frontational, she was not just lusty, but "shocking," "outrageous"; and that her success depended on it. On her next and to-date final release, *Crashin' from Passion,* aka *Hangin' Out in Hollywood,* she experimented with more conventional pop/dance forms that didn't play to her strengths, like the mutant aspects of her shape-shifting singing.

Throughout this search for Betty Davis's smile, there is the nagging sense that she was a woman without a context. Her shows were banned by religious groups in certain American towns and many of her catchier tracks were too specifically sexual for radio. So many young lions are chewed up and spat out by the music business's greedily grinding maw; what does one silver space-suited lioness matter? But a large lacuna has been left by the absence of Betty's forceful, raspy-voiced, strong-thighed, sassy spirit.

The outrageousness of rap artists like L'il Kim seems closest to Davis's template; but their infinite varieties of fetish gear suggest a specific, cal-culated correlation between flesh showed and money earned, pandering to male/femme fantasies, aiming to please to squeeze a few dollars more. But when Betty sings that people think she's different, she's not talking about her barely there outfits. She just likes to wear them and look good. Instead, she boldly claims her place as a daughter of the blues and refer-ences Bessie and Leadbelly, not Gucci and Pucci.

To quote Betty herself—Don't call her no tramp, no skeezer. And so, don't call Betty no ho.

# KANDIA CRAZY HORSE

# INTERVIEW WITH
# VENETTA
# FIELDS

**V**enetta Fields, a former Ikette and a member of both female vocal combos the Blackberries and classic rock outfit Humble Pie, is a rock 'n' roll pioneer in her own right. From an early 1960s recording with the Ikettes to the 2000 release of her solo debut *At Last* (Drum

Lake), Fields's inimitable soulful sound has indelibly shaped our sonic space. Assembling her remembrances at home in Australia, Fields breaks down the role of the black woman in rock for her humble fan, Kandia Crazy Horse.

## BEGINNINGS

KANDIA CRAZY HORSE: Please tell us a bit about your background.

VENETTA FIELDS: I was born in Buffalo, New York. My mother and father were both gospel singers in different groups. I used to get out of bed when my mother's group was rehearsing at my house and watch them sing. My mother was saved, and we went to church often. We lived with my uncle and aunt, and my uncle was a preacher and had a church first in Oakfield, New York, then built one in Rochester. I went to church a lot and sang with many choirs and groups throughout my childhood. I remember singing solo at first, then sang with a girlfriend named Joan Austin. From there I joined another church, and the choir director put me in the choir and a group called the Templeaires. I was the youngest member. I also started playing piano and directing a few choirs around town. I directed one choir on the first and third Sundays and another choir on the second and fourth Sundays. I also sang with a 100-voice choir from a Baptist church as well. Just before the end of high school I joined another group called the Corinthian Gospel singers and was with them until I left one night with Ike and Tina Turner and never looked back. I was also very active in my school and always sang for assembly and other things.

KCH: Did you always want to be a singer and aspire to get involved with the music business?

FIELDS: I never thought I would be doing what I have done. I wanted to be a hairdresser, because that was all there was at the time to aspire to. The churches frowned on singers that would sing songs other than gospel so that was not in my mind.

KCH: How specifically did you get started in the music business?

FIELDS: I was a hairdresser and would listen to the radio in the shop. There was a black station from sunup to sunset that I listened to with all the black singers. I had been listening to Ike and Tina's record called "You're Just a Fool in Love," and many other artists. Eddie O'Jay was a disc jockey and was well known around town for promoting acts as well. He came into my shop and put in some placards and gave me two tickets to Ike and Tina's show. I had never been to a dance before and asked one of my friends to go with me. I got to the skating rink and Eddie O'Jay asked me where Flora was. She was a singer in my gospel group that would sing rock and roll on the side. She was in New York at the time and I asked Eddie why he wanted her. He said that the Ikettes were looking for a new girl. I asked Eddie if I could audition for them. Eddie was surprised, because I never indicated that I could or would sing anything other than gospel. He said that he would find me at intermission and take me to the dressing room. He did and I auditioned for Ike. He gave me cab fare and told me to go home and get my clothes.

Kandia, I intend to write my own book so I won't go into too many details. I went home got my clothes and turned up back at the skating rink. We rode in a Cadillac all the way to Boston. The next night I was on stage, shakin' my tail feather!

KCH: What was the rock scene like when you were beginning? Which women were the main players?

FIELDS: During my Ike and Tina Turner days, I didn't know that backing singers existed. I was totally into the Motown sound. With the Supremes, Martha and The Vandellas, etc. Just girl groups, since I was in a girl group.

When I left Ike and Tina, I wanted to stay in L.A. That is when I discovered that singers were getting paid to do backing vocals for other acts. The Blossoms were the best singers at the time and were recording for and with a lot of groups. Soon after I met Merry Clayton and others.

KCH: Was there any particular black woman singer that influenced and/or mentored you as you started out?

FIELDS: Merry Clayton and Patrice Holloway at that time. I loved people like Etta James and Aretha Franklin even then.

KCH: Please talk about your experiences as an Ikette.

FIELDS: Working with Ike and Tina for five years was the beginning and the highlight of my career. It would take a book to explain. I'll have to talk more about that when I can think more.

KCH: What about forming the Blackberries, your deal and recording for Motown. Why was the Blackberries' album never released?

FIELDS: Sherlie Matthews was the motivator for the Blackberries. After Clydie [King] and Sherlie and I started to sing together, we seemed to create a sound of our own that was very unique. We started getting a lot of work, and after a while it was suggested that we record. Sherlie suggested the name Blackberries. We recorded an album that was produced by Sherlie and Deke Richards, who was the upcoming producer for the Jackson Five. Motown was a very political organization at that time, and everyone was vying for Berry Gordy's attention to get a release. I don't know why it did not get released in the end.

# LOS ANGELES, LONDON, AND THE CLASSIC ROCK HEYDAY

KCH: How did you enter "The Clique" and figure out how to navigate the heart of the rock business in Los Angeles?

FIELDS: There were cliques at that time. My first session, I was called by Merry Clayton, and Clydie and Sherlie and Gloria Jones and Edna Wright were there. After that first session I got calls from the other cliques to see where I would end up. Patrice Holloway was on the way out, which left an empty space and voice. Merry Clayton called me a few times. But it ended up with me Clydie and Sherlie.

KCH: Describe your experience working with Humble Pie.

FIELDS: I went to a Clairvoyant early this particular week and she told me that on that Thursday I would get a phone call that would change my life. It was a call from Dee Anthony at the time, telling me that Steve Marriott had been following my career and admired me a lot and would I get two other girls and come to London to record. I got Clydie King and Billie Barnum. It was a whirlwind experience. We worked so well recording that Steve asked us to tour North America. I had never experienced rock 'n' roll before, and it was a great experience.

KCH: What do you think attracted rockers like Steve Marriott to your style of singing and your talents as a whole?

FIELDS: I realized when we got there Steve and the other Pie members were over the moon that we were there. They couldn't do enough for us. Every time we opened our mouths and sang or made up a part and sang it, they would get so excited. I thought about it and came up with the answer. They were the ones that started me to thinking about our blackness in the rock field. That was the time when every act had to have three *black* American singers in the band. They wanted to feel and hear the blackness. They would do anything and pay anything to get it or experience it. That was also the time when James Brown released "I'm Black and I'm Proud."

KCH: What memories do you have from Pink Floyd's Dark Side of the Moon Tour?

FIELDS: That was another great experience. We were already in London with Humble Pie when Dave Gilmour asked Steve if they [the Floyd] could borrow us for a few dates in Europe. They didn't want to send for their girls from America and they had heard about us. Steve said yes, reluctantly. Dave came to our motel and brought a tape of *Dark Side of the Moon* for us to listen to. I had never heard of the Floyd before and the music sounded fun to me. There were hardly any words and they were weird except for Dave Gilmour. We also saw a performance by them to watch what the other girls were doing. I found the music to be boring and did not know what to do. Their singers would come out and sing a song, then go back off stage. And wait for another song and come back out on stage. I told my girls that when we got on stage we were not coming off. We did the two dates in Europe and got to know each other. When they were about to tour America with *Dark Side,* they asked us to tour with them. They were so kind and generous. We flew first class, had 5- and 6-star accommodation and limousines. It was the best. They had state-of-the-art equipment and lots of things that I had never seen before. "Great Gig in the Sky" was the big hit along with "Money." It was a great privilege to sing "The Great Gig in the Sky." It sounded awesome with Quadraphonic sound throughout the venue. I had never sung to such big crowds before.

KCH: Steely Dan are notoriously "difficult" and revered in rock-crit circles. What was it like to record with them?

FIELDS: Recording with Steely Dan was another big experience in my life. We had recorded almost all of their albums before I got it. I had no idea that they were going to become one of the most respected groups in the U.S. and that we would become well known because of it. Donald [Fagen] is a very meticulous person, but very kind and patient. I didn't realize what was happening until we did *Aja.* There I found out a lot of things and every thing came full circle for me and I knew that my time was over for doing backing vocals. I had sung with the best and there was no one else coming up that could give me what I had learned and experienced. The *Aja* album was the hardest for me. People had been asking me what it was like to work for Steely Dan. I was just doing session after session then and had no time to assess what I had been doing until that time. Donald would have us work on "Deacon Blues" for about three hours, send us home, call us back two weeks later, and continue. I didn't know what he was looking for, until I heard the album. That is when I found out what it was that I had been doing all those ten years and that it was time to go. He wanted us to have our own individual sound, but together. I would never learn another thing, if I stayed, it would all be redundant. I made up my mind then that it was over. Even though I was still trying to get work and even though the record industry was rapidly changing.

KCH: Performing in *A Star Is Born* and working with Barbra Streisand must have been a high point of your career.

FIELDS: Early in January 1976, I got a call from a contractor for an audition for *A Star Is Born.* As I answered the phone I said to myself, This call is going to change my life again! Since it was early in the New Year, we think in terms of resolutions—that is why I thought about it. I went to the audition and all the girls were there. We waited for a while for Barbra. When she came through the door, she spotted me and Clydie. She walked up to me and said, "I know you, come on!" She took us into another room and the auditions were over! We had sung on two of her albums and she remembered us. It would take another book to tell you about my feelings during that time. But she was kind, gracious, and very generous. She is also a perfectionist and very particular about what she wants. I thought that she would not like the backing parts that Clydie and I made up and sang. She liked everything we did and only called us back once to fix something. Clydie and I did all the backing vocals on the soundtrack. The only thing that I did get a little upset about was that she didn't give us gold or platinum albums. Steely Dan and Boz Scaggs and a few other artists had given us gold albums. Steely Dan gave us platinum albums for *Aja*. But, all in all, it was a great experience.

KCH: What is the story behind your album, which featured the participation of Clydie King, Marriott, and Billy Preston?

FIELDS: I never made a solo album in the U.S. It was only a Blackberries' album on the A&M label. It was a very disappointing experience working with Billy Preston as the producer.

KCH: But you had your own band, Venetta's Taxi.

FIELDS: When I came to Australia I put a band together. I wanted to try to create my own sound through my experiences. I had worked with so many artists and seen how they created, I wanted to try that out myself and for myself. I put a pretty good band together. I was learning and bringing back what I had learned all at one time. It was a crazy experience! When I moved here [to Oz], all the things that I wanted to happen started. I had to get far away and clear my head and start again. Venetta's Taxi stayed around for a few years. We recorded and worked live. I was still learning.

## SEX, DRUGS, ROCK 'N' ROLL

FIELDS: I done and seen a few things, but nothing to the extreme.

KCH: The sad reality is that a lot of black women's oppression and misperception in the rock biz centers around sexuality.

FIELDS: I have certainly experienced it! I don't think that it was anything out of the ordinary. We were all oppressed then. I noticed that the white singers were getting all of the commercials. Commercials brought residuals. It was just starting to happen that a few commercials were sung by blacks. We had a very unique sound, and it was in the first stages of breaking out to what it is now. If a producer wanted a black sound, he would still call a white contractor. The contractor would call everyone in her clique, and one black singer to carry the sound of blackness instead of all black singers or at least two or three more. Now that is all changed.

KCH: You participated in the recording of *Exile On Main Street* with the Rolling Stones. That must've been madness.

FIELDS: *Exile On Main Street.* It was a midnight session. That was late for me. It was also a cash date. Which was good for me. I was leaving the next day for two weeks with Nancy Sinatra in Las Vegas. I had seen a coat that I wanted, and the cash I got for the Rolling Stones session would be for the coat. Remember, we were session singers, and we weren't thinking of the artist's fame at that time. We were working.

Sometimes we did two and three sessions a day. When we got there, Mick [Jagger] was still putting on a guide vocal. What I noticed the most was that he had the sound in the earphones with lots of echo and very loud. He showed us what he wanted and we did it. I went to Las Vegas the next day with that coat! I never gave it another thought until Steve Marriott reminded me that I had sung on the album and that it was a classic. I've only heard it a few times.

KCH: Some say you were romantically linked to Mick Jagger in the wake of the *Exile* sessions. Any comments about him?

FIELDS: I read that recently on the Internet. That is not true.

KCH: Sorry, but on the sister-friend tip, you have worked with some of the finest men in rock, like Kris Kristofferson and Gregg Allman. You got to give it up!

FIELDS: That is for my book!

KCH: In the interest of candor, is there perhaps anything you want to share about unpleasantness with sex and drugs and the dark side of the rock biz?

FIELDS: For the most part I was blessed and lucky that through my career I was never in danger or put in a compromising position. I have loved all the people that I have worked with, and thank them for the experience.

KCH: Any blatant episodes where you felt you or musicians working with you were being objectified due to fantasies about "red-hot mamas" and the like?

FIELDS: No! We all loved and respected each other and never got into pettiness. We had music!

## CULTURAL MATTERS

KCH: Interestingly, you recorded with several Native American performers prominent in the rock arena—Rita Coolidge, Buffy Sainte-Marie,
Jesse Ed Davis. Were they conscious of cross-cultural connections, and
what did you learn about the position of "Indians" in the industry?

FIELDS: I wasn't paying attention at that time, but I noticed on the Gram-
mys last year that there was not only a category for North American
Indian Music, but they had a few very good groups.

KCH: Also, you seem to have played with many folk types (Gene Clark, Arlo
Guthrie, Tim Buckley) and country-rock/southern boogie acts (Allman,
Wet Willie, Delaney Bramlett, Richie Furay and Poco, Joe Walsh, Tanya
Tucker). I'm interested in your experiences with them because these are
two genres rarely associated with black performers and audiences.

FIELDS: I loved working for Arlo Guthrie and Dr. John. Delaney and Bonnie and I were good friends during that time. As I said before, almost
all artists had to have black singers at that time. That is how we
seemed to have crossed over. They wanted to meld the two sounds together. They usually liked what they heard and called us back. We had
a great sound, and we were fast, creative, and professional. Joe Walsh,
Tanya Tucker, Bonnie Raitt, etc. really respected and relied on us. They
always had a smile on their faces when we sang something really beautiful with perfect pitch and harmony.

KCH: Since Shuggie Otis has recently been "rediscovered," could you
please shed some insight on working with him around *Freedom Flight?*

FIELDS: Sorry, I don't remember much.

KCH: Allen Toussaint is a legend and probably one of the most revered
black music figures of the era we're dealing with. What did you learn
from him?

FIELDS: He was he first black producer I worked with and has great
charisma. His songs were complicated but had great soul. He carried
his blackness with style. Just singing his backing vocals, which were
so intimate, was a thrill.

## BLACK WOMEN IN ROCK

FIELDS: Tina Turner is the only one I can think of. Everyone else went
R&B or pop, or disco.

KCH: Please talk about any black women beyond the Blackberries that
you might have known in the industry.

FIELDS: I worked with Ella Fitzgerald once. It was the biggest thrill! The other ladies that you have mentioned weren't around long enough, with the exception of a few, like Rita Coolidge, etc.

KCH: What was the scene and living situation like for you and others, like your fellow Blackberries, in Los Angeles and other cities where you were based? And what networks did you forge among yourselves?

FIELDS: When we were hired to travel, we were accommodated in the best hotels and ate the finest foods, had limos and the like. Personally, we all had nice apartments, then we all bought houses.

KCH: Do you think the black women singers and performers that you came up with were self-conscious about wanting to play rock?

FIELDS: At the time all we wanted to do was work. We never encountered anything like that. Music was music and we had no preferences, with the exception of Motown. We all wanted to do sessions for Motown.

KCH: What are your views on how the press and other media have perceived you and your career (especially in the 1970s)?

FIELDS: [Back then] we were always glad to see our names in interviews and reviews. We didn't have managers or agents that would keep our names out there, like a spin doctor. We never solicited it and were always surprised when we saw our names mentioned along with the artists.

KCH: How has life on the road and in a male milieu affected you personally?

FIELDS: I realized early that you had to be the band's sister, mother, confidante, dresser, advisor, and singer, etc. That is the one thing that I realized early. It was always fun and interesting about how boys and men never really grow up, and that they had to have a mother figure all the time.

KCH: Do you think racism, sexism, and other issues might have limited your choices in your profession?

FIELDS: I think so, but that was the norm then. We can look back in hindsight, but we didn't think so at the time. It was just the opposite. We were needed by the men in the rock field. And when they needed us, they gave us love and support as women and singers.

KCH: How did the Blackberries (and offshoots) differ from, say, the Merry Clayton Singers and the Waters (Maxine and Julia) sisters in terms of work and style?

FIELDS: There was not that much of a difference since we came from the same environment. We used each other for backing vocals and support. I don't think that there was much of a difference.

KCH: What is your opinion of the male rock stars of the era (especially black rockers like Jimi Hendrix, Sly Stone, and Arthur Lee of Love)?

FIELDS: At the time, I didn't think much of them, though I loved Sly [Stone] and thought it was more R&B than rock. Motown was happening then along with gospel, so I didn't pay much attention to black rock artists.

We were also singing with the best white rock bands—Humble Pie, Pink Floyd—and didn't think about the other black rock groups. I am not a music fan of anyone, with the exception of a few women singers throughout my time. Black and white.

KCH: Do you think there was a big double standard about women in the rock field having groupies or casual relationships and especially living on the road? Did you prefer the "nightbird" lifestyle, or did you want stability?

FIELDS: I didn't travel with many female rock artists so I don't know. I didn't have any relationships on the road because I didn't want to go out with a stranger in a small or big town and no one knew where I was. After performing, I would mostly go to my room and watch TV or read or do crossword puzzles.

KCH: Have black women had the same opportunities as others to become rock stars? [If yes, why can the average rock fan typically only name Tina Turner?]

FIELDS: Yes, I think that black women have the same opportunities, but are from different backgrounds and not interested in rock. Tina Turner is the only one. She was smart!

KCH: Is there some element in black culture that discourages young musicians from pursuing the rock field and black audiences in general from claiming rock music as their own?

FIELDS: No, I don't think so. You can do or be whatever you want to be nowadays. It is not like it was in the 1960s and 1970s.

KCH: Do you think an organization like the Black Rock Coalition is vital, or is it merely separatist and wrongheaded?

FIELDS: I think that it is unnecessary. There are not enough women that want to be rock singers. The time has passed for rock music. The number of black women in music now is far greater than it was years ago. As long as you have good material and a gimmick, you can get over, whatever color you are.

KCH: How would you like to see the story of black women in the rock world treated?

FIELDS: I'd like to see the story depicted in a strong positive manner. Especially dwell on the changes we made when they started using black female backing vocals. What an art form we created, and what great singers in our own right we are.

## NOW

KCH: What are you doing now and do you still associate with the rock scene in any form?

FIELDS: I have my own band. I teach vocals. And in my repertoire, there are all kinds of songs, from gospel to rock. I keep in touch with Boz Scaggs, Kris Kristofferson, Dave Gilmour, and a few more.

KCH: Discuss your new album *At Last* and the process of recording, dealing with the label, and touring behind it.

FIELDS: More than being white or black was relevant to my situation and with women that are my age that have been in the business. It is the age factor now! I could not get a record deal because of my age, regardless of my reputation and skills. It was a very disappointing experience financially and emotionally. What I did get out of the project was the fact that I got the project done. I felt that with the knowledge I have, I should be able to record my own CD. From that point of view, I had a great time. I had a coproducer who was there for me right from the beginning, and working with him was a treat. His name is Michael Wade. I put the CD on an independent label. I never promoted myself or had agents or managers to help and it never got off the ground. I financed it myself. Michael recorded on Pro-Tools, which was the latest digital recording facility. What was interesting to me was going from analog to digital. No more tapes! It is much faster as well. I remember splicing, and now we don't have to and many other things I learned while recording my CD. It is a novel by itself! It was meant to be because, for the most part, the recording of the CD was interesting and exciting, and to think that I was doing it for myself. I loved all the songs that I chose, and I really loved the songs that I wrote and they came so easily. Just to get the chance to use the knowledge that I had acquired throughout my experiences with all the artists that I have ever worked with [was rewarding].

KCH: How does the Australian music industry differ from that of the States? Do you feel your audience down under is receptive and cognizant of your subjectivity as a black woman?

FIELDS: The Australian music industry in small compared to the U.S. But it is also so familiar to me that I can see at lot clearer because it is so small but the goals are the same. The U.S. still dictates what Australia does, because the artists here want to be on American labels. The U.S. labels are here waiting to grab up any acts that they think are ready for the" big time."

KCH: You've worked in film, musicals, and theater, as well as performed with the Melbourne Symphony Orchestra. How has participation in the wider arts world differed from the industry?

FIELDS: Not that much. You have to either learn lyrics or words. The rest is about the same. It is about the business as a whole, not just rock. I think that rock is dying out now and as a word "rock" will soon be something else.

KCH: What recording or event would you describe as a highlight of your career and why?

FIELDS: I have a few milestones. Working with Barbra Streisand. She has one of the finest voices and careers of my time. Working with her on *A Star Is Born* was truly a wonderful experience. Aretha Franklin, my idol from when I was a little girl. I wanted to sing gospel just like her. And still do! I was disappointed by how her organization was run, but when she sang all was forgiven for a while. I finally got tired of the disorganization of her and her company, so that I quit after two years. Pink Floyd, the biggest rock band of my time, was the very best. I saw, lived, and ate the very best. Had the biggest crowds and the weirdest music that I soon learned to love and get into. In the beginning, touring with them, I didn't understand the music and laughed about it. But I soon learned and took it seriously and got a great deal out of the experience. Steely Dan, Humble Pie, Steve Marriott, more or less, put me on the map as far as giving me many opportunities in the rock field. Working in the musical *Big River.*

KCH: If you had your career to do over again, what different choices might you make?

FIELDS: I would not be so lazy and understand my experiences early enough to do something with them.

KCH: Which black female singers of today interest you?

FIELDS: I don't get a chance to hear a lot of them because they don't reach over here. But what I do hear I love. I can't even remember their names, but I've seen a few on Oprah's show and love them!

KCH: What do you feel your legacy is?

FIELDS: I think that my legacy is my voice and sound.

## PLUS

KCH: How can people get your record in the States and the UK?

FIELDS: Sorry! Impossible.

[Not quite so. Check out Venetta Fields's website at www.drumlake.com.au]

# MICHAEL C. LADD

# HARDCORE JOLLIES
## IN THE HIMALAYAS, STARING AT THE
# COSMIC SLOP:
## THE MOTHERSHIP CONNECTION BETWEEN TRIPLE AND QUADRUPLE
# CONSCIOUSNESS

I went to high school 7,000 feet above aqua boogie. A boarding school in northern India thought it prudent to let two American kids run rampant on their mountainside with some postcolonial fantasy of finding the most tripped-out place on earth. I brought two tapes with me, *Cosmic Slop* and *Hardcore Jollies*. Our school was high enough to see the snows to the north and to the south, what seemed like a million miles of plains rippling in the heat like high-speed ether. It was a vantage point that made the earth feel infinite.

Snowcaps on a wall of mountains turn purple when the sun starts to doze. That's when the guitar would come out, Gary Shider coaxing strings into colors in the sky; twisting the blue, pulling in lavenders, emeralds, and lapis to fill a purple and paint the snows above. [Cordell] Boogie

Mosson's bass lines would rumble to light behind storm clouds. Trouble. The terrible joy of watching the world do its thing with no permission so all you can do is serenade. So they did; Funkadelic did their thing, no permission. "Looking back at you I got a lot. . . ."

At sixteen, I was not happy in the United States. The type of analysis espoused in *America Eats Its Young* had become a solid worldview before I had heard the record. I had grown with the music influenced by Funkadelic, Grandmaster Flash and the Furious Five, Kool & the Gang's bass and kick coming through the ceiling from my cousin Dean's room while I watched *Sanford and Son,* both at full blast. The high-end AM radio crackle of Boston's only black music station in the kitchen fused with the drone of Cronkite's last days as anchorman in the living room. Auntie C. yelling at Diane and Uncle Jimmy chiming in on his way to the night shift. Me worried about El Salvador and ducking my mom, crack simmering in the street like popcorn with steel inside, about to go off. "Wars of Armageddon"–lite. I was already enthralled by the decadent apocalypse. Naturally, I was also terrified and disgusted by it.

Race, too, was an annoying gnat with humongous teeth. I was brought up in Cambridge, Massachusetts, a slice of non-America in the middle of racist Boston. The Boston black community was relatively conservative. It was not easy to fit in without the right creases in the right jeans; it was offensive if you didn't care. My mother, like any sensible black woman of her age, was big on appearance. Getting me to dress well was a constant struggle. Attempting to drag a comb through my afro was near impossible. I'd pull a William and Ellen Craft and just start running. I would run until I had exhausted my mother and my aunt's energy and the pick would slip from their hands. But I felt like the world was against me on this one. Everybody was snap tight Up South. Needless to say, when I saw the Funkadelic covers I felt I had finally found some company—big bushy muthafuckas. They were the masters of the margin, right in the middle.

I actually discovered Sly Stone first. My mother had a massive record collection made up of what my father left when he died and what my brothers and sisters left when they moved out. I pulled out *Stand!* one day. I heard 'Sex Machine' and knew I had to hear everything that sounded like that. Funkadelic record giggling in the hide 'n' go seek closet, trying not to give itself away, thinking, "Man, wait 'till he finds us. It's gonna be over." Grit, nappy and ashy kneecapped grit is what I needed. I didn't wash already, that's whom I was, a complicated black kid bouncing from a faux ghetto to suburbia and back, in the same town. Parliament was too clean for that shit. Parliament was definitely too clean for India.

I found *Cosmic Slop* at my cousins'. It did not save my life. It just gave me the map so I knew how. First thing to do was to get the hell outta

Dodge. My friend Toby had gone to elementary school in India. He knew of a high school called Woodstock in the foothills of the Himalayas and asked me if I wanted to go. I was effectively paying my own way through an overrated boarding school in Massachusetts. School in India was going to cost considerably less. I didn't take long to say yes.

## OPEN UP YOUR FUNKY MIND AND YOU CAN FLY

When I left for India, I did not know if I would return to the United States. I was more interested in becoming a member of what, in my neo-colonial black American gaze, was the psychedelic bizarreness of the southern hemisphere. It seemed more interesting than being American and less complicated than being black American. Of course, in the tradition of all black American expatriates, the one thing I could not escape was myself. Funkadelic knew that already. ". . . your ass will follow."[1] "The Funk is synonymous with finding oneself."[2] Nevertheless, by leaving, I had entered into a long tradition of Black Americans in transit. In essence, we are a people invented in transit. William Wells Brown put it simply: "The act of fleeing is an existential act of self creation."[3]

Funkadelic is one of several groups that took that concept to the fullest, out of the atmosphere and back in fact, but they were riding on some old grooves. The Flying African, the people could fly. "Say that long ago in Africa, some of the people knew magic. And they would walk up on the air like climbing up on a gate. And they flew like blackbirds over the fields. Black shiny wings flappin' against the blue up there."[4]

Flight was a necessity for black Americans in ways unparalleled by few groups in the last 500 years. Our concept of flight, the way we negotiate our sense of place has been intensely complex. The Mothership Connection helps clarify and testify.

I did not get a lift on the Dogon ark or chill with Elijah on Ezekiel's Wheel.[5] I wasn't in the car with George and Bootsy when the wheel almost dented their grille.[6] I took a Dutch 747, not a far cry from a sailing ship. Dubious like the assumptions I carried, dangerous like the ones about me that arrived before I did. The first day of school was a trip. A kid named Pavan sauntered over to me and gave me the standard teenage interrogation. He asks me my name, pauses, and asks me if I drink, I say, "Yeah." He says, "Do you smoke?" I say, "Yeah." "Do you like porn?" "Yeah," I say. Excited, he interjects, "I love porn except for *Emmanuelle II* with the niggers." I give him a severe look that lets him know that my high yellow shade should not be mistaken for anything other than black and he starts backpedaling like he has no breaks. "The colorless monster of RACISM is gleefully unchained by garroted gibbons and hirsute hooligans, whose abbreviated mentalities cripple their own minds. "[7] I told him to fuck off. I couldn't even hear his apologies. I thought, "Damn, I travel 12,000 miles to get called nigger by a kid darker than me." I was beat by Hollywood: "Specific inspisstated ignoramuses of cankerous audacity [. . .] engage professionally and/or morally in the unique practice of PIMPAFICATION."[8] There is no better language for dealing with such bullshit. The philosophy carried by this lingua funkadelica was crucial to how my worldview was revamped in the Himalayan foothills. Funkadelic focused on flight but not escape.

Psychedelia and neocolonial travel share an odd kinship. Probably best exemplified in Coppola's *Apocalypse Now,* a strong film on American colonial expansion and arguably one of the best to see on acid. I would walk through a Dhobi ghat, a washing village where untouchables live, with a Walkman worth the equivalent of $10,000 playing "Funky Dollar Bill." A washerwoman with a load on her head the size of three of her grown children would look at me as if I had a gun. This was not far from the truth. I was a carrier infested with American customs, music, and a severely distorted sense of monetary value. "Yea, though I walk through the Shadow of poverty, I must feel their envy for I am loaded, high and all those other goodies that go along with good god big buck."

In India, with my comparative wealth, I often felt absurd. Delving into absurd music was sometimes my only recourse. America eats its young and everybody else's. India is one of many places where the young, the old, and even the unborn were eaten by the British and subsequently by U.S. multinationals. One can witness the consumption on the roadside, kids with knees the size of softballs compared to their legs, their stomachs bloated from all the food being eaten away from them. I was on both sides of the coin, as a black American, I had felt America's teeth sink into me. As a black American in a "third world" country, I was sinking my teeth into the disenfranchised Indians around me. I was beginning to develop a triple consciousness. Simply by being American, despite the African and the hyphen, I was associated with American imperialism. No matter how many people I tried to convince of my African roots, my build alone said well fed, well paid. I used Funkadelic as my flight pattern for understanding the global dilemma I was experiencing.

Funkadelic, the ultimate expatriates, are from space. "By the way, my name is Funk/ I am not of your world." They come down to earth as the repatriating Astro-Afro-conquistadors, space messengers here to save us from eating our young. Funkadelic's image used such a hodgepodge of influences that they do not evoke the same cultural impositions that someone like Michael Jackson or even James Brown do. First, they never endorsed American values, they consistently indicted America, and second, even when on Warner Brothers, Funkadelic did not enjoy the worldwide recognition that some of their colleagues did. On an international scale, they were relatively obscure. Most important, they genuinely portrayed an otherworldly image with an otherworldly sound that allowed them to be universal. "Space people universal lover." They got their image from everywhere but primarily the broom closet or the trash. They were beyond "third world"; they were out of this world. My friend Mikel, horn player and flutist, remembers seeing them at the Apollo Theater in 1977: "Shider was wearing a diaper like he always did, and he had these elevator boots on but they weren't fly, they were worn, like really worn. Then out comes George in a baby-blue sheet with Roadrunner and Wily Coyote on it and the sheet is not clean. He's got a bike chain around his waist for a belt. I mean it looked like he grabbed the first thing he saw when he was walking out the door and was like, 'Fuck it, I'll wear this.'"[9]

Like members of a cargo cult, George Clinton and Shider are accessorizing with benign trinkets of western excess to symbolize their affinity with an off-world order. They did this every night, all within the context of the Mothership, for the Mothership, and of the Mothership.

Their Astro-Afro epistemology may have sourced the cult called "the Process"[10] on early albums. However, Funkadelia is its own thing. It is part of a tradition of elastic history fused with social critique fused with science fiction, from the Dogon ark to Elijah Muhammad's beef with the mad scientist Yacub to Sun Ra. But Funkadelic got to people like a sales pitch, like an inside joke we could all get. You knew you could get off the Mothership if you had to. You could always phone home because you had never left, one simply had a better view. Kodwo Eshun waxes,

> Funkadelia impeaches the universe, confronts reality, sets out to destroy an insane world over and over. Back in his mind again after tripping out, George Clinton realized that "I could not get mad enough at the world and how it was treating people to wait in an alley and kill some muthafucka. But there ain't no winning situation like that, so once we got out of there I'd take acid and make sure I didn't get that mad no more. I'd start looking at, you know, alternate realities."[11]

To impeach the universe, one must have authority over it and a mastery of alternate realities. Sometimes this may have gone too far. I heard this from a friend: One time when on tour, Sly Stone and George Clinton were beamin' up in the bus, not just beamin', but that was the main event. So much so that they ran out of water. They were in the middle of nowhere, in the desert I suppose. A real classic situation, so they used the next best thing available, Hawaiian Punch. Big red rocks of Hawaiian punch and something just under yellow. Funky, outer space, Arizona, or Xgatze it doesn't matter—it's universal ghettomars. Three-sixty perspective in all its pain. Some say Sly has gone mad. People talk about him as if he is dead but he is alive. Space is limitless but it's fuckin' cold.

As a black westerner in search of my "third world" origins in a country my origins had little to do with, I was in quite a postcolonial quagmire. The absurdity of my intent beat out the absurdity of my perceptions of the place. However, in my U.S. teenage gaze, Uttar Pradesh was romantically absurd. Many of my assumptions were centered on anticipating bizarre experiences and aligning myself with a global brown community. Funkadelic provided a perfect guide. They had explored realms of blackness that had not really been touched, outside of jazz. They made the afro-existentialist questions posed by Coltrane and Sun Ra even more accessible. This was the first time these questions were posited in a way I could relate to. I was also relating to the nostalgia of the music. Funkadelic came from the time that I had missed, a mysterious better time, which I had spent in the sandbox. A time before all the optimism of the 1960s had dissolved into Carter's demise and faded into the Reagan Era. By 1986, 10,000 miles west of India, Black America was experiencing the biggest influx of drugs and violence to date. My friend Spencer sent me a tape of *Maggot Brain*. I was tripping.

## ROLLING ON THE ONE, TAPE'S IN MOTION

Memories are better in present tense. Looseness makes them work, like hearing recording instructions during "Hit It and Quit It": "Okay play that from the top," just before Eddie Hazel's solo. The engineer on "Mommy What's a Funkadelic" says, "Rolling on the one," and the rest is discography. Even fans have pooh-poohed the first albums for the poor recording quality and the mistakes. For me, it is the mistakes and the mud that makes them perfect. There are the Process liner notes, too: the fact that they were definitely the wrong people to be quoting, but Funkadelic didn't seem to care. When you look at the *Maggot Brain* gatefold check the brick in the hand. The freakiness of all of it is enough to give you loose booty, forget a bundle. So loose that it's tight again, so tight that you can't get that loose without being tight. *So high you can't get over it, so low you can't get under it.* That's what Motown and James Brown boot camp did. That is how they were able to bubble like that, at least that's how they made me bubble, happy to be comfy that close to the sky.

Smoked out at the haunted house: Toby, Ranjit, me, and dead British sprawled on a ghost lawn 1,000 feet above school. *Hardcore Jollies* blared out of a broken boom box like Bollywood on a bus, the ultimate rugged-rugged music. It turns woofers to sawdust and rides the tweeter like a junkie on luck. The grass is like a backrub; it's all around my neck. Gary Shider is playing guitar like he's saying, "Take that and that!" giving Eddie Hazel a run for his money, not quite, but good enough for us. We don't know any better. We are closer to the stars than we have ever been before. We see them shoot across the sky that night, more than we can count. God bless the Slop in all its grandeur.

*What is soul?* Malaria mosquito in your dhoti, a high school with no toilet paper, that's soul. A Worrell solo falling from a pine tree, a *bidi* in my mouth, buggin' out on pan. The smell of burnt rubber and gasoline will always be funky, the entire, afro-sensation on a dark-skinned straight-haired people funky, Dalit funky.[12] Soul is ashy kneecaps, and both South Asians and Africans got that. Shade relations are always funky. Pande looks at me like I was crazy when I put on *Maggot Brain,* "Black people listen to this?" We watch *Platoon* on the VCR and go to the roof to throw rocks at cobras. It is summertime in Katmandu; smoke in the air, somewhere in the grass a cobra rises. I have the sound of Eddie Hazel's mother dying filling my body. He plays out the pain in "Maggot Brain," and it is euphoric.[13] It picks me up and floats me in a womb, above Pande's house, above the burning ghat, and I am solid on the ground.

*Let's Take It to the Stage* gets me open one day. I'm in the courtyard of our dorm sitting on the railing, look straight down, 900 feet. We are waiting on dinner. "She'll Be Coming Around the Mountain" is on my Walkman. I forget that I had eaten about an inch of Afghani hash two hours earlier. We are looking out at vegetated forever and the mountains beyond that, talking shit, basketball and cricket, when the cable in my back lobe connects with my frontal. I am a lightning cloud of laughs. Big bold bellows like a giant, 'It will blow your funky mind' type laughter. Nonstop.

There is something about the way the drums on "Hit It and Quit It" come in crooked and deliberate. There is a road that cuts through school. Coal trucks, big TATA trucks, with Vishnu stickers dead in the middle of the windshield, grind up the road with 1,000 shriveled saffron flowers lining the outside. A paint job of stripes and images of Ganesh, Hanuman, and the hardest of hard, Kali, grace the side panels and dapple the cab. The workers on these trucks look like war veterans from the war of poverty 1498 to the present.[14] These trucks are these workers' homes—the cab and maybe a plastic tarp down in Dhera Dun. Life is trying to bend them. They walk crooked but deliberately. I heard one time that

Funkadelic were going get to the essence of funk by not washing at all. I mean, just letting it all cake on until the record was done or the tour was over, allowing the essence of funk to accumulate to an overwhelming degree. These coal truck coolies were funky by default, not by choice. As work beat them, they beat back as bodies of men do. You can see the tension of the fight in their arms, their muscles creating ravines and ridges stretching to tributary hands.

"Super Stupid" is perfect when you are sixteen. Rugged, driving from your dome down to your tail. I dub the song five times in a row so I can get at least twenty minutes of it. I stick it in my Walkman, tape my Walkman to my chest, and tape up the wires and everything like I'm a Navy SEAL or some action-out white kid (which I half was). I go running down the mountains. The mountains are so steep and I am running so fast that when I grab hold of a sapling my feet kick out from under me and I spin 360 around the tree. I try and time that with the chorus:

> Oh Stupid with your ups and downs
> Your maggot brain, your grins and frowns
> Super Stupid you're here today
> You've lost the fight and the winner is fear.

All that but in negative, a super-stupid pastime. I am alone in space, in the khud, in the cut.

Cosmic slop begins in tricky outer space. It is tricky because it is a low-tech space with very organic drums. The toms are dirty; everything in Funkadelic space is dirty. They know. They have been there, like Sun Ra they are not seeing space through a telescope and claiming there is nothing there. Unlike their richer half, Parliament, and their imitators, Funkadelic do not make the mistake of equating space with western space technology. Just because you visit Cape Canaveral or sit in the space shuttle does not mean one has been to space. One has only become familiar with a form of space travel. Funkadelic shows up dusty, brushing himself off, "not of this world," talking about his moms. I don't know if you need plastic and metal, whizzes and blips to be from space; you do, however, need a Mother Nature, jealous of her own shadow or not. The toms are open in space. The snare is like the wooden controls on a spaceship made of space wood and space stone. The crash symbols come in light like space dust and Tibetan dust mixed together. Then the track opens. It is a small flower, the reverb is essentially over, and it doesn't take you under like Funkadelic or "Maggot Brain." It seeps in you like space scag and, like any scag, it's womblike comfy, making you think of home no matter where you are.

# WE ARE BACK IN OUR MINDS AGAIN

It can be argued that black Americans are the only four-dimensional people on the planet. Double consciousness is whipped up and beat down in every essay; I maintain that triple consciousness is the view the black American has of him- or herself in a neocolonial context. One examines one's self as an oppressed person of color who, in a "third world" context shares an imperialist position with whites of the United States. Ugly but true. A fourth consciousness, however, allows the black American to reinvent him- /herself from space and therefore rearrange her/his gaze to that of the ultimate outsider and simultaneously the ultimate insider. A fourth consciousness allows one to bypass the other three. "P-Funk transcended this conundrum [double consciousness], as the notions of intellect, education, or sophistication were totally removed from white status."[15] Fourth consciousness view exposes the absurdity of race and simultaneously continues to focus solely on the Diaspora. It runs the risk of slipping into universalism—"space people universal lover"—but the tradition is deeply connected to home and the soul, and as others have stated, culture and particularly our music is propelled by the wannabe "raceless" yet politically complex computer chip.[16]

The origins of this perspective may begin in Mali with the Dogon ark, which is said to have shuttled aliens to Africa. More concrete evidence is available in the mythology born of slavery and the aforementioned tale of the Flying African. We flew to escape bondage. Kelefa Sanneh writes, "The notion of voyaging through space mirrors and exaggerates the dislocation of the Middle Passage, and it echoes the plaintive song of slaves entreating one another to 'follow the drinking gourd'—the Big Dipper—to escape bondage."[17]

On a more temporal level, black Americans' sense of time also alludes to a supernatural or otherworldly quality. Since the moment of enslavement, black Americans have had to be distrustful of the histories provided for us. Whether they be the European lies that have supported white supremacy over the past five centuries, the damaging lies of an overseer, or even those of a fellow African selling his brother to a white man. This profound feeling of betrayal alters one's belief in everything, including time.

Black America's sense of time had to become elastic as we were. And we are constantly maneuvering around white people's attempts to confine us both mentally and spiritually. One of the primary ways we eluded whites was with language; James Baldwin: "Negro Speech is vivid largely because it is private. It is a kind of emotional short-hand by means of which Negroes express, not only their relationship to each other, but their judgment of the white world."[18]

An elastic language allows one's sense of history to be elastic, similar to how one's sense of history is subjective.[19] Subsequently, our collective spirit becomes mobile; we feel connected to an ancient king, farmer, or shepherd from Benin and even Egypt, where hardly any slaves from the Americas came from. If we are able to experience this in some profound way ontologically, then it is not much of a stretch to assume that African Americans are perhaps capable of a fourth consciousness, a nontemporal view of the world and history. Kodwo Eshun is helpful here as well: "From Sun Ra to 4 Hero [Funkadelic is right in the middle] today's alien discontinuum therefore operates not through continuities, retentions, genealogies or inheritances but rather through intervals, gaps, breaks. It turns away from roots; it opposes common sense with the force of the fictional and power of falsity."

I would take it one step further, as Eshun also does, and state that we gain the freedom of reinvention that turns this power of falsity into reality. A postcolonial Afterfuture is the only perspective that allows the black Americans to bond with the international community of color. Funkadelic is at the core of that perspective. This is not a collective perspective by any means. However, if one feels inclined to subscribe to the Talented Tenth paradigm, than why not Omni-Terrestrial Tenth? *Can you get to that?*

This intergalactic epistemology is useful when the African-American begins to travel. In the case of this chapter, for example, it may well be what saves it from tumbling down a postcolonial slope of western assumptions. This perspective may provide some sort of authenticity to this gaze, since it is the only perspective that acknowledges all cultural and historical aspects of being black American from a view so high above the earth that it is unavoidably global. Mr. Eshun, if you please, "P-Funk's connection forward in time to the Mothership allows an equal and opposite connection back in time to the Pharaonic connection, both of which converge on the present."

You got to understand your mother's kitchen as directly connected to the Mothership. In order to make sense of Funkadelic's Afro-futurism, it is important to note that it is born out of a science fiction very dedicated to home (down home in particular). Not just a place of origin, but how one was grown in that place of origin; and then how that pertains to the intergalactic window dressing. There is nothing like a little escape to let one properly understand home.

I had traveled to India to find the farthest thing from home as possible, to identify with black and brown people who, prior to my visit, seemed like a welcoming mass of southern hemispheric partygoers with a collective revolutionary consciousness. I thought Funkadelic would aid me in my escape. I thought they were so out there that if I followed them I would never have to return. In both cases, the opposite was true. India, Uttar Pradesh really, was not a psychedelic or spiritual playground but a place with enough social complexities to make U.S. race relations feel like kindergarten. I did not find myself spiritually enlightened on a mysterious Vedic path but involved in the day-to-day rhythms of (relative) labor and leisure, from making omelets for Ramadan with Rehan to rhyming over tabla with Jivaid at the high school talent show. In addition, the distance allowed me the perspective to see how bizarre and mysterious America can be. Funkadelic does the same thing; they take you all the way out to show you home. What one fantasizes to be a totally out-of-body psyche- delic experience is, at the end of the trip, completely about the body. It is about the body you came from. It is about your grandmama's body. It is about my mother's kitchen and the women in it. It's about all the porce- lain Jesus' on Aunt Honey's mantel, it's about cousin Lynwood in Vietnam, it's Granny singing, "Oh What a Friend We Have in Jesus" playing the piano off key, almost in reverse with Hazel on top. It is about home.

Music For My Mother
(G. Clinton)

*Man, I was in a place*
*Called Keeprunnin', Mississippi, on time*
*And I heard someone on my way by*
*Sounded a little something like raw funk to me*
*So I slowed down and took a listen*
*And this is all I could hear baby*

*Whoa-hah-hey*
*Whoa-hah-hai*

*It got so good to me, man, that I stopped runnin'*
*My feets was tired anyhow*
*So I reached in my inside pocket*
*And got my harp out*
*Sit down by that old beat-up railroad train*
*And get me get myself*
*A little of that old funky thang . . .* [20]

# NOTES

1. Lyrics from "Free Your Mind And Your Ass Will Follow," from *Free Your Mind and Your Ass Will Follow* (Westbound, 1971).

2. Ricky Vincent, *Funk* (New York: St. Martin's Griffin, 1996), p. 260.

3. William Wells Brown, *The Travels of William Wells Brown* (Princeton, NJ: Markus Wiener Publishing).

4. Virginia Hamilton, *The People Could Fly: American Black Folk Tales* (New York: Knopf), p. 166.

5. In a discussion with the author, Kandia Crazy Horse mentioned the Dogon ark. The Dogon, of what is now Mali state, believe they were once visited by aliens in an ark that came from space. This claim is more intriguing when one examines the Dogon's knowledge of astronomy, especially of the Dog Star, Sirius and Sirius B. *Africana.com.* Elijah Muhammad envisioned a flying saucer, which inspired the Nation of Islam, *Transition,* vol. 7, no. 2.

6. In *Funk,* author Ricky Vincent retells the story of Bootsy Collins and George Clinton encountering a flying saucer on the road near Toronto. This incident helped them conceive their version of the Mothership (p. 240).

7. Liner notes to *Cosmic Slop* by Funkadelic (Westbound, 1973).

8. Ibid.

9. Incidentally, the night Mikel saw them they were opening for Rare Earth, who was booed following Funkadelic.

10. "The Process" Church of the Final Judgment was a major cult in the 1960s and 1970s founded by Mary Ann McClean and Robert DeGrimston. Fugs frontman Ed Sanders was exposed as having a connection to Charles Manson and other limited white people in California. Check Gary Lachman, "Sympathy for the Devil," in *Fortean Times,* June 20, 2000.

11. Kodwo Eshun, *More Brilliant than the Sun: Adventures in Sonic Fiction* (London: Quartet Books, 1998), p. 53.

12. In *Everybody Was Kung Fu Fighting,* Vijay Prashad writes about the connection between black Americans and Dalit people of India. Historically they are both considered the untouchables. They are sometimes darker-skinned, and there is an intellectual movement, led mostly by African Americans and Dalit to prove their connection to Africa. (See Vijay Prashad, *Everybody Was Kung Fu Fighting: Afro-Asian Connections and the Myth of Cultural Purity* (Boston, MA: Beacon Press, 2001).

13. George Clinton told Eddie Hazel to think of his mother dying when he recorded the solo for the song "Maggot Brain."

14. Also in Vijay Prashad: 1498 is the year Vasco de Gama arrived in South Asia. One can assume the war of poverty was waged prior to that but global expansion really heated up the game.

15. Vincent, *Funk,* p. 235.

16. Some of the many others are Beth Coleman, Paul D. Miller, Kodwo Eshun, Greg Tate, and an army of young, gifted, black, beautiful smarty-pants.

17. Kelefa Sanneh, "The Secret Doctrine," *Transition,* vol. 7, no. 2.

18. Harry Allen cited this quote in his article "Eminem," *The Source,* no. 161, February 2003. It was excerpted from an article titled "Sermons and Blues," *The New York Times Review of Books,* March 29, 1959.
19. I know this would not hold up in even the jivest of jive universities, but my library is not helping and since this chapter is for George Clinton University, one has a little more leeway than at Jivus no-onus Academeeum. (See the bottom of the liner notes for Funkadelic's *Let's Take It to the Stage* (Westbound, 1975).
20. George Clinton, "Music for My Mother," from *Funkadelic* (Westbound, 1970).

# JENNIFER RICE

# LORRAINE O'GRADY Q & A

**L**orraine O'Grady's brief yet distinguished journalism career began after spending some time among New York's top-line music indus-trati. Bored by the endless parties and her position as "the girl-friend," O'Grady parlayed her experience as the lone African American woman in a predominately white male orbit into some of the most pre-scient rock criticism of the 1970s. Her coverage of southern rockers, par-ticularly the Allman Brothers Band, articulated the cultural melange that was her New York existence. It would be twenty-five years before another African American woman wrote extensively about southern rock.

After writing criticism and features for the *Village Voice, Rolling Stone,* and other outlets for a year, O'Grady retired from music journalism. O'Grady is best known for her conceptual art, which also focuses on the place she oc-cupies—between the worlds of black and white, male and female—as a contemporary artist. Citing influences from Toni Morrison to Man Ray, O'Grady has been the recipient of the Bunting Fellowship in Visual Art and the National Endowment for the Arts emerging artist fellowship. An assis-tant professor of art and African American studies at University of Califor-nia at Irvine, O'Grady now splits her time between New York and California. We spoke about her former career as a rock critic and the state of music during the 1960s and 1970s.


JENNIFER RICE: You went to the University of Iowa for creative writing. How did you get involved in music journalism for *The Village Voice?*

LORRAINE O'GRADY: I was writing features and criticism at the same time, but all as an amateur. I wasn't a musician, I wasn't a critic, I was only somebody's old lady. Basically, I had broken up a marriage and come to New York because I was dating a guy named Ron Oberman who was very very big in the record business at that time. After a certain number of parties it was getting very lame and tired to just be his girl-friend. That's when I started writing. I wrote two pieces; I didn't know which one was going to get published because I didn't know anybody at the *Voice,* but they both got published the same day. One was a cri-tique of *Soul Train* and the other was about the Allman Brothers Band. Nobody knew who I was except I was Ron Oberman's girlfriend. But suddenly there I was with a piece of criticism and a feature. It was not a career, it was just a world that I entered accidentally.

JR: What kind of music did you listen to growing up?

O'GRADY: I actually was raised listening to race music. Not rock and roll, not rhythm and blues, race music. I grew up with Louis Jordan and the Tympani Five and with [ballad singer] Savannah Churchill. My re-lationship to rock and roll was total awareness that it was white cover music.

JR: White cover music?

O'GRADY: The only time you could hear race music in Boston, except at parties, was once a week at midnight. They played Wynonie Harris's

"Around The Clock Blues" so when Bill Haley and the Comets covered "Rock Around the Clock" I suddenly realized, "Oh, white people are interested in this music, too."

JR: What was your reaction to hearing Elvis Presley for the first time?

O'GRADY: I remember being in a car and we had pulled over to the side of the road. We were in this car, my friends and I, and we heard this voice from the radio, and like I told you, you only could hear black music in Boston at midnight on either Friday night or Saturday, and this was the middle of the week, three-thirty in the afternoon, and we heard this voice and we pulled over to the side of the road because we couldn't believe that we were hearing a voice like this in the middle of the day, in the middle of the week. We thought he was black.

JR: When you realized Elvis was white, were you put off?

O'GRADY: No, I wasn't put off. I loved it; I loved the fact that it was happening. But I was with these people, all white people—most of my people were white then—and they were all still into Broadway show tunes. I was so bored by everybody's musical tastes I could scream. People were horrified, not I think by the sound of Elvis Presley or rock and roll, but they were horrified by the fact that they didn't know what it was. Their idea was that it was a fad and my idea was, it's not going to be a fad. Once you hear this, once your body feels this, there's no going back to Broadway show tunes. You're only going to go from here to maybe jazz. I thought it was going to go that way—I didn't know it would sort of swoop into rhythm and blues or race music and stay there.

JR: What do you think was the first departure among white musicians from "black cover music"?

O'GRADY: I think the first real original white [rock] music made was the Beatles. I really thought of the Beatles as pioneers in terms of taking the black impulse in music and putting it together with a white impulse and making something move. But all that time, there was this other stuff that was happening, like Chuck Berry and Little Richard. There were so many different kinds of music, there were so many different kinds of black music, and there were so many different kinds of white responses to black music, i.e., covers, that I think there was a long period, from about 1953 to 1963, where music didn't quite know what it was doing or why it was doing it.

JR: You came to New York several years after that. How would you classify the state of music when you arrived?

O'GRADY: I didn't follow [Ron Oberman] into the world of Woodstock; I had known people who'd gone to Woodstock, but I wasn't one of those. I was married, I was just listening to this music, it wasn't transforming my life. Most of the people who went to Woodstock felt their own lives being transformed by this music, and that wasn't—even though I liked the movie afterward and was seeing a lot of those people for the first time, actually, in that movie, I came to New York when rock had already become money.

JR: Everyone realized there was money to be made in the cultural revolution?

O'GRADY: Record companies were cashing-in in a way that they never would have imagined was possible. I came into the world of promotion, where every day was a PR party. I have seen the inside of every supper club, every music venue in the City—paid for, wined and dined, what can I tell you? It was about money. I never paid for a drink or meal for months.

JR: Do you think this was unique to New York's record industry? Was Motown any different?

O'GRADY: There were two kinds of music, fully money-oriented. They were dividing the audience up between them. There was the rock-and-roll world and there was the Motown world. Everything that Berry Gordy was doing out there in Detroit was as much about money as what the people on Sixth Avenue were doing.

JR: Was the segregation of music—the dividing of audiences—intrinsically racist, or just a consequence of business or geography?

O'GRADY: I knew that in New York, in this all-white world—because I was the only black person that I ever saw, basically, in those parties—I loved the Allman Brothers; the only other thing that I *loved* was Motown. In New York rock and roll, there was tremendous racism. There was a kind of unconscious hatred of Berry Gordy and Detroit and Motown.

It couldn't come out as that, so it had other ways of coming out. . . . I'll never forget—I will not mention his name but this rock critic and I were sitting in Ron's office at Columbia waiting for Ron and, somehow or the other, we got on to the topic of Motown and Berry Gordy and he started running it down. He ran it down in the way that they always ended up running it down—they would run it down ad hominem that Berry Gordy was involved with the Mafia, that that was how he got the money, and I said, "He can't go to the country club and play golf, so what the fuck's the difference?"

JR: Wow.

O'GRADY: They [also] talked about the packaging. Everybody in New York, instead of being able to come out and say, "I hate James Brown; I hate Motown," would say, "I hate the packaging." They said the album covers were crude and amateur and unartistic and whatever, and I remember saying to this guy that they could put it out in brown paper bags and it would still have been the best stuff that came out in the 1960s.

At the most sophisticated levels, it was making those kinds of critiques. At the less sophisticated levels, people refused to acknowledge that [rock music] ever had any connection to black people. You'd be shocked at how many people really didn't know and if they were told wouldn't believe that this music ever had anything to do with black people.

JR: Where do you place rootsy bands like the Stones on this spectrum?

O'GRADY: I never have enjoyed the Stones. I remember [during] graduate school, I was in a bar and we were dancing and this kid that was living on the hall where I was living went crazy and started dancing to "(I Can't Get No) Satisfaction." He thought that was the greatest lyric he'd ever heard, because he was the frustrated, pimply kid. I remember thinking, "I can't dance to these people."

JR: That's interesting, especially since that's Mick Jagger's criticism of all other white music. Why do you think the Rolling Stones are not danceable?

O'GRADY: It sort of sounds like black music—but with no rhythm to move your body to. I always thought they were musically impossible—physically impossible and musically. Because you couldn't move to their music. The only way you could move to the Stones was if you were still at the level of following those Arthur Murray foot patterns on the floor. That's how you would have to dance to the Stones. So actually—there was a lot of interesting psychedelic music that I thought was interesting, but I didn't hear any white music that I thought was really great until I heard the Allman Brothers.

JR: What was your introduction to their music?

O'GRADY: [Ron] was always getting these albums, and so I think it was either the Allman Brothers self-titled or *Idlewild South* that I was listening to.

JR: So it was discovered amid his pile of—?

O'GRADY: He liked them and I liked the way he introduced me to them. We used to play it in bed, but that was like—and you could actually move to them. You really could, as opposed to the Stones. But I said, "I like them," and Ron said, "Well, that's interesting, because I think they're a real American band." Their musical attitudes were so totally American even though some of the stuff that they played—they did Donovan!—was British.

JR: And they weren't playing black cover music.

O'GRADY: I hadn't heard white people playing black-inspired music so totally in their own way. Some of the Righteous Brothers you'd have to say was really brilliant, but it was so deep a cover that the southern white Righteous Brothers weren't there. They didn't exist in the work that they were doing; they had become black, whereas the Allman Brothers had remained white but had totally synthesized the black thing and that I found—well, because I felt it was what I was. I felt it was the future of the United States.

# DARRYL A. JENIFER

# PLAY LIKE A WHITE BOY: HARD DANCING IN THE CITY OF CHOCOLATE

**B**lack rock, blacks performing rock: What does this all mean? Well, being a full-fledged, bona fide "brother" born as the fires engulfed civil rights movement–era Chocolate City. Me and my mom lived on Bruce Place—southeast D.C., to be exact, in a cinder-block, four-story apartment just adjacent to the more projectlike, two-leveled barracks that my ma often referred to as "the projects"—living in these smelly-ass buildings wasn't that bad when you knew better, but after a couple afternoons watching the Brady Bunch livin' it up in their suburban split level, I began to fantasize about living the white life. The "good" life.

Reflecting on back in the day when I was just a kid, I vividly recall listening to Aretha Franklin, the Temptations, and Sly Stone on the ever-crackling WOOK—D.C.'s own black-supported radio station. Music somehow always seemed to be in my life. Strangely enough, neither of my parents played or sang, but my father was nevertheless a very talented artist, thrilling my nana and me at least once a week with a hot buttered sketch.

Living in D.C. on certain levels can be very tribal when you're black, because you are constantly surrounded by all that is Babylon: the government, the monuments, even the alleged so-called leaders of the so-called free world reside there. The White House? Ha that brings to mind, if the White House is white and the black rock is black. Anyway, one day while being baby-sat by my cousin Jack (who was and still is a brilliant guitarist), I fondly remember him saying, "Darryl, you wanna learn to play guitar, man?" Me being the knucklehead that I was, I smart-assly spit back, "I already know how to play." Then Jack broke into "Light My Fire" on some ol' Wes Montgomery type shit; I was in awe of the sound and magic of the chords. It was amazing how the sound of his then vintage Bradley Les Paul deluxe filled the air, not to mention my soul. This, I believe, was the day I fell in love with music and instruments.

Years would pass, my skills would grow, and through some twisted, bizarre turns of fate, I have become the self-elected "dropper of jewels" on matters of "black rock." I have come to recognize just exactly how this black rock term evolved (peep this): As we all should know by now, rock and roll has its roots in blues—the original swamp-bucket styles that were (unfortunately) rooted in slave field hymns, which I'm sure came across the sea from Africa. Okay, I'm not gonna leave out the styles rooted in bluegrass and hillbilly-type shit, which I'm sure were imported across the seas by the Irish and other assorted Euro types (kids: learn your American history).

But how about the first time Little Richard stomped on his piano in them pointed-toe, hurtin'-ass shoes? Or when Mr. Berry duck-walked across stage while shredding some mangled guitar solo? It seems to me that rock and roll has been on the "take"—raided by bands of British invaders, who wound up biting and pillaging all that is rock, to the degree that now the passionate primal screams of musical abandonment have been deemed, um, "white music." How is this so? Is it because blacks like to dance, like to "get dey groove on," and the abrasive, often awkward rhythms of today's rock ain't cutting it (the rug, that is)? As we all know, dancing is essential to African culture, so trying to Harlem shake to some Hendrix might get kind of crazy (unless you're tripping on acid).

Have you ever noticed the dance that the Anglos created for their own punk rock music, a.k.a. the pogo? Yes, the pogo is a dance rooted in white culture; when early punk forerunners the Buzzcocks would rip into their power punk–driven joints, the crowd had no choice but to bounce up and down like a gang of deranged lemmings, creating the perfect dance for punk rock: jumping up and fucking down (big up to Eater). Now (y'all still wit me?) who, what, when, and how did this mosh thing come along? And what does it mean to mosh? Well, I'm going to drop some original, hardcore history on you about the origins of mosh. Check it: Once there was a group of black teens from the Washington, D.C., metro area. These teens were always on the lookout for different and new horizons in life—especially when it came to music. They loved all sorts of sounds—from the smooth psychedelic jazz flavors of Lonnie Liston Smith to the complex musical corridors of Return to Forever. These guys were young, black, and eclectic with their ears wide open.

And don't mistake them for just a band, for they were a clan, always living their daily lives under the premise of PMA (positive mental attitude); concepts derived and practiced by cats like Andrew Carnegie and the Rockefellers during the industrial age. These concepts that promoted the power of positive thinking would go on to fuel the fires of musical exploration and inventiveness in each one of the Brains for years to come/years to cum.

"Go-Go" was the music of their youth, but these cats were just straight tired of it and found it to be not so much boring, but *normal*. Then one day, thanks to Channel 13, a special on "British rock" came across the airwaves. The uninhibited sounds and fashion of the wild punk rock seemed to be the perfect deflection from their everyday D.C. existence, which in turn inspired the four young brothers who were the band Mind Power to change their musical approach (abandoning jazz fusion) and name (to the undisputed Bad Brains); their poster for their first gig billed them as "the greatest punk rock band in the world." The powers of positive suggestion came in handy when it was time to capture the attention of the sparsely cool alt-rock crowd of the era; these scene players are cats who would go on to become "extreme" show hosts on cable television and green punk rock icons.

Anywaze, one day the Brains were performing at the famed 9:30 Club in D.C. (the venue's load-in area was the same alleyway John Wilkes Booth fled down after poppin' the prez in the back of the head—Honest Abe, that is; it was the same alley dudes would puke in after running offstage). This was during the time when the Brains were discovering that their beloved PMA was really Rastafari: a way of life, not a religion, not a philosophy, but a way of life. With this divine discovery came the ever-colorful, widely imitated, never underrated Jamaicanisms.

Jamaica is the birthplace of Rastafari essentially because her people were the first to find a link between "the gods must be crazyish" coronation of Ethiopia's emperor Haile Selassie and the second coming of Christ; thus we have Rastafari. It has been written in the Christian text that a king will be crowned—king of kings, lord of lords, the conquering lion of the tribe of Judah. Lo and behold, the Jamaican daily gleaner ran this very prophesy on its front page, divinely hailing Haile Selassie's coronation and launching the Rastafarian faith.

Now let me return to clearing up this "mosh" crap. The very second the relationship between PMA and Rastafari was overstood, the Brains would introduce its all-white, black dot–spec'd crowd to the true and living jungle (not that French synth-wank sound of yesteryear, but the original kings music: roots rock reggae). Reggae music opened the eyes and spirits of the Brains as they spent months to years living the Rastaman vibration.

One of the early songs to be dropped on the pre–straight-edgers was "I Love I Jah," a tune penned by H.R., inspired by a clash he had with a gang of our sisters—D.C.'s own—at a Salvation Army. Them sisters didn't understand the rip tear Rasta, and the Brains were not trying to hear about their "neck poppin'," hence the song's lyrics: "My lovely sister judge me by my cloth/only to learn to her mistake—not everyone's alike." "I Love I Jah" was the first reggae song ever to bring hope and humility to our lives, and we would perform it every show like some special request sent down from the king himself. But I digress.

I remember one particular show at the 9:30 Club in which the four black rebel teens from the District arrived in full Rasta spec khakis and Clark's, with a vast adornment of pins and medals that celebrated the glory of their newly found father H.I.M. (His Imperial Majesty) Haile Selassie. The crowd was used to the Brains' way-out fashion sense (inspired, of course, by the Sex Pistols), but this new rebel Jah solider look was something to behold. And to top that all off, the Brains would find it hard to slide all of two weeks' worth of dreadlockage into those knit crowns of Rasta recognition (which created a sort of elfish, Papa Smurf sleeping hat appearance; Ian "Minor Threat/Fugazi" McKaye and Henry "S.O.A./Black Flag" Rollins would come to imitate this steelo).

But back to the mosh. The early D.C. crowd would severely slow down their pre–slam dance routine while jockeying along to our reggae songs; their movements came off sorta like a goofy, satirical interpretation of the ska skank. I remember laughing as I watched my friends skanking in a circle with their knit ski caps flailing, as if to say "we are down with y'all Brains. Do it Jah!"

Then there was the song "Banned in D.C."—at the end of which the Brains would switch the gears of their revolutionary sound, causing the whole house to drastically change their slam tempo. Well, it was at some point in either late 1979 or early 1980 that H. R. of the Bad Brains yelled a Rasta/reggae inspired "mash it—mash down Babylon!" Add a little Jamaican accent to the mix and the untrained ear hears "*mosh* it—mosh down Babylon."

There you have it, from the lion's mouth. It was during this time that the pogo grew into slam dancing and slamming morphed into moshing; the front row begat the pit and the pit begat the mosh pit. So the next time some tribal band tattoo-wearing knucklehead tells you Metallica or some other ass-biting hair band invented mosh, you tell 'em to go look up the Brains.

Black rock? A few quick thoughts: Was Jimi Hendrix black rock, or was he an ill-ass blues guitarist who happened to dig altered states? (Yell at me about that when you see me.) Being a so-called black rock brother, I always had reservations about brothers attempting to appear white when performing rock. It seems to me that unless a brother breaks with the spandex, extensions, and wrestling boots, the wide white world of rock won't really have it. I've come to this conclusion based on the black folk who appear in the media reppin' rock. So I've gotta say to the new school of rock and rollers, be yourself, invent and expand the music, expand the *art* form; you don't have to dress like Motley Crüe or play like Hendrix to be rock, all you have to do is rock the fuck out from your heart.

Rock and roll is about the liberation of the spirit, about one's musical soul—and rock has no rules. Actually, the only true rule to rock is really to mean what you are exalting—whether you're kickin' it about girls, cars, parties, whatever. I'm personally a fan of conscious rock—word sound, power (except for when I moonlight wit the White Mandingos. Look out, world); a sound with a purpose, not just loud amps and a party. Then again, all music has its purpose.

Man, the next time someone says "black rock," you should say "white rock," or how 'bout "just rock"? The youth of today should continue to destroy all that is Babylon and thrive for a new way; a way absent of all this black/white nonsense. Just like H.I.M. said to the League of Nations many moons ago: "Until the color of a man's skin is no more significant than the color of his eyes, there will be war." And I say until the sounds that soothe our very souls and nourish our beings are absent from issues of color, there will be wack-ass bands, concepts, and organizations out to taint the blessed magic that is music.

Simply music.

## NOTE

1. "I Love I Jah," written by P. Hudson, D. Jenifer & G. Miller. Bad Brains Publishing.

**SACHA JENKINS**

# HOW THE BAD BRAINS INSPIRED TWO GARDEN-VARIETY BLACK DOTS FROM QUEENS TO BE AS ROCK 'N' ROLL AS THEY WANNA BE (AND PROBABLY YOU TOO)

In the middle 1980s, hip-hop was everything in Astoria, Queens. The Queensbridge Housing Projects (which was about a mile away from Astoria's very own waterfront public housing development) is the place where rising stars like beat-banger extraordinaire Marlon "Marley Marl" Williams and supreme microphone controllers like MC Shan and Roxanne Shanté lived. Astoria PJ's had her own rappin' big willies in a duo known as Supa Lover Cee and Casanova Rud; back in '87, you'd always hear their hit, "Do the James," pumped out of the back of cars back to back with the Audio Two's "Top Billin'." These party slayers made all of the kids on the corner of 9th Street and 27th Avenue nod with immense pride—especially since we all knew Supe and Rud from around the way.

Things were crazy back then; crazy like the frontier Wild West, only our gold rush was fueled by the crack rush. In other words, crack dealers sold their wares in order to buy dookie rope chains, like the kind that rich rap icons like Run-DMC and Jam Master Jay used to rock. Moms and daddies were smoked out; VCRs were bought for twenty dirty bucks, blow jobs were three smackeroos if you caught the right fiend at the right time. Me? I appreciated the major savings on electronics and major appliances, but I was more interested in a way out. Someway, somehow.

Graffiti, believe it or not, would encourage me to leave the 'hood. I'd ride out with a backpack swollen with Krylon, my magic carpet flowing me out to the surf—the cloud had four wheels and grip tape. Don't get it scrambled: I was down with my hip-hop, but I always admired Hendrix on the side. I was down with the brainy, corduroy-donning white kids who, back in the third grade, read detective novels and liked Rush (as in the band from Canada). I was one of *those* brothas. And you know how it is with us kinds of brothas: We usually bump into the other brothas who are like us brothas. My brother from another mother turned out to be this brotha named Chaka Malik. He was from the Woodside Projects. He, too, was a graffiti writer. I'd met him in the hallway at Bryant High School because we both looked like graffiti writers.

At the time, Chaka had an interest in skating; myself and a friend from my 'hood were way more up on it than he was. I could tell that he appreciated the fact that me and my homie were brothas, because back in 1987, it really wasn't cool for brothas to be riding skateboards—because that was considered to be "whiteboy" shit by the heads. It's safe to say that the three of us formed a brothahood. Then again, we weren't on some Black Skaters Coalition type trip or anything. Our crew—Team Stage Dive Skates—was racially and ethnically diverse (word to Dominican Fred, the Keefe brothers, and the Korean brothers).

Chaka was also heavily into hardcore punk. He was forever trying to get me to come out to the Sunday matinees over at CBGB's and the Saturday gigs at the Pyramid. Punk seemed so fucking utterly nuts. Skinheads (who were probably racist) punching each other, kicking out each other's necks? Spitting on one another? (at least that's what it all looked like as I spied a videotape of a Sick of It All show in his living room). Moshing? Hell, no! But a brotha like me wasn't totally close-minded: Chaka made me a few mix tapes comprised of hardcore's hardest; put me up on Spermicide's show on WNYU. I started tuning in. Shit was still sounding nuts to a brotha like me.

On more than a few of the tapes Chaka hit me with, there was a band that really struck a chord, so much so that I had to ask who was who. Sure enough, the band that came up again and again was the Bad Brains.

Bad Brains from different eras even, different albums altogether. He pulled out their *I Against I* album; there were two black faces on the cover, faces obscured with dreads fighting to be seen. These dudes were even ill on the reggae tip. Hmmm. Versatility. I had to have that album right then and there. Duke sold me his worn and weathered and scratched copy for eight bucks!

Chaka was the hardcore expert; he had everybody's first seven inch. The only one he didn't have was the Brains' first 45 donut, "Pay to Cum," backed with "Stay Close to Me." This little gem was released by the Brains themselves back in 1980. Rare as fuck, although it could be had for $50 if one were at Bleecker Bob's at the right time. One day up at Bryant, my guitar teacher, Mrs. Dux (who was a duck, I might add), was out and knocked out by the flu. Chaka, who was out roaming the halls with one of those piss-stained hall passes in tow, decided to check into my room, because clearly, things were off the chain where I was (being a substitute teacher ain't easy). Chaka comes in, sits down. Substitute teacher asks if Chaka belongs there. Chaka tells no lie. Teacher says he can chill if he stays chill.

Me, Colombian skinhead Randy, and Chaka get to talking about hardcore and record collecting. Chaka mentions that the only record that he needs to make his collection complete is "Pay to Cum." Substitute teacher butts in: "I produced that record." All three of us: "Fuck you!" Substitute teacher: "Bring me $20 tomorrow and a copy of the record will be yours." We laughed, kicked out a few "Yeah, rights," and high-stepped into the next period. The next day Chaka bought "Pay to Cum" off my substitute teacher—he really was Jimmi Quidd, producer of the Bad Brains' first record. That was almost like meeting Rick Rubin. That chance meeting really rocked our bells.

Even though it was the Public Enemy era, I decided that pro-blackness shouldn't stop me from flexin' my head with the whiteys: I finally broke down and went with Chaka to a hardcore show at this place on the Lower East Side called the Lismor Lounge. Bugout Society played; they did a song called "Lees and Pumas," and they were throwing White Castle hamburgers at the sixty of us who watched in the dark. Lismor was a dirty fucking basement that you entered via those steel trapdoors that lead to the street level. People are starving, and these white boys are throwing hamburgers? I didn't get it.

Then Absolution played. Chaka was friends with that band. The singer, a cat named Djinji Brown from the Bronx, was a brotha. They were dynamic. With Djinji on the mike, a brotha didn't feel so foreign. Gavin was an amazing guitarist. I started to pick up on the sonic esthetics of hardcore. I knew what I liked, and I was liking more and more. I learned more about the Brains, caught up on the back catalog. Me and Chaka and a stupid posse would go to see a reunited Bad Brains play L'Amour's in Brooklyn (they really like to break up, those Brains) with Living Colour. Living Colour had a bigger marquee value then. The whole club was a mosh pit during the entire abbreviated set. H.R. came out playing the horn; Living Colour frontman Corey Glover dove into the crowd like he just didn't care, flying his arms and fists like helicopters. Everyone in that room knew that they were participating in something sacred.

Chaka—even though he was only six months older than me—graduated from Bryant High two years before me (he started school early and, because of chronic truancy, I was forced to play out the movie called the eighth grade twice). He had moved to Williamsburg with Gavin and they started a new band called Burn. Chaka was a front man now. Now Chaka was gonna step up like Paul "H. R." Hudson did along with fellow Bad Brains Gary "Dr. Know" Miller, Darryl Jenifer, and Earl Hudson ten years earlier.

Burn toured up and down the East Coast hitting the same venues that the Bad Brains had opened up a decade before. I roadied for the band, so I got to sleep in vans and get into fights and steal on behalf of that band. Burn were heavy hitters in the scene; I rolled up to parties outta state with the MVPs. The scene had its own media outlets—'zines—so I bought in and started my own.

After a couple of years, Burn burned out. Chaka would go on to front yet another hard band, Orange 9mm. They were signed to East/West Records at one point for a nice chunk of change. Dave Jerden, the dude who produced Jane's Addiction, produced their first album, *Driver Not Included.* Chaka got to tour the states and Europe several times over. Made videos. He hasn't had a "real" job since. And I would go on to publish my own music magazine and write about rock and roll and hip-hop for magazines like *Spin* and *Vibe.*

Then again, never mind the bollocks about our résumés. The point I'm looking to make here and now is this: If it wasn't for the strength and determination and the innovations of the Bad Brains. . . . The Bad Brains gave at least two regular brothas I know the power of identity and self-determination. They showed us that the righteous way is the route that's truest to self, and that what's truest to self is the purest, most potent form of creative energy there is. It's the kind of power that'll make you a Fearless Vampire Killer. The Bad Brains let us know that it was possible for brothas to hold on to their cultural identities while contributing to a whole new movement that was culturally foreign. The Bad Brains taught us how to get involved. The Bad Brains taught us that, hey, if you can't beat the scene, join the scene and *run* the stinkin' scene—with dignity and superior skill and integrity. The Bad Brains weren't black rock, they were *the* rock; their music touched lives from all walks of life. Every white dread in America needs to drop the Brains—who were steadfast ambassadors of peace, unity, and Rastafari—a little thank you note. Seen?

They were just four regular brothas from D.C. who made the most incredible Mars music you've never heard. Music that is still unfadeable twenty-five years later. Although the Brains haven't had the smoothest career in the music biz (thanks in part to H. R.'s unpredictable behavior; whether he's the realest punk in history or clinically out has yet to be determined); that much isn't too hard to believe because there is nothing easy about their rhythms. Their boom is the kind that breathes in the moment; recoils after the blows have retracted. Besides, the business of money and success will never be able to siphon away the influence that Paul and his brother Earl and Doc and Darryl had on peeps like Kurt, Perry, Flea, Vernon, and Chino.

Salute these brothas when you see 'em, punks—for everyday is Veteran's Day when you're a Bad Brain.

# LESTER BANGS

# THE WHITE NOISE
# SUPREMACISTS[1]

**T**he other day I was talking on the phone with a friend who hangs out on the CBGB's scene a lot. She was regaling me with examples of the delights available to females in the New York subway system. "So the train came to a sudden halt and I fell on my ass in the middle of the car, and not only did nobody offer to help me up but all these boons just sat there laughing at me."

"Boons?" I said. "What's boons?"

"You know," she said. "Black guys."

"Why do you call them that?"

"I dunno. From 'baboons,' I guess."

I didn't say anything.

"Look, I know it's not cool," she finally said. "But neither is being a woman in this city. Every fucking place you go you get these cats hassling you, and sometimes they try to pimp you. And a lot of the times when they hassle you they're black, and when they try to pimp me they're always black. Eventually you can't help it, you just end up reacting."

Sometimes I think nothing is simple but the feeling of pain.

When I was first asked to write this article, I said sure, because the racism (not to mention the sexism, which is even more pervasive and a whole other piece) on the American New Wave scene had been something that I'd been bothered by for a long time. When I told the guys in my own band that I was doing this, they just laughed. "Well, I guess the money's good," said one. "What makes you think the racism in punk has anything special about it that separates it from the rest of the society?" asked another.

"Because the rest of society doesn't go around acting like racism is real hip and cool," I answered heatedly.

"Oh yeah," he sneered. "Just walk into a factory sometime. Or jail."

All right. Power is what we're talking about, or the feeling that you don't have any, or how much ostensible power you can rip outta some other poor sucker's hide. It works the same everywhere, of course, but one of the things that makes the punk stance unique is how it seems to assume substance or at least style by the *abdication* of power: *Look at me! I'm a cretinous little wretch! And proud of it!* So many of the people around the CBGB's and Max's scene have always seemed emotionally if not outright physically crippled—you see speech impediments, hunchbacks, limps, but most of all an overwhelming spiritual flatness. You take parental indifference, a crappy educational system, lots of drugs, media overload, a society with no values left except the hysterical emphasis on physical perfection and you end up with these little nubbins: the only rebellion around as *Life* magazine once labeled the Beats. Richard Hell gave us the catchphrase "Blank Generation," although he insists that he didn't mean a crowd with all the dynamism of a static-furry TV screen but rather a bunch of people finally freed by the collapse of all values to reinvent themselves, to make art statements of their whole lives. Unfortunately, such a great utopian dream, which certainly is not on its first go-round here, remains just that because most people would rather follow. What you're left with, aside from the argument that it beats singles' bars, is compassion. When the Ramones bring that sign onstage that says "GABBA GABBA HEY," what it really stands for is "We accept you." Once you get past the armor of dog collars, black leather, and S&M affectations, you've got some of the gentlest or at least most harmless people in the world: Sid Vicious legends aside, almost all their violence is self-directed.

So if they're all such a bunch of little white lambs, why do some of them have it in for little black lambs? Richard Pinkston, a black friend I've known since my Detroit days, tells me, "When I go to CBGB's I feel like I'm in East Berlin. It's like, I don't mind liberal guilt if it gets me in the restaurant, even if I know the guy still hates me in his mind. But it's like down there they're striving to be offensive however they can, so it's more vocal and they're freer. It's semi-mob thinking."

Richard Hell and the Voidoids are one of the few integrated bands on the scene ("integrated"—what a stupid word). I heard that when he first formed the band, Richard got flak from certain quarters about Ivan Julian a black rhythm guitarist from Washington, D.C., who once played with the Foundations of "Build Me Up Buttercup" fame. I think it says something about what sort of person Richard is that he told all those people to get fucked then and doesn't much want to talk about it now. "I don't remember anything special. I just think that most people that say stuff like what you're talking about are so far beneath contempt that it has no effect that's really powerful. Among musicians there's more professional jealousy than any kind of racial thing; there's so much backbiting in any scene, it's like girls talking about shoes. All musicians are such scum anyway that it couldn't possibly make any difference because you expect 'em to say the worst shit in the world about you."

I called up Ivan, who was the guy having trouble at the pinhead lunch counter in the first place. "Well, I was first drawn to this scene by the simple fact that a lot of the people with musical and social attitudes more or less in common. No one's ever said anything to my face, but I overheard shit. A lot of people are just ignorant assholes. I don't think there's any more racism at CBGB's, where I went every night for about the first year I lived here, than anywhere else in New York City. Maybe a little bit less, because I find New York City a million times more racist than D.C., or Maryland and Virginia where I grew up. There's racism there, outright killings around where I lived, but here it's a lot more insidious. You get four or five different extremes, so many cultures that can't stand each other. It's like, when we toured Europe I was amazed at the bigotry between people from two parts of the same country. They'd accept me, but to each other they were niggers, man. And at CBGB's it's sorta the same way, sometimes. Mutants can learn to hate each other and have prejudices, too. Like Mingus said in *Beneath the Underdog:* forty or fifty years ago, in the ghetto, the lighter you were the better you were. Then you'd turn another corner and if you were somewhat light, like Mingus, there'd be a buncha guys saying 'Shit-colored mutha' ready to trash your ass. My point is, regardless of how much people might have in common they still draw away. There are certain people on the scene, like say this girl in one band who's nothing but a loud-mouthed racist bitch—it's obvious we want nothing to do with each other, so I stay away from her and vice versa.

"I'll tell you one thing: the entrepreneurs, record company people, and shit are a hell of a lot worse. People like Richard Gottehrer, who produced our album, and Seymour Stein and a lot of other people up at Sire Records. They were *totally* condescending, they'd talk to you differently, like you were a child or something. I heard a lot of clichés on the level of being invited over to somebody's house for fried chicken."

I was reminded instantly of the day I was in the office of a white woman of some intelligence, education, and influence in the music business, and the subject of race came up. "Oh," she said, "I like them so much better when they were just Negroes. When they became blacks. . . ." She wrinkled her nose irritably.

"Race hate?" says Voidoids' lead guitarist Bob Quine. "Sure, it gives me 'n' Ivan something to do onstage: *The Defiant Ones*."

But the ease and insight of the Voidoids are somewhat anomalous on the New York scene. This scene and the punk stance in general are riddled with self-hate, which is always reflexive, and anytime you conclude that life stinks and the human race mostly amounts to a pile of shit, you've got the perfect breeding ground for fascism. A lot of outsiders, in fact, think punk is fascist, but that's only because they can't see beyond certain buzzwords, symbols, and pieces of regalia that (I *think*) really aren't that significant: Ron Asheton of the Stooges used to wear swastikas, Iron Crosses, and jackboots onstage, but I don't remember any right-wing rants ever popping up in the music he did with Iggy or his own later band, which many people were not exactly thrilled to hear was called the New Order.

In the past three years Ron's sartorial legacy has given us an international subculture whose members might easily be mistaken at first glance for little brownshirts. They aren't, for the most part. Only someone as dumb as the Ramones are always accused of being could be offended when they sing "I'm a Nazi schatze," or tell us that the first rule is to obey the laws of Germany and then follow it with "Eat kosher salami." I've hung out with the Ramones, and they treat everybody of any race or sex the same—who *they* hate isn't Jews or blacks or gays or anybody but certain spike-conk assholes who just last week graduated from *The Rocky Horror Picture Show* lines to skag-dabblings and now stumble around Max's busting their nuts trying to be decadent.

Whereas you don't have to try at all to be a racist. It's a little coiled clot of venom lurking there in all of us, white and black, goy and Jew, ready to strike out when we feel embattled, belittled, brutalized. Which is why it has to be monitored, made taboo and restrained, by society and the individual. But there's a difference between hate and a little of the old *épater* gob at authority: Swastikas in punk are basically another way for kids to get a rise out of their parents and maybe the press, both of whom deserve the irritation. To the extent that most of these spikedomes ever had a clue on what that stuff originally meant, it only went so far as their intent to shock. "It's like a stance," as Ivan says. "A real immature way of being dangerous."

Maybe. Except that after a while this casual, even ironic embrace of the totems of bigotry crosses over into the real poison. Around 1970 there was a carbuncle named Wayne McGuire who kept contributing installments of something he called "An Aquarian Journal" to *Fusion* magazine, wherein he suggested between burblings of regurgitated Nietzsche and bad Céline ellipses that the Velvet Underground represented some kind of mystical milestone in the destiny of the Aryan race, and even tried to link their music with the ideas of Mel Lyman, who was one of the proto-types for the current crop of mindnapping cult-daddies.

On a less systematic level, we had little outcroppings like Iggy holler-ing, "Our next selection tonight for all you Hebrew ladies in the audience is entitled 'Rich Bitch'!" on the 1974 recorded-live bootleg *Metallic K.O.,* and my old home turf *Creem* magazine, where around the same time I was actually rather proud of myself for writing things like (in an article on David Bowie's "soul" phase): "Now, as we all know, white hippies and beatniks before them would never have existed had there not been a whole generational subculture with a gnawing yearning to be nothing less than the downest baddest *niggers.* . . . Everybody has been walking around for the last year or so acting like faggots ruled the world, when in actuality it's the *niggers* who control and direct everything just as it always has been and properly should be."

I figured all this was in the Lenny Bruce spirit of let's-defuse-them-epithets-by-slinging-'em-out—in Detroit I thought absolutely nothing of going to parties with people like David Ruffin and Bobby Womack where I'd get drunk, maul the women, and improvise blues songs along the lines of "Sho' wish ah wuz a nigger / Then mah dick'd be bigger," and of course they all laughed. It took years before I realized what an asshole I'd been, not to mention how lucky I was to get out of there with my white hide intact.

I'm sure a lot of those guys were very happy to see this white kid drunk on his ass making a complete fool if not a human TV set out of himself, but to this day I wonder how many of them hated my guts right then. Because Lenny Bruce was wrong—maybe in a better world than this such parlor games would amount to cleansing jet offtakes, and between friends, where a certain bond of mutual trust has been firmly established, good-natured racial trade-offs can be part of the vocabulary of under-stood affections. But beyond that trouble begins—when you fail to real-ize that no matter how harmless your intentions are, there is no reason to think that any shit that comes out of your mouth is going to be under-stood or happily received. Took me a long time to find it out, but those words are *lethal,* man, and you shouldn't just go slinging them around for effect. This seems almost too simple and obvious to say, but maybe it's good to have something simple and obvious stated once in a while, espe-cially in this citadel of journalistic overthink. If you're black or Jewish or Latin or gay those little vernacular epithets are bullets that riddle your guts and then fester and burn there, like torture-flak hailing on you wher-ever you go. Ivan Julian told me that whenever he hears the word "nig-ger," no matter who says it, black or white, he wants to kill. Once when

I was drunk I told Hell that the only reason hippies ever existed in the first place was because of niggers, and when I mentioned it to Ivan while doing this article I said, "You probably don't even remember—" "Oh yeah, I remember," he cut me off. And that was two years ago, one ostensibly harmless little slip. You take a lifetime of that, and you've got grounds for trying in any way possible, even if it's only by convincing one individual at a time, to remove those words from the face of the earth. Just like Hitler and Idi Amin and all other enemies of the human race.

Another reason for getting rid of all those little verbal barbs is that no matter how *you* intend them, you can't say them without risking misinterpretation by some other bigoted asshole; your irony just might be his cup of hate. Things like the *Creem* articles and partydown exhibitionism represented a reaction against the hippie counterculture and what a lot of us regarded as its pious pussyfooting around questions of racial and sexual identity, questions we were quite prepared to drive over with bulldozers. We believed nothing could be worse, more pretentious and hypocritical, than the hippies and the liberal masochism in whose sidecar they toked along, so we embraced an indiscriminate, half-joking and half-hostile mindlessness that seemed to represent, as Mark Jacobson pointed out in his *Voice* piece on Legs McNeil, a new kind of cool. "I don't discriminate," I used to laugh, "I'm prejudiced against *everybody!*" I thought it made for a nicely charismatic mix of Lenny Bruce freespleen and W. C. Fields misanthropy, conveniently ignoring Lenny's delirious, nigh-psychopathic inability to resolve the contradictions between his idealism and his infantile, scatological exhibitionism, as well as the fact that W. C. Fields's racism was as real and vile as—or more real and vile than—anybody else's. But when I got to New York in 1976 I discovered that some kind of bridge had been crossed by a lot of the people I thought were my peers in this emergent Cretins' Lib generation.

This was stuff even I had to recognize as utterly repellent. I first noticed it the first time I threw a party. The staff of *Punk* magazine came, as well as members of several of the hottest CBGB's bands, and when I did what we always used to do at parties in Detroit—put on soul records so everybody could dance—I began to hear this: "What're you playing all that nigger disco shit for, Lester?"

"That's not nigger disco shit," I snarled, "that's *Otis Redding* you assholes!" But they didn't want to hear about it, and now I wonder if in any way I hadn't dug my own grave, or at least helped contribute to their ugliness and the new schism between us. The music editor of this paper [*Village Voice*] has theorized that one of the most important things about New Wave is how much of it is almost purely white music, and what a massive departure that represents from the almost universally blues-derived rock of the past. I don't necessarily agree with that—it ignores the reggae influence running through music as diverse as that of the Clash, Pere Ubu, Public Image Ltd., and the Police, not to mention the Chuck Berry licks at the core of Steve ones s attack But there is at least a grain of truth there—the Contortions' James Brown/Albert Ayler spasms aside, most of the SoHo bands are as white as John Cage, and there's an evolution of sound, rhythm, and stance running from the Velvets through the Stooges to the Ramones and their children that takes us farther and farther from the black-stud postures of Mick Jagger that Lou Reed and Iggy partake in but that Joey Ramone certainly doesn't. I respect Joey for that, for having the courage to be himself, especially at the sacrifice of a whole passel of macho defenses. Joey is a white American kid from Forest Hills, and as such his cultural inputs have been white, from "The Jetsons" through Alice Cooper. But none of this cancels out the fact that most of the greatest, deepest music America has produced has been, when not entirely black, the product of miscegenation. You can't appreciate rock 'n' roll without appreciating where it comes from, as Pinkston put it.

Musical questions, however, can be passed off as matters of taste. Something harder to pass off entered the air in 1977, when I started encountering little zaps like this: I opened up a copy of a Florida punk fanzine called New Order and read an article by Miriam Linna of the Cramps, Nervus Rex, and now Zantees: "I love the Ramones [because] this is the celebration of everything American—everything teenaged and wonderful and white and urban. . . ." You could say the "white" jumping out of that sentence was just like Ornette Coleman declaring This Is Our Music, except that the same issue featured a full-page shot of Miriam and one of her little friends posing proudly with their leathers and shades and a pistol in front of the headquarters of the United White People's Party under a sign bearing three flags: "GOD" (cross), "COUNTRY" (stars and stripes), "RACE" (swastika).

Sorry, Miriam, I can go just so far with affectations of kneejerk cretinism before I puke. l remember the guy in the American Nazi Party being asked, "What about the six million?" in PBS's California Reich, and answering "Well, the way I heard it it was only really four-and-a-half million, but I wish it was six," and I imagine you'd find that pretty hilarious, too. I probably would have at one time. If that makes me a wimp now, good, that means you and anybody else who wants to get their random vicarious kicks off White Power can stay the fuck away from me.

More recently, I've heard occasional stories like the one about one of the members of Teenage Jesus and the Jerks yelling "Hey, you bunch of fucking niggers" at a crowd of black kids in front of Hurrah one night and I am not sorry to report getting the shit kicked out of him for it. When I told this to Richard Hell, he dismissed it: "He thinks he's being part of something by doing that—joining a club that'll welcome him with open arms, trying to get accepted. It's not real. Maybe I'm naive, but I think that's what all racism is—not really directed at the target but designed to impress some other moron."

He may be right, but so what? James Chance of the Contortions used to come up to Bob Quine pleading for Bob to play him his Charlie Parker records. Now, in a *New York Rocker* interview, James dismisses the magical qualities of black music as "just a bunch of nigger bullshit." Why? Because James wants to be famous, and ripping off Albert Ayler isn't enough. My, isn't he *outrageous?* ("He's got the shtick down," said Danny Fields, stifling a yawn, when they put James on the cover of *Soho Weekly News.*) And congrats to Andy Shernoff of the Dictators, who did so well they're now called the Rhythm Dukes, for winning the *Punk* magazine Drunk as a Skunk contest by describing "Camp Runamuck" as "where Puerto Ricans are kept until they learn to be human."

Mind you, I like a cheap laugh at somebody else's expense as well as the next person. So I got mine off Nico, who did "Deutschland Über Alles" at CBGB's last month and was just naive enough to explain to Mary Harron, in a recent interview in *New Wave Rock,* why she was dropped by Island Records: "I made a mistake. I said in *Melody Maker* to some interviewer that I didn't like negroes. That's all. They took it so *personally* . . . although it's a whole different race. I mean, Bob Marley doesn't resemble a *negro,* does he? . . . He's an archetype of Jamaican . . . but with the features like white people. I don't like the features. They're so much like animals. . . . it's cannibals, no?"

Haw haw haw, doncha just love them dumb kraut cunts? And speaking of dumbness and krauts, my old pal Legs McNeil has this band called Shrapnel, who are busy refighting World War II onstage in dogtags, army surplus clothes, and helmets that fall over their eyes like cowlicks, while they sing songs with titles like "Combat Love." Personally I think it's not offensive (well, about as offensive as *Hogan's Heroes*) that they're too young to remember Vietnam—it's funny. The whole show is a cartoon (it's no accident that they open their set with the "Underdog" theme) and a damn good one. Musically they're up there, too—tight dragstrip guitar wranglings that could put them on a par with the MC5 someday, combined with a stage act that could make them as popular as Kiss. The only problem, which has left me with such mixed feelings I hardly know what to say to them, is that the lyrics of some of the songs are nothing but racist swill. The other night I sat in the front row at CBGB's and watched them deliver one of the hottest sets I've seen from any band this year while a kid in the seat right next to me kept yelling out requests for "'Hey Little Gook!' 'Hey

Little Gook!'" the whole time. Christgau, who considers them "proto-fascist" and hates them, told me they also had lyrics on the order of "Send all the *spics* back to Cuba." I mentioned this to Legs and he seemed genuinely upset: "No," he swore, "it's 'Send all the *spies* back to Cuba.'"

"Okay," I said (Christgau still doesn't believe him), "what about 'Hey Little Gook'?"

"Aw, c'mon," he said, "that's just like in a World War II movie where they say 'kraut' and 'slants' and stuff like that!"

I told him I thought there was a difference between using words in dramatic context and just to draw a cheap laugh in a song. But the truth is that by now I was becoming more confused than ever. All I knew was that when you added all this sort of stuff up you realized a line had been crossed by certain people we thought we knew, even believed in, while we weren't looking. Either that or they were always across that line and we never bothered to look until we tripped over it. And sometimes you even find that you yourself have drifted across that line. I was in Bleecker Bob's the other night, drunk and stoned, when a black couple walked in. They asked for some disco record, Bob didn't have it of course, a few minutes went by, and reverting in the haze to my Detroit days I said something about such and such band or music having to do with "niggers." A couple more minutes went by. Then Bob said, "You know what, Lester? When you said that, those two people were standing right behind you."

I looked around and they were out on the sidewalk, looking at the display in his front window. Stricken, I rushed out and began to burble: "Listen . . . somebody just told me what I said in there . . . and I know it doesn't mean anything to you, I'm not asking for some kind of absolution, but I just want you to know that . . . I have some idea . . . how utterly, utterly *awful* it was. . . ."

I stared at them helplessly. The guy just smiled, dripping contempt. "Oh, that's okay, man . . . it's just your head. . . ." *I've run up against a million assholes like you before, and I'll meet a million after you—so fucking what?*

I stumbled back into the store, feeling like total garbage, like the complete hypocrite, like I had suddenly glimpsed myself as everything I claimed to despise. Bob said, "Look, Lester, don't worry about it, forget it, it happens to everybody," and, the final irony, sold me a reggae album I wondered how I was going to listen to.

If there's nothing more poisonous than bigotry, there's nothing more pathetic than liberal guilt. I feel like an asshole even retelling the story here, as if I expected some sort of expiation for what cannot be undone, or as if such a tale would be news to anybody. In a way Bob was right: I put a dollop more pain in the world, and that was that. There is certainly something almost emetically self-serving about the unreeling of such confessions in the pages of papers like the *Voice*—it's the sort of thing that contributed to the punk reaction in the first place. But it illustrates one primal fact: how easily and suddenly you may find yourself imprisoned and suffocated by the very liberation from cant, dogma, and hypocrisy you thought you'd achieved. That sometimes—usually?—you'll find that you don't know where to draw the line until you're miles across it in a field of land mines. Like wanting the celebration of violent disorder that was the Sex Pistols, ending up with Sid and Nancy instead, yet realizing the next day that you still want to hear Sid sing "Somethin' Else" and see *The Great Rock 'n' Roll Swindle,* and not just because you want to understand this whole episode better but to get your kicks. These are contradictions that refuse to be resolved, which maybe is what most of life eventually amounts to.

But that's begging the question again. Most people, I guess, don't even think about drawing the lines: They just seem to go through life reacting at random, like the cab driver who told me that the report we were listening to on the radio about Three Mile Island was just a bunch of bullshit dreamed up by the press to sell papers or keep us tuned in. And maybe if you go on like that (assuming, of course, that we all *don't* melt), nothing will blow up in your face. But you may end up imploding instead. A lot of people around CBGB's are already mad at me about this article, and the arguments seem mostly to run along the lines of Why don't you can it because there's not really that much racism down here and all you're gonna do is create more problems for our scene just when this Sid Vicious thing had blown over. I mentioned Pinkston's experience and was told he was paranoid. Like the people at Harrisburg who didn't wanna leave their jobs and actually believed it would be safe to stick around after the pregnant women and children were evacuated, these kids are not gonna believe this stuff exists until it happens to them. Hell, a lot of them are Jewish and still don't believe it even though they know about the neighborhoods their parents can't get into.

When I started writing this, I was worried I might trigger incidents of punk-bashing by black gangs. Now I realize that nobody cares. Most white people think the whole subject of racism is boring, and anybody looking for somebody to stomp is gonna find them irrespective of magazine articles. Because nothing could make the rage of the underclass greater than it is already, and nothing short of a hydrogen bomb on their own heads or a sudden brutal bigoted slap in the face will make almost anybody think about anybody else's problems but their own. And that's where you cross over the line. At least when you allow the poison in you to erupt, that can be dealt with; maybe the greater evil occurs when you refuse to recognize that the poison even exists. In other words, when you assent by passivity or indifference. Hell, most people *live* on the other side of that line.

There is something called Rock Against Racism (and now Rock Against Sexism) in England, an attempt at simple decency by a lot of people whom one would think too young and naïve to begin to appreciate the contradictions. Yippie bullshit aside, it could never happen in New York, which is deeply saddening, not because you want to think that rock 'n' roll can save the world but because since rock 'n' roll is bound to stay in your life you would hope to see it reach some point where it might not add to the cruelty and exploitation already in the world. In a place where people are as walled off from one another as we are in America now, all you can do is try to make some sort of simple, humble, and finally private beginning. You feel like things like this should not need to be said, articles like this should perhaps not even be written. You may think, as I do of the sexism in the Stranglers' and Dead Boys' lyrics, that the people and things I've talked about here are so stupid as to be beneath serious consideration. But would you say the same thing to the black disco artist who was refused admittance to Studio 54 even though he had a Top Ten crossover hit that they were probably playing inside the damn place at the time, the doorman/bouncer explaining to a white friend of the artist, "I'm not letting this guy in—he just looks like another street nigger to me"? Or would you rather argue the difference between Racist Chic and Racist Cool? If you would, just make sure you do it in the nearest factory. Or jail.

## NOTE

1. Reprinted from the *Village Voice,* 30 April 1979.

## BARRY WALTERS

# PRINCE
## LEADS BLACK POP
## THROUGH THE BACK DOOR

The year is 1982 and you've just bought a copy of *1999*. You pull off the shrink-wrap, examine the inner sleeves that contain both vinyl discs, and there, between your hands, is Prince's half-naked ass.

If you'd been following Prince Rogers Nelson's career up to this point, you'd already seen him riding a winged white horse nude and blurry on the back of his 1979 album *Prince,* lying on a bed wearing thigh-high leggings, a raincoat, and not much else on the back of his 1980 *Dirty Mind* LP, and standing in the shower covered only by a skimpy pair of leather briefs and a dainty gold chain that wrapped around his waist for the poster that accompanied 1981's *Controversy.*

But this was different. This was a man's extremely round and possibly hairy butt. Although a sheet coyly covered half of it, you could clearly see the beginnings of a crack. Surrounded by neon and fog, Prince's heavily made-up face was dimly lit, but his body shined as he lay in bed and stared at the camera, a paintbrush in his hand, an empty page in front of him waiting to be filled with portraiture. It was a sign o' the times that said: Check out this fine black ass and I'll paint a picture of your curiosity/desire/repulsion.

Prince in 1982 lay somewhere between the pleasure principles of R&B-oriented dance music and the eccentric individualism of New Wave. It's usually overlooked that when his first album appeared in 1978, Prince was first promoted as a disco do-it-yourselfer. His initial singles, "Soft and Wet" and "Just as Long as We're Together," were keyboard-dominated dance tracks delivered mostly in a falsetto that allied him with Sylvester, the pioneering gay disco diva who shrieked gospel-schooled cries in sequin-encrusted gowns and who'd unsuccessfully launched his recording career as a black glitter rocker in the wake of David Bowie. When Prince first appeared on *American Bandstand* to lip-synch his first pop hit, "I Wanna Be Your Lover," MC Dick Clark briefly interviewed a barely clothed singer who could only utter a few mumbled words in a whisper that made Michael Jackson's boy-squeak sound butch.

"I Wanna Be Your Lover" arrived late in 1979 at that exact moment when the media suddenly backed away from all things disco. This abrupt cultural reversal rejected every rhythmic and uptempo genre that wasn't rock 'n' roll, and it put a freeze on up-and-coming black artists with nat-ural crossover appeal. Unless one was already Diana Ross, Kool & the Gang, the Commodores, or a Jackson, most black musicians suddenly had to abandon thoughts of reaching a mainstream that had been eager for dance music only a few months earlier and adopt a black-music-for-black-folks strategy. It was either funk or die, or take your chances with New Wave.

By the time Prince dropped his *1999* opus, he'd lost the disco tag, but retained its ambiguously gay connotations, while bolstering his connec-tions to New Wave and funk with his *Dirty Mind* and *Controversy* LPs. De-spite his guitar skills and free-spirit similarities to Jimi Hendrix, Prince wasn't about to penetrate the pale world of traditional rock just yet; that would soon come with his next album and first film, *Purple Rain*. Not one to hold back the freak card, Prince knew electro-funk and neo-punk were the broadest platforms for his aesthetic sprawl that the era could offer, even if they couldn't entirely contain him.

The 1980s truly began in 1982: Madonna released her first single. Michael Jackson let loose *Thriller*. Culture Club's "Do You Really Wanna Hurt Me" and the Human League's "Don't You Want Me" were heard on New York black radio months before they went pop, back to back with paradigm-shaking future rap classics like Grandmaster Flash & the Furi-ous Five's "The Message" and Afrika Bambaataa & the Soul Sonic Force's "Planet Rock." A new R&B sound and presentation, first heard on Evelyn "Champagne" King's 1981 post-disco comeback "I'm in Love," had begun: the sound of soul being stripped down, overdubbed in the studio by a drastically reduced cluster of musicians and a growing number of machines. Although Stevie Wonder birthed this approach a decade earlier with classic albums like *Innervisions,* it wasn't until R&B's prototypal producer/songwriter/multi-instrumentalist and future solo star Kashif replaced the conventional electric bass with keyboards on multiple black radio smashes for King, Melba Moore ("Mind Up Tonight"), himself, and others that the one-man funk groove had come of age. Given the fact that few uptempo R&B successes were now crossing over, Kashif's strategy of cutting out the lavish string orchestras of disco and the sprawling horn sections of funk may have been in pursuit of musical modernity, but it was also a cost-cutting measure that record labels large and small soon loved.

Technology made the switch possible. Synthesizers were suddenly much cheaper and easier to play than only a few years before. Listen to the sequencer on Donna Summer's pioneering 1977 disco anthem "I Feel Love" and hear it subtly and repeatedly go out of sync with the drums. The new keyboards heard on Kraftwerk's 1981 *Computer World* album (another left-field but hugely influential black radio hit) were precise, eager to please, and their deeper bottom end connected with the b-boys who lugged around those monster ghetto blasters with the giant woofer speakers. Suddenly the thumb-popping electric bass guitar that fed the previous decade's funk no longer fueled the hippest, most hypnotic breakdancers. Urban teens now craved electro-jams with the latest synth-driven space-bass.

Prince gave it to them, yet cut it with New Wave. Prince's restless, boundless songwriting ability suited the style's addiction to bubblegum novelty, cheap nostalgia, outré statements, and nervous plastic rhythms. His one-man-band approach to funk didn't swing, didn't sweat like the live-in-the-studio, James Brown–led jams of yore, but that wasn't its intention. New Wave shared electro's celebration of stiffness—the up-and-down pogo of punk, or the accelerated side-to-side skank perfected by Belinda Carlisle—that has come to epitomize white folks' dance moves in the 1980s. Prince reveled in mechanical beats, and his rigidity helped set him apart from the fluidity of disco, the looseness of garage band rock 'n' roll. Funk celebrated The One, the initial downbeat, the jungle pulse that pushes. Prince instead accentuated the upstroke, the clattering snare drum, the metropolitan impulse that pulls. It's the overpowering *snap* of his productions that was soon picked up by the early beat-box rap hits, like Run-DMC's "Sucker MCs" and that whole New Jack Swing Teddy Riley/Bobby Brown/New Kids On the Block sound that closed the decade with deliberately cheap and easily duplicated kiddie R&B.

Whether wistfully bopping with "When You Were Mine" (a future Cyndi Lauper cover) or laying down a new-school party manifesto with "D.M.S.R.," Prince put his purple paws on so many styles with such a recognizable sonic signature that he ended up creating his own genre. By 1982 he'd already branched out with his sleazy girl group Vanity 6, recorded two albums with (some say for) his more traditional funk alter-ego, the Time, and had more on the way with less important but still status-reinforcing releases on his own Paisley Park label (the Family, Apollonia 6, Sheila E., Mazarati, Madhouse, Jill Jones, Taja Savelle, etc.). Together with Tina Turner, Lionel Richie, Quincy Jones, and Michael Jackson, Prince created the mid-1980s sound of black pop. But unlike his peers, Prince, despite his versatility, truly and singlehandedly authored an aesthetic, one that would be elaborated on by associates (particularly early Time members Jimmy Jam and Terry Lewis, who'd soon write for and produce the SOS Band, Janet Jackson, Cheryl Lynn, and others, as well as Revolution members Jesse Johnson, Wendy & Lisa, and Bobby Z) and imitators (Ready For the World, Dreamboy, Jermaine Stewart). This Midwest crossover funk-pop became so omnipresent that it didn't even need a name, and no one did it better than its originator. It was simply Princemusic.

Although they were solely made possible by the recording studio's infinite potential to dub and redub, Prince's productions weren't sonically sophisticated in the more-is-more Phil Spector tradition. Play them next to the lush disco productions they followed, or today's digitally perfected hip-hop, and many of Prince's classics seem thin, crude, even tacky. Prince found the groove he was looking for on what would be the biggest hit of his career and quite probably his greatest achievement, 1984's "When Doves Cry," when he dropped the bassline he'd originally created for this late addition to *Purple Rain*. Maybe he was influenced by the radical rap tracks of the time that turned the volume of his clattering snares even higher and offered little more than rhythm machines and rhyme. Nowadays, anti-corporate rock acts like the White Stripes and the Yeah Yeah Yeahs transform the absence of bass guitar into a positive, as if to say that they're so punk that they don't need bass. Prince's statement on "When Doves Cry" was even more extreme: He was so funky that he didn't need the foundation on which funk is built, the instrument that is to funk what an electric guitar is to rock.

Prince was like that: He didn't need to be macho. He didn't need to be street. He certainly didn't, as the expression goes, "represent." When he tried years later to close the gap between himself and hip-hop, he simply and emphatically represented himself: The title of his most notable rap track is "My Name Is Prince."

That's what made Prince so rock 'n' roll. Even after decades of mainstreaming, rock still loves those who stand out from the crowd—misfits and renegades and deviants and sexually ambiguous straights who might as well be bent. Hip-hop generally does not, and it's taken a decade-and-a-half of gangsta-isms and Puff Daddy–dominated designer R&B to coax black music into welcoming the weirdoes back to the 'hood. If you listen closely, you can hear the echo of Prince's vibe in records produced by Timbaland and the Neptunes, and it's even more overt in those retro-futurist club records by Felix Da Housecat and other electroclash mutants who party like it's 1982.

When I think of Prince, I think back to that year, and his butt in that bed. This was not now, when prominent and barely clad female buttocks adorn every other hip-hop video, and we talk about Jennifer Lopez's rear section with the same reverence with which we regard Marilyn Monroe's smile. Reagan was in office, the New Conservatism had begun, and what soon became recognized as AIDS was then known as "gay cancer." It was a dangerous time to put your butt on the line, and that's what made Prince's pose so liberating. Like Lopez, Kylie Minogue, and other short people, Prince had a butt that didn't stop. It was geometrically balanced, so childlike, so feminine, and clearly his best feature. As if they'd been greased up and ready for entry, Prince's buttocks shined: You could practically see yourself in those cheeks.

And that, today, remains radical. Prince invited fans and foes alike to find their reflection in what we're still told shouldn't be shown. Aside from Nelly and his sagging athletic wear, when was the last time a black man successfully dropped his drawers in the face of pop culture? It's a transgression that literally goes beyond the pale: Even a veteran white hunk like George Clooney spooked reviewers and filmgoers alike when he bared his bottom through long stretches of the 2002 sci-fi film *Solaris*, as if he violated an unwritten law stating that naked male posteriors should not float through space. Prince went one further two decades earlier by putting his butt into the bedrooms of a growing multiracial audience, and he did it in an era when album art really did mean something, just before CDs would shrink such gestures to near-irrelevance and MTV would learn to systematically sell sex and race and shock. To be sure, Prince wasn't always sexually progressive. Half the time he seemed as if he was pimping Vanity, Apollonia, Sheila E., and the other lingerie-clad women of his Revolution. But he backed up his booty music by emancipating his own posterior, and did so with a ridiculous enthusiasm that's gone sadly out fashion.

# MARK ANTHONY NEAL

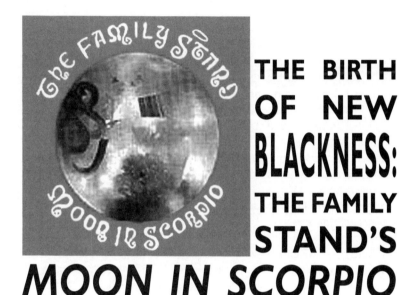

# THE BIRTH OF NEW BLACKNESS: THE FAMILY STAND'S MOON IN SCORPIO

I n May 2001, the exhibition *Freestyle* opened at the Studio Museum in Harlem. The show featured twenty-eight artists who were described by the show's curator, Thelma Golden, as reflecting the "post-black" aesthetic. According to Golden, "post-black" refers to artists who are "adamant about not being labeled as 'black' artists, though their work [is] steeped, in fact deeply interested, in redefining complex notions of blackness." Golden's notion of the "post-black" owes something to Trey Ellis's much–debated essay "The New Black Aesthetic," which initially gave rise to the perception that the post–civil rights generation of black artists and critics—the Soul Babies—represented a distinct break from "modern" blackness. The aesthetic that Golden identifies in the "post-black" could have been used to describe the music of the Family Stand. Beginning with their debut *Chapters: A Novel by Evon Geffries and the Stand* (1988) and followed by *Chain* (1990), *Moon in Scorpio* (1991), and *Connected* (1998), the music of the group embodied a style that consistently challenged efforts to define it. Perhaps none of the group's recordings captured that style better than *Moon in Scorpio*. Released the year after Living Colour's *Time's Up*, it would be easy to characterize *Moon in Scorpio* as quintessential black rock (at least according to mainstream taste). Still, it's commonplace to think of the trio as the progenitors of what later became "neo-soul"—a casual reference to their clear devotion to the soul music that came before them. What *Moon in Scorpio* really marked was the birth of Newblackness.

In an interview with Greg Tate, Golden traces the roots of post-black art to the 1980s and the "moment of multiculturalism, a moment of discovery when people said, Let's explore; let's discover and expand. It had this real frontier quality."[1] No doubt there was a sense of discovery associated with mainstream assumptions about the very concept of *black* rock bands, particularly in an era, the late 1980s, in which black expression became synonymous with hip-hop culture. For folks unfamiliar with the likes of Mother's Finest and Bad Brains (or the Isleys and Funkadelic for that matter), groups like 24–7 Spyz, Living Colour, the Black Rock Coalition, and the Family Stand were indeed novelties—fly boys and girls in the buttermilk. Useful as Golden's depiction of post-black is, I'd like to gently nudge the concept even further in consideration of what I call newblackness. The "newblack" (uttered in a cadence reminiscent of the sound of be-bop) is a term coined by poet and Audre Lorde biographer Masani Alexis De Veaux to describe the contemporary moment of blackness—one that represents a distinct fracture from previous eras. Taking some liberties with De Veaux's concept, newblackness embodies a radical fluidity within the spheres of blackness that allow for powerful conceptualizations across black genders, sexualities, ethnicities generations, socioeconomic positions, and socially constructed performances of "black" identity (like Dunbar said, so long ago, "We Wear the Mask"). The collapsing of the term "new black" into one word ("newblack") distances itself from Ellis's previous pronunciation of fractured black aesthetic(s) by heightening the sensations of fluidity and hybridity that the concept aims to illuminate.

In some sense it's about conceiving of blackness in the absence of the black racial subject—what happens to blackness when the need (and desire) to acknowledge the physical presence of black folk is removed. Without having to acknowledge the social realities of the black subject, black artists can be freed to explore rich hybrid notions of blackness without the risk of such work being viewed as some unspoken erosion of blackness. Me'Shell NdegéOcello's "Six Legged Griot," which posits a singular black subject that contains the spirit and talents of three radically different black artists, Etheridge Knight (the quintessential prison poet), Claude McKay, and June Jordan, is but one example of the kinds of fluidity that a newblack aesthetic actualizes.

The Family Stand's *Moon in Scorpio* embodied many of the attributes of newblackness before such a language existed to conceive of it as such. Though their previous release, *Chain,* began to chart some of the terrain that *Moon in Scorpio* covered, the most commercially successful track from the album was "Ghetto Heaven," which hit on the basic conventions that made New Jack Swing and the Soul II Soul shuffle the flavors in the hood's ear. In his review of the group's late 1991 performance at Wetlands in New York City, Peter Watrous suggested that *Moon in Scorpio* "sounds new, as if it were the product of an imagination that hadn't been hindered by the racial politic of genre."[2] What distinguished *Moon in Scorpio* was not simply the musical fluidity that it signified, but the fluidity of thought that allowed the group to openly confront issues within the mainstream of black life that are usually rendered as unspoken. Of course the fact that the group's musical style was largely unnamable and thus jettisoned to the margins of black life and culture emboldened them to provide the kinds of progressive commentary that have become their signature.

"New World Order," the opening track from *Moon in Scorpio,* gives early indication of the project's ambitions. The title is of course a reference to the Reaganesque mantra that shorthands American imperialism in the late twentieth century. The song was one of the few produced by black artists at the time that lit a fire under Papa Doc Bush (shout to Bruh Gil Scott-Heron) for the politics of the Gulf War. Though "New World Order" never received the attention of Paris's "Bush Killa," the song's lyrics speak powerfully to Bush Sr.'s bankrupt foreign policies. But what the song really highlights is the disconnect between Bush et al.'s attempts to control world events and the organic nature of revolution—the phrase "world in the midst of revolution" dutifully repeated throughout the song to buttress the point. So whether riffing about the rotation of the earth or the movable stages of political resistance (both as localized acts of personal politics and more widespread efforts to bring systems like the pre-Mandela South Africa to its knees), these folks weren't in control of nothin' despite what CNN told ya. It's like Fela Kuti once said, "water no get enemy"—here the notion that the politics of resistance and struggle were natural and organic is reinforced in V. Jeffrey Smith's improvisational rant on his tenor sax.

Lest folks think that the title of the song was also a reference to a "new world order" where bands like the Family Stand could get MTVed, the constant refrain that things are always in the "midst of revolution" is a not-so-subtle reminder that black folk had always been getting their revolutions on—the praxis of the "changing same," if you will (Sly and the Fam are all up in the mix). The project's title track also hints at a world more defined by randomness than control. The music on "Moon in Scorpio" wildly fluctuates between a speedball metal groove and the power rock anthem—a metaphor for the competing realities of insanity and clarity ("Bouts with insanity are good for the soul / It kills the façade of being in control"). And it is in this moment of clarity—when the "moon is in Scorpio"—that "new world orders get seen for what they are / the same old folks trying to hold on to power."

For all the talk that the Family Stand was bred in some alternative universe without an intersection at Malcolm Avenue and King Boulevard, much of the action throughout *Moon in Scorpio* takes place right around the way, up the block. Some of the strongest tracks cut across the grain of straight-up Afro-diasporic crisis, placing a mirror up to the folks who might otherwise view the Family Stand perspective as born of a world both unknown and unwanted. And there *was* something foreign about black folk giving a critical eye to some of the demons that befall the weak and the privileged, particularly after decades of unwashed linen piled in the collective closets of too many New Negroes–cum–Black Power nationalists. So like some of their black women writer peers, the Family Stand got to the core of the ongoing pain and despair that murked the streets of too many ghetto nation-states, while a bunch of other folks held their collective crouches (or mikes), sipped Old E, and postured about Malcolm's revolution two decades too late. Nowhere was the Family Stand's newblack power on better display than on a trio of songs that dealt with the pitfalls of post-soul aspirations, the issue of sexual violence against children, and the lack of a womanist foundation for young brown girls living in a world that has little regard for them.

Written by Peter Lord, "The Education of Jamie" is a cautionary tale for those who believed the hype about a postrace America as they pursued the "upper, middle, middle, upper, upper class life." Jamie had the classic late 1980s Buppie profile—the MA, the Beemer, and the love (or lust) of a high-ranking politician's son. In a world defined as much by an unspoken racial caste system as it is by a clichéd glass ceiling, Jamie got a taste of reality when word got around that the governor's son didn't just want a sprinkle of brown sugar in his life but wanted to break ranks and marry her (you down with BPP?). With shit hitting that ceiling (now a shit ceiling, I guess), the Family Stand offers this advice: "Get black it's your resurrection / the white lies hold no protection / know this it's your one salvation." Lord even manages to drop a little Du Bois on the 'groes no longer around the way, giving a twist to homie's double-consciousness trip ("And if you've ever seen yourself / through their eyes / You know you've never seen yourself at all.") While the Stand might be given a slight nudge for some trite essentialist politics, where middle-class aspirations equate to some fictive state known as the un-black, "The Education of Jamie" counters the time-tested idea that somehow the so-called Affirmative Action era was gentler and kindler to sista-girls on the rise (still remember that episode of *Good Times* where Florida got offered the job that James wanted 'cause it filled a double quota). Not quite a blacker-than-thou intervention, the fact of the matter is Sandra St. Victor's vocals get all up in an negress's ass, as she is literally screaming "get black, it's your salvation" by the song's close.

The action is no less dramatic on the project's most poignant song, also written by Lord, who sings lead on "Quiet Desperation." Some eleven years before everybody pointed a celebrity finger at R. Kelly and then an accusatory finger at his underage victim (everybody forwarding links to the Kelly sex video without any regard for the fact that they were trafficking in child pornography and thus no better than Kelly), Lord painted a portrait of the ways that young girls become prey to the desires (and lust) of male adults ("little NaNa's got a problem / Mister Uncle like to touch her / And she better not tell"). In the context of Lord's lyrics, "Quiet Desperation" is not just a metaphor for NaNa's condition but for his own efforts to address her situation publicly. The song's chorus finds Lord trying to put NaNa's story in a context that folks can understand, portraying the insidiousness that sexual abuse would be visited on a small child whose perspective is measured by "ocean[s] in teacup and a great big world with little hands." Featuring string arrangements by Clare Fischer, the song's brilliance lies not only in its vividness, but in its sparseness.

The music is even more stripped down on Sandra St. Victor's "Where Does Mommy Live?" The song details the life of a young girl (the proverbial church girl), raised by her father who "taught her that to be alone / was better than to feel." Unprepared, baby-girl heads out into the world "with her womanhood aglow" and gets pregnant. She ends up giving her own baby-girl for adoption. Thus there are now two generations of these woman/girls asking the question "Where Does Mommy Live?" The opening moments of the song are performed a capella, with St. Victor backed only by her own background voices. Suddenly St. Victor is joined by the Daryl Douglas Workshop Choir, figuratively placing the overall narrative out of isolation and into a broad community, with whom the question "Where Does Mommy Live?" resonates powerfully. And even though baby-girl eventually finds a "man with so much soul . . . an angel from the sky" (a metaphor for a man of the cloth perhaps, particularly given the song's conscious gospel inflection), she is still committed to finding her mother. In its essence, "Where Does Mommy Live?" fashions a womanist politics that never forgets the value of women in a woman's life.

The Family Stand reserved their harshest critique for the hands that fed them—the recording and radio industries. In his well-circulated critical diatribe, Norman Kelley recently described the recording industry as a form of neocolonialism.[3] Kelley's depiction of the recording industry and Courtney Love's equally vivid description of the same industry as a version of "sharecropping" neatly bookend the ongoing drama that many black acts still face when trying to garner support for urban (read: black) radio outlets whose concept of "diversity" in black music runs the slim gamut between The Neptunes and Timbaland *and* the more traditional pop–Top 40 outlets, which get confused when Negroes can play more than four chords on their instruments ("yo, dude . . . where's the turntablist?"). Long before the Viacom twins (dat be BET and MTV) and Clear Channel became the A-list target of *Brave New World* conspiracy theoricians, the Family Stand gave their own spin on the racial politics of the music industry.

In a review of *Moon in Scorpio,* Janine McAdams cited "Plantation Radio" as a "danceable, sly commentary on current programming habits." No, "Plantation Radio" was more like a forearm in the grill, one that the Family Stand knew they could offer because there would be no retribution to be made if folks weren't trying to get them in the mix in the first place. In the process, the group takes shots at Milli Vanilli (you know the lip-synching Grammy winners), Black Box, and C&C Music Factory (who both fronted vocals of a full-figured Martha Wash with skinny-ass model types), the Great White Hopes—in this case misters Jagger, Simon, and Sting, who respectively "discovered" Living Colour, Ladysmith Black Mambazo, and Vinx, and even manage to throw some ill rhythms in Christopher Columbus's direction, a year before that *damn* five-hundred-year celebration. The song is brilliant in its polemics and brave in its willingness to call a spade a spade. In his much-slept-on classic *Development Arrested: The Blues and Plantation Power in the Mississippi Delta,* Clyde Woods opines that "Slavery, sharecropping, mechanization, and prison, wage, and migratory labor are just a few permutations possible within a plantation complex. None of these forms changes the basic features of resource monopoly and extreme ethnic and class polarization,"[4] and it is this critique of the political economy of the music industry that the Family Stand fashioned in dance floor–friendly terms ("we need Lincoln to come and free the slaves / From the clutches of the radio airwaves").

Twelve years after the release of "Plantation Radio," acts such as Lenny Kravitz, N.E.R.D. (the T. S. Eliot–like alter-egos of the Neptunes), Stew and the Negro Problem, Reece, and Res still can't get no love from so-called black radio and video outlets, while Justin "cry me a river" Timberlake and Remy "take a message to my love" Shand (who both happen to be white) had top 10 videos on BET. Such bankrupt industry politics left Dionne Farris without a record company, when she wanted to get back to the groove of her damn-near-brilliant debut *Wild Seed Wild Flower* (1994), while her company wanted a disc full of "Hopeless," the neo-soul ditty that she contributed to the *Love Jones* soundtrack in 1997. A year after the release of *Moon in Scorpio,* the Peter Lord, Sandra St. Victor, V. Jeffrey Smith version of the Family Stand went the way of the automatic turntable. Reporting on the demise of the group, Janine McAdams cited "lack of record company promotion that clearly understands [the] band's vision . . . an insufficient budget with which to effectively convey that vision" and "lack of radio support, on the part of both urban and rock radio."[5]

Sandra St. Victor resurfaced four years later with a major label solo recording, *Mack Diva Saves the World,* which included some production by Lord and Smith. She returned in 2001 with *Gemini,* which was independently released on her own label. Lord and Smith regrouped with a new version of the Family Stand that featured Jacci McGhee. Their 1998 release *Connected,* like *Mack Diva Saves the World,* contained the elements of what made earlier Family Stand releases such cultural events, but when all was said and done, both lacked the genius of *Moon in Scorpio.* The group laid a fertile ground for a next generation of artists to emerge in the spirit of the newblack. Me'Shell NdegéOcello's *Plantation Lullabies* was released two years after *Moon in Scorpio;* some critics misnomered the project as a hip-hop recording simply because she engaged in some spoken word on the joint. A decade later, four releases strong, NdegéOcello's music is the best example of the fluidity that *Moon in Scorpio* first captured in 1991. The Family Stand will never get the props that they deserve, but in retrospect mass commercial appeal was never the reason we dug them. What the band stood for was a vision of black music and a black world unfettered by the constraints of mediocrity and essentialism (antiessential-essentialism, as Mr. Tate refers to it), and the recording industry simply isn't ready for that just yet.

## NOTES

1. Greg Tate, "The Golden Age," *The Village Voice,* May 22, 2001.
2. Peter Watrous, "They Like Their Sound Intense and a Mite Loud," *The New York Times,* December 16, 1991, C11.
3. Norman Kelley, "Rhythm Nation: The Political Economy of Black Music," Norman Kelley, *Black Renaissance/Renaissance Noire,* vol. 2 no. 2 (1999), p. 10.
4. Clyde Woods, *Development Arrested: The Blues and Plantation Power in the Mississippi Delta* (London: Verso, 1999).
5. Janine McAdams, "Family Stand Decides to Sit Down," *Billboard,* August 1, 1992, p. 17.

# HARRY ALLEN

# INTERVIEW WITH VERNON REID

**V**ernon Reid has proven himself an eclectic maverick as an artist, guitarist, and composer, from his formative years with the Decoding Society as part of New York City's downtown funk/punk/jazz scene through his project Yohimbe Brothers. Reid cofounded the Black Rock Coalition in the mid-1980s and has enjoyed fruitful collaboration with artists as diverse as Salif Keita, Donald Byrd, Carlos Santana, and choreographer Bill T. Jones. Best known for leading multiplatinum rock band Living Colour (founded ca. 1985), Reid piloted the group through a decade featuring the albums *Vivid* and *Time's Up* for Sony; two consecutive Grammy Awards for Best Hard Rock Performance; and touring with the Rolling Stones and the debut Lollapolooza outing in 1991. Currently, Living Colour mk. 2 have reunited in the studio and Reid remains involved with a plethora of composing and scoring work.

HARRY ALLEN: How do you feel that your story—either Vernon Reid's story, musical story, or Living Colour's story fits into the larger story of African Americans in rock music?

VERNON REID: I think we're part of the, we're a branch, a leaf [*laughs*]. I think we're part of, you know, the time line of bands and performers and troubadours and characters, I think that we're a part of history, we're part of the ongoing, still-evolving history of American music—and not just American music, music on the planet—we're just that big a part, you know, we're influenced by mentors and elders and we're influenced by people who are our contemporaries, as well, and it's been a very interesting trip.

HA: Why do you say that?

VR: You know that I started out as someone from a family that wasn't . . . I'm like the first professional musician in my family and, as far as the business and all like that goes, I was a complete—unlike many people, you know—complete outsider to it. I had no clue as to how it operated, I totally came in as a fan of music, a fan that became a musician, and it's just been very interesting. I've like met a lot of people that I grew up as a child listening to and the people that influenced me: I'll never forget meeting Santana at a Living Colour gig in San Francisco—it was pretty astounding, and when Carl was jamming with us, you know we played for the Stones and the various times I've played with him, you know, at concerts—and this is the person that influenced me to pick up the guitar, at least as a kid, that was the first time I heard the guitar and said, "Oh, I like that sound," so to go from listening to "Black Magic Woman" or "Oye Como Va" to standing on stage in a club and seeing that person standing on the side of the stage, I mean, that's pretty magical and I've just had—

HA [*Interrupting*]: You said standing on the side of the stage; you mean standing looking at you, you mean?

VR: Yeah, on the side of the stage.

HA: Watching you play?

VR: Yeah, I mean that's—there really aren't words to adequately describe that feeling, and I've had that feeling again and again and again and that's been a magical thing. I've stood next to Eric Clapton and played guitar, I've chatted, I've presented an award with George Benson to Charlie Christian at the Rock and Roll Hall of Fame, I've jammed with Prince more than once. I mean, these are things that are just, for me, a turnaround and more than anything else the greatest part of it was to interview George Clinton and jam with him. I've played with Bernie Worrell in Jack Bruce's band (Cuicoland Express), I mean, it's pretty . . . it's an astounding thing because I came into it as a fan, and I'm still a fan, and so that's been the most extraordinary part of it for me, and it's funny because it's interesting to run into people that are quite accomplished musicians, who say "Oh, you know, I heard Living Colour and that made me want to pick up the guitar or the saxophone" or "I knew that it was possible for me to go forward with what I wanted to do because of what you did," and so on and so forth. So we're part of a continuum, and as human beings we learn by imitation, we learn by looking at what other people are doing and adopting, and we're influenced by the things other people do and we're attracted to the sounds or the images or the structures that other people build, for whatever reason, and occasionally there are those of us who take upon ourselves to investigate what that is and then we go and do that same thing, we put brush to canvas or we sit behind the piano and begin the arduous task of learning what it is to play like Jelly Roll Morton or Herbie Hancock or whoever, or maybe not even that. Maybe someone sits behind the piano and starts doing whatever they do, and in the process of discovery, because of using whatever capacities they have, they're able to affect things, to create things. So we're just part of a community and we're part of history.

HA: What would you have liked to have seen Living Colour do that you never got to do? What did you not get to do with it? And I don't mean playing with this person or that person, I mean, in terms of an effect?

VR: I would have liked to done a black rock opera [*laughs*] or some such thing, I think, a black rock science fiction opera [*laughs*]. You know, a concept album. I would have liked to have done a record that took one theme or one story and—like a *Tommy*. Black Tom [*laughs*].

HA: Uncle Tom?

VR: Uncle Tom. You know, it's funny, Uncle Tom is an interesting figure because he's, you know, Uncle Tom has become something different that what Harriet Beecher Stowe—

HA [*Interrupting*]: Originally meant.

VR: Originally meant. There are so many things that are like that. I recently learned the story of the kazoo, and it's so interesting because the kazoo is actually an instrument that was created in Africa, but what it meant originally was something very different than what it's become—what it's come to mean, and that's how things change, things start in one place and they end someplace completely different.

HA: What did it mean and what has it become?

VR: Well, it was used by priests, uh, you know, to imitate the voices of the dead and the original kazoos, some of them were made out of—were priests blowing into a human skull with a membrane to create this buzzing sound, and so the buzzing of the kazoo which we take to be kind of very kitsch and zany and tacky was originally, before it was brought in the Migration, the forced migration here, it was originally—

HA [*Interrupting*]: It was sacrament.

VR: Yeah, it was for rituals and it was quite a terrifying thing. It was like "Now I will communicate with the dead," and that buzzing sound was the sound of—

HA [*Interrupting*]: Terror and dread.

VR: Yeah, and it became something completely different, but that's part of what we do.

HA: Do you think that that parallels Living Colour as well? In terms of what you intended to do, and then how you were ultimately perceived, or—

VR: Well, I don't know how it was ultimately perceived.

HA: Well, what's your sense of that?

VR: The ultimate perception of the band . . . there are people who have differing things to say. In the pop music world, your assessment is your Sound Scan or having gigantic hit records or whatever. The band had a kind of layoff that broke the band up in '95.

HA: Why?

VR: Because I was very unhappy with . . . It became just very difficult to work with the members of the band—to work with one another. There were a lot of emotional stresses that kind of came together from inside and outside that led to it becoming very—it fell very far away from what I wanted the band to be. And I realized that on the other side of it, I was holding on to it because I was afraid of what the alternative would be and communication was at a null point.

HA: Between the band members?

VR: Yeah, between the band members. Between at least three of the band members.

HA: Which three?

VR: Oh, me, Will Calhoun, and Corey Glover. Muzz Skillings, the original bass player, had left. It's funny—when you're in the middle of this thing, and the band is popular and it's ongoing, there's sort of a kind of pressure to keep going; what we should have really done I think, in hindsight, is to take a long layoff, because there were a lot of things that were just not good and I was breaking up my first marriage at that time, so it was an unhappy time.

HA: Was this about money?

VR: It was not really about money as much as it was about not really being able to communicate or be in a situation . . . hmm. It's funny, because I'm so not in that place right now—it's hard to go back and turn around and say, "Oh, I was in this place and at that time it seemed as if there were no way out" [laughs]. I can look back and psychoanalyze myself or psychoanalyze the people and say, "Oh, well, what you should have did was this or that," and you can always go back after the event and be completely calm and be completely "Oh, it was really simple. You coulda did this or you coulda did that, or all we needed to do was this or all we needed to do was that."

HA: I'm not clear—why did the band break up? You said you weren't communicating; what was it that you wanted to talk about or that you guys needed to talk about?

VR: About directions in the music, to be able to talk about how decisions were made, a lot of it was just male stuff—guys don't like to talk. You get on stage and sort of act out whatever and do the gigs and then you don't want to talk about anything. It may be hard if you're the kind of person that always talks about everything, but a lot of it was that kind of thing. And as I said, I mean, it may not be clear to you, and I don't know—I spent a lot of time explaining myself [laughs] and trying to explain the unexplainable, it's what it was at the time. It wasn't flowing and the language wasn't there to talk our way out of it. And there were all kinds of internal stresses, you know when you have a group of people that have all kinds of different relationships that happen within any group of people that are supposed to be doing a particular thing, like a sports team or a band or whatever. And different people have different motivations for why they're doing what they're doing. If everyone had the same motivation for doing the same thing, then maybe everyone could see things the same way. But we're different from each other, we have different lives and different experiences, we have different techniques for dealing with things. Dealing with conflict or dealing with disagreements or dealing with what works and doesn't work in a relationship and that if you don't have this—if you're with this other person and communication is like "Oh, I see what you're going through with this, well, maybe I can help you with this, help you with that." But say when you ask me—it's kinda funny when I hear that. "Why did you break up with her? She was beautiful and intelligent and great, why did you break up with her?" You know what? If you would've lived with her, or if you'd went out with her, or if you'd have been the person that I was when I was with her, maybe you'd understand. I don't know . . . do you get what I'm saying?

HA: Someone once wrote on a bathroom wall, "No matter how beautiful she is, there is some guy who's sick of her crap."

VR: You know, it's a funny thing because all the external things: success, beauty, money, having money, being given the best table in the restaurant when you walk in the room—all those things are illusionary things to me. They're all part of the illusion, and even having to define what I'm meaning—it's like "walk a mile in my shoes." Anyone can look at someone on the outside and I could look at one of the bands that was contemporary to us, Public Enemy, I could turn around and say, "Why couldn't they do that, why couldn't Flavor Flav do that solo record that was, that everybody wanted him to do? Why couldn't that happen?" Well, there were reasons why, but, you know, ultimately it didn't happen because whatever else was going on in the background was more important than what was going on in the foreground.

HA: Going back to the kazoo metaphor, you talked about how it starts as an instrument of extremely serious intent, something maybe kind of awe-inspiring in a certain way, but then over the time, for various reasons, it becomes this kind of thing, light-hearted, I guess you could say flippant—you used the word "kitschy." I'm not saying Living Colour became kitschy, but what I'm saying is that when one starts a project there is always a lot of passion, and "Yeah, let's go get 'em" and "Let's do it" and then, at the end, it's kind of like "Pffssh, whatever."

VR: You know, the thing about it is, the passion—you see, I am really proud of what Living Colour did on its records. Of course, I could turn around and look at certain things that we did, touring or whatever, and there were times that the band could be extraordinary, and there are times that the band could be "What is going on here?" like literally, you know, like acting out of something that isn't maybe completely well thought out or whatever—you know, the band could be . . . I don't know. When I saw the first Public Enemy show at the World and they were completely awful—there was no rhythm to the show and the pacing was really bad, and I remember seeing them, actually doing a show with them and Fishbone and Public Enemy didn't even get a chance to finish its set because they essentially sparked a riot in the audience.

HA: You mean at a later time . . .

VR: No, during the show that we did with them.

HA: Right, but I mean that show took place some time after the first one you saw.

VR: Oh, yeah, this took place quite some time [later]. I saw them kinda right after *Yo bum rush the show!* and literally it was the first thing they were doing and I saw them in between *It Takes a Nation of Millions to Hold Us Back* and *Fear of a Black Planet* and they were on this completely incredible other level—it was "Wow," it was incredible, they'd really become a great [act] . . . and they only played about twenty minutes before all hell broke loose.

HA: What I think I wanted to ask was in terms of these dynamics, to what degree do you believe that . . . how did race or racism effect Living Colour's development?

VR: Well, we live in America, and racial dynamics and racial politics and racial identity and all of these things are part of what we live with, it's like the great American question that's either in the foreground or in the background. And definitely, as far as it pertains to—between African Americans and Caucasian Americans, whatever hyphen-hyphen slash thing you want to say—those relations in terms of culture and business and media are certainly thinking about things from the twentieth century, they played a consistent and important role and certainly, I feel, in terms of culture, and in terms of our daily lives. Being an African American slash African Caribbean American is something that I grew up with. I grew up in the '60s and '70s, and it was a dynamic time in terms of the national debate about race and opportunity and equality and all of those questions. It was a dynamic and contentious time, and that was the backdrop and certainly the music I was listening to, that I grew up with, spoke to all of that. I remember songs like Donny Hathaway's "Someday We'll All Be Free" and how heartrending his rendition of that song was, and part of that had to do with the fact that he was also dealing with debilitating mental illness as well as having the extraordinary talent and was also called to be a witness for the collective pain of his race, and also in so doing transcended even that and spoke to really anyone who had ears to hear it, because really, the story of the blues and the story of R&B, and I mean R&B as music that's connected to blues and connected to rock and roll.

HA: But more pointedly, I think what I'm trying to ask is how did racism effect the direct development of your group, either retarded or . . .

VR: One of the expectations, I mean, one of the definitions of what rock and roll had become for us, perhaps it was off point, but rock and roll is defined as a white person's—more of a white person's music than a collective music, and All-American. In my mind, the history of rock and roll is a multiracial history and, at some point it became the definition of a rock and roll band became cemented in the public mind as "This is a music of white guys with long hair."

HA: And guitars.

VR: And guitars. And the guitar, after the death of Hendrix, was basically to be played by talented white males and if a black male should come, or a black person—you see, I'm defining it as male, but that's sort of what the definition became—and if a black male *did* come into the role of playing the guitar, then that person would have be someone that was trying to copy Jimi Hendrix. Jimi Hendrix became the glaring exception to the rule. And so that perception of what—and certainly the great rock bands, and a lot of this is about media and promotion and where the industry chose to market and the people's willingness to identify with something outside of themselves.

HA: I agree with what you're saying. I see how these are outgrowths of race or related to race, but I'm not clear on how you're saying this impacted Living Colour.

VR: Well, it impacted Living Colour because, like that whole definition thing, it impacted what the band encountered in terms of getting gigs, in terms of doing stuff, but, you know, at the same time we were very fortunate in that we had people who came to really just appreciate it as music. Some of the club owners in New York, one in particular, Hilly Kristal, who's the owner of CBGB's. You see, early on, there were places where it was really tough, the old kind of post-punk clubs and things. I had a really hard time at places like Danceteria.

HA: You mean getting gigs there?

VR: Getting gigs and stuff like that, but Hilly Kristal who, in a way, is one of the people you heralded in the new wave and the last wave of punk and new wave thing by putting on bands like the B-52's [etc]. I mean, it was just hard for the band to get signed to a record contract, because that was the paradigm at that time: You put together an act, you get a record deal. Hard to do it because they said, "Well, we don't know what to do with this, we can't—I don't know how to market it." It's "rock is white."

HA: That's what I don't understand, what are the kinds of things that people say that . . .

VR: You already know that. I don't know if there is anything new I can add to it other than, hey, hard to get the band to the next [level] people. Okay, I encounter racism like this: Frankie Crocker had us on to WBLS and interviewed me and Corey Glover and wanted to talk to us about what we were doing, 'cause we were hard to ignore because we had cracked the top twenty, you know.

HA: This was when "Cult of Personality" was out?

VR: Yeah. Frankie Crocker was one of my heroes, and I think he might have played "Cult of Personality" once, literally one time. But there was no way that Living Colour was going to be added to that radio station.

HA: WBLS?

VR: Yeah. I remember going to a station, I forget which one, it was a big rock station, and the jock really was excited about the band coming through, but at the outset of the interview he said, "Man, I can't add your record." Before "Cult of Personality" became a hit record, but this is when we were early touring on—we'd already been signed, made a record, and we were traveling, and I heard this time and again. The record could not be added to the play list because it was . . . whatever it was. But it was really clear that a black band doing this music was a challenge.

HA: When they said that to you, what would you say back to them?

VR: Well, the people who would say it to me, I would thank them for their honesty. I would thank them for being honest and not just smiling in my face and then having me think that something's happening that's not happening. Because generally the jocks were very sympathetic, and really into it, and the program directors, they had their whole other thing, they have to answer to the general managers, and the general managers answer to the owners, and the owners answer to the advertisers and tada, tada, tada.

HA: What you're saying is that these are two different stations, one's a station that plays "R&B" or, as it was called, "urban contemporary music," and the other one's a rock station. In one case they're not going to add you because, even though you're black like most of the musicians on the station, you're playing a genre that they don't play, and the other, they play your genre, but you're black, so they won't add you.

VR: Right, so to me, both of those things, they're very different, but both of those things are indicative of the same thing.

HA: And that is?

VR: And that is that there's a definition, there's a sort of artificial performance of blackness, there's a certain thing that's expected of black people and unless you were performing in the particular role that was excepted and marketed to people, there would be no place for you. That's why most people don't know anything about the great L.A. rock band, Love featuring Arthur Lee, because what he did was just freaky and psychedelic. It was 1967 and nobody knew what to do, it's also why, to me, the Isley Brothers aren't listed as a rock and roll band. The Isley Brothers are a band, to me, that, in a way its own development became totally affected by that dynamic because, they had this range, this incredible range, you know they were doing everything from "It's Your Thing" to "Between the Sheets" and "Who's That Lady" and "Fight the Power," I mean, this was one group. This is a group that is arguably as important as the Rolling Stones, in terms of what it's done. In my mind, I wonder if it will ever be accorded its real importance, I mean, it's basically seen as this R&B band and is a band that is remarkable because it was a band that evolved—it was an R&B band that became this powerhouse rock and roll band, and had hit records as a rock and roll band, had rock songs.

HA: When you say rock songs, you mean in the traditional mode? Because, see, this is for a book about black rock, but I find this term "rock" to be extremely slippery.

VR: Oh, "rock" is a very slippery term. Rock is . . . that's why I say rock. Rock when you look at the genre and groups like Emerson Lake and Palmer, and Iron Maiden and Steely Dan—that's all included in the rock and roll genre.

HA: Yes, but then also you'll see "Women in Rock" on the cover of *Rolling Stone* and it will have Britney Spears, Shakira, and Mary J. Blige.

VR: Right, well that's like a very "now" kind of thing, it's become really, really slippery, and . . .

HA: Let me just also add, also, in the definition—in the Black Rock Coalition, the group talks about its forebears, they talk about George Clinton and they talk about Hendrix and the Isley Brothers and these are groups that even sonically are very diverse, as you said. Diverse within themselves and so it's like, so I'll hear that and I'll say, Well, I could play "Flashlight" in Harlem, in central Harlem, and get a reaction, I might not be able to play [Hendrix's] "Star-Spangled Banner" in central Harlem and get much interest.

VR: Well, it's a funny thing. But that's what we do in America, we struggle with the definitions of things, we struggle with the definitions of what—I mean, this whole thing is, we're talking about . . .

HA: I said the "Star-Spangled Banner," but really "Wind Cries Mary" or something like that. "Star-Spangled Banner" people would react just because it's the "Star-Spangled Banner," but I'm saying that any of Hendrix's more better-known "obscure" songs . . .

VR: Yeah, well, it's kinda like the whole idea of how do we deal with the people that step off, and this is true—how do we deal with the people who are essential but are not in the mainstream or are on the edges of things, it's a very unique thing, because the Harlem of now is not the Harlem of ten years ago or fifteen years ago, or twenty years ago. Nothing is static.

HA: That's true, as well.

VR: You say that, if you go up to Harlem now there are cuts that, say, we grew up with and we recognize as important cuts, but unless that cut is connected to a car commercial, there's a whole generation of people who have no idea.

HA: I think you're correct, but what I think—there's a fundamental issue here that I'm trying to get to, and that has to do with the question of this definition of rock and this whole question—and it's the same one that you've been addressing through the Black Rock Coalition and in your work, and in this example you gave about WBLS specifically, on one hand I can look and say, Well, the rock station that won't play a rock record by black people, that's just like some southern 1935 kinda stuff to me, but the R&B station that says, Well, we don't play this kind of music—you could say, well, they don't play André Watts either, you know what I'm saying?

VR: Well, that's exactly right, there's a world of difference between BLS and—BLS used to be called the "total black experience." The BLS of the 1970s and early '80s was a very different station than what it was by the late '80s and early '90s, a very different thing. I mean, I remember hearing jazz-rock fusion on WBLS, they would play really adventurous things, they played black rock . . .

HA: And you were correct, you see this is the thing, not to cut you off, Vernon. Something like "Black Magic Woman," like that would never get on the air nowadays, but for a lot of people who end up hearing that music, that stuff hits real hard and real close to home. You see, the thing I'm trying to get is this: Unless you're playing the "blues" for most black audiences—and does this divide by age, or geography? If you stick a guitar in it, a guitar tone, and then, let's say you have varieties with the guitar tone, straight guitar tone and then you just move it up toward—then you start distorting it, grade zero-one-two-three-four all the way from zero to nine, and nine is the most outrageous distortion. As you put these sounds into records, does this music become more or less relevant to black audiences? Because there's a perception, there's an argument that rock is the heritage of black people that the Black Rock Coalition makes, etc., and even that this book puts forward and it can be argued as well, but it seems that most black people are like, "I don't care about this stuff."

VR: Yeah, but most black people don't care about jazz, so why—you see, this is my problem with that whole line of thinking, in a way. It's because, see, people seize on rock and go, "Oh, It's like this and that," and I turn around and say, "You know, black people are not supporting jazz," no one's going to argue, no one's gonna fight if you put Duke Ellington up and say Duke Ellington is black music. But you go to see these concerts, you bring up André Watts—you know, I could bring up John Coltrane or I could bring up Thelonius Monk—and the question is about the disconnection, the disconnect between black people and their own heritage, and guitar tone and all like that notwithstanding. It's the issue that goes really beyond that, and it really deals with how we value, how we value our own thing, the remarkable things that we've done, the remarkable work of the interpretations of an André Watts or an Awadagan Pratt at the piano—you know Awadagan Pratt, cat like bench presses 300 pounds and plays Rachmaninoff and shit like that. These are deeper questions about how we see ourselves when you look at it from our place, on the other side it's all about identification. How willing are we to identify with another human being beyond the illusion that they're different? Like, you look at the person and they're an Eskimo, because when we talk about racial dynamics, we are stuck in this black-white thing because of these very difficult relationships in the past, we've let that define it, as if there aren't other people on the planet. Black people and white people in America get so hung up about what we're doing, and there are a whole host of other people that are on the playing field now, there are a whole host of people that are on the playing field that don't have that history that we're obsessed with. How do we fit in black people from other countries? Black people from South America? How do we fit in the black Latin people? How do we fit in black people from the Caribbean? From Indonesia and things like that, that have completely other references. It's all about this kind of narrowness, narrowness in willingness to experience. The thing that Hendrix did, the "Hendrix Experience," that's the gauntlet that he threw in everybody's face. He said, "Are you willing to experience something beyond yourself, outside of what you normally hear or do?" He went there, that's his real value. He's a great, great guitarist and all of that, but beyond that, his importance as a songwriter, as a creator, part of it was that he was trying to connect, he connected the past to the future, and scared a lot of people along the way, and that to me is the part of the rock and roll equation that gets left out, it's really not about doing, being able to do what white people can do, it's really not about that at all, it has nothing to do with that. I mean, that's something that you can see on the surface, it's like, everything is mutating and changing and what's my part of this human experience, and what can I contribute to this ongoing thing? Because I think a lot of us are stuck in a dynamic that's: Things are changing but we're still stuck in the conversation of 1975, we don't realize that shit is shifting, it's shifting around. And not just us, but the other people that are also obsessed with that conversation on the other side, don't realize that shit is moving. And we try and barricade ourselves in tradition, "Well, this is how it has to go down," and "This is how this went down, this is how it's done." It's like, well, "Keep it real." We live under the tyranny of the "real" as opposed to imagining new and different and other worlds to inhabit, and new and different ways of hearing and doing, we're shackled, sometimes, to the past. The beauty of traditional forms is their dynamism, their dynamic things—but we lock everything in cement, "Oh, this is the way it is, white people can't dance and they never gonna be able to dance." That's bullshit. Now we've got at least two generations that have grown up with hip-hop and funk music, and it's their music, it's the music they grew up with. Certain dynamics—things ain't what they used to be, but the more things change, the more things stay the same, at the same time.

HA: Why did you call your band Living Colour? What did the name mean?

VR: What the name means to me? Well, part of it was about the arcane, because it's spelled in the English way, c-o-l-o-u-r, which has something tangential to do with the fact that . . .

HA: British? Born in England?

VR: I was born in England, but I'm also a fan of H. P. Lovecraft, who was a writer of weird—

HA: Cthulhu.

VR: Yeah, the Cthulhu Mythos, which, in my mind, ultimately that would be a great subject for a black rock opera. The Cthuhlu Mythos. Because H. P. Lovecraft was grappling with and struggling with his fear of black people and his fear of Africa. This is me just interpreting. Because you look at some of his early writing and he's clearly a racist, but if you read any parts of the Cthulhu Mythos, the very name Cthulhu is an African-sounding word and, well, that's a whole other interview. [*laughs*]

HA: Great stuff.

VR: You know, but that's my—and this is a totally novel interpretation of Lovecraft, but he came up at a time in the 1920s when African exploration and African art was an obsession in America and the whole idea of going to Africa to, you know, the African safari was in its heyday then, and they were also discovering dinosaurs. This was around the time they were discovering some of the first dinosaur remains, and this was electrifying stuff.

HA: What does this have to do with Living Colour? I'm just trying to understand how you're connecting—I mean, I understand the British allusion, but . . .

VR: One of H. P. Lovecraft's stories is called "The Colour from Space," which—he's an American writer, but he spelled it with a "u." And, you know, the word stuck in my mind. And the other thing is that I remember when TV's went from black and white—I'm old, huh?—to being color on NBC, "the following program is in living color."

HA [*Mimicking an announcer's voice*]: "Is brought to you in living color" and the peacock goes *pvvvffft* . . .

VR: Yeah, and they'd have the peacock feathers. And I was like "Wow!" So that just stuck in my mind, "Living Color," and then spelling it with the "u." I could have called it the Black Dragons, but, you know, I didn't.

HA: We spoke earlier about the Black Rock Coalition. What is your sense of what the organization accomplished?

VR: It accomplished—it raised the debate about the definition and the terminology, about language, and language is reality. It basically served as a springboard for a community. That's what it did accomplish, that's what it did.

HA: Do you think it accomplished anything else?

VR: I think it gave people a lot of information about practical stuff, like information about the music business and how things go down and what have you. It was all on a volunteer basis.

HA: What do you make of the charge that your group was the one that benefited the most from the Black Rock Coalition?

VR: You know what, the only thing I can say is that the Black Rock Coalition—someone who would make that charge has no idea of the actual history of the Black Rock Coalition. It would seem to be, on the surface, that Vernon Reid set up this thing and then he benefited, his band benefited the most, but you have to understand, when I called that first meeting, there was no plan in mind to start and organization. It didn't become an organization—I didn't say "Let's start an organization, guys, and my band will be the first thing." That's not what went down at all. I called together a bunch of my friends and I was just needed to talk to somebody other than myself to say "Am I crazy, or is this a real thing?" I only raised the question. It becoming an organization—I didn't suggest that it become an organization, it was like, I believe it was like Greg Tate who suggested there be an organization. The name Black Rock Coalition came from Craig Street, I believe.

HA: [The producer] Craig Street?

VR: Yeah, because I was thinking we'd call it The Black Rock Collective and that sounds like communism [*laughs*]. That was my name for it, The Black Rock Collective, then Craig said, "Nah, what about 'coalition'?" and then it was like, "Well, who's going to be in charge?" And then every one got quiet and looked at me. I didn't put myself—I didn't start an organization and put myself at the head of it. That's not what happened.

HA: What is your relationship to the organization today?

VR: It's mostly in an advisory capacity, like, "This is happening, that's going on." I was president for its first five years. Bruce Mack is the current president, and I believe he's talking about stepping down. I have very little to do with the day-to-day affairs of the organization now, but it continues, the people that want it to continue and want to keep the conversation alive.

HA: What's your favorite record, or album?

VR: You know it would be difficult for me to say—you know, I'd have to give you a list of records.

And give them equal weight and, also, my favorite record of all time changes, I could turn to you and say, oh, *Mysterious Traveler*—Weather Report, but that's also a sixteen year-old, a fifteen- or sixteen-year-old talking. And I go back to that record now and I still love it, I could say *It Takes a Nation of Millions to Hold Us Back,* but that's a twenty-eight-year-old or a twenty-seven-year-old talking.

HA: What is it that you're listening to right now, that you're passionate about?

VR: I really like the Queens of the Stone Age—*Songs for the Deaf.* And there's this band called Sigur Rós. And there's something—you know, it'd have to be a rainy night [*laughs*] and it's really good driving and you're suddenly in the middle of your own Dogme 95 movie. [*laughter*]

HA: Real quickly, what are you working on musically right now?

VR: Well, Living Colour is together again, the second version of the recording band with Doug Wimbish on bass. We're working on songs for a record that's gonna be on Sanctuary Records. And I have a commission to write an orchestral piece for the Dutch Metropol orchestra that I'm gonna do in June.

[I've also been] composing for film. I just did Charles Stone's first movie *Paid in Full.* I did the score for Thomas Allen Harris's latest movie, *É minha cara / That's My Face.* And for *Ghosts of Attica,* which is a film by Brad Lichtenstein about the Attica prison riot—brilliant film that was shown on Court TV and won a DuPont award.

# DARRELL M. MCNEILL

# ROCK, RACISM,
## AND RETAILING 101:
## A BLUEPRINT FOR CULTURAL THEFT

I'm tired of people saying, "Bitter wasn't black radio music." Who the fuck are you to tell me that? White people telling me, "It's not a 'black record.' You forsook your black audience." Fuck you! If I was Sarah McLachlan, you would have played my record! But then they have black people tell me I'm "not black"? That shit's crazy! Y'all have bought into this crap! Like my music 'cause you like the music, not because of what color I am or where you think it fits in your parameter! They've turned us all into one huge demographic!

—Me'Shell NdegéOcello, interview with *BRE* magazine, April 2002

Fuck what people think at this point. This is the most I've had to explain myself about any project. And if I was [*sic*] a White boy doing it, I wouldn't be going through this questioning. I'm treated like I'm approaching something that's foreign to me. My artistic pockets are being patted down because I want to do rock 'n' roll. My attitude is that the natural progression for my generation would be to do rock 'n' roll music.

—Mos Def on his rock project, Black Jack Johnson, interview with *Vibe* magazine, February 2002

Rock 'n' roll has long been affirmed as one of the most significant cultural phenomena of the twentieth century. It's also a locus of perpetual controversy and conflict. Forged in America's social cauldron of the 1950s—arguably its most conservative and xenophobic climate since the Civil War—rock music was considered the bane of the predominant white society due to its origins in the Afro-American underclass. This was the music of "ignorant, oversexed and violent lower-class Negroes," and whites (and privileged-class blacks) would have no part—or so it seemed at the outset.

This resistance proved decidedly hollow in a decidedly short period of time. Rock records catapulted from 15.7 percent of the market in 1955 to 42.7 percent in 1959. Revenue exploded from $213 million in 1954 to $603 million by 1959.[1] Cut to half a century later: According to the Recording Industry Association of America (RIAA), rock was the top-selling musical genre in 2001, representing 24 percent of the market and generating nearly $3.3 billion in sales revenue.[2]

Rock music—once impugned as a host of a nation's evils—became the foundation for the modern music industry and remains the fabric of popular American culture. However, while rock has permeated every media and evolved into a myriad of subgenres—pop, punk, New Wave, southern, metal, grunge, rap rock, rave, thrash, Gothic, hardcore, art rock, "emo"—the vast majority of its performers, producers, gatekeepers, tastemakers, historians, and consumers are white males.[3]

Only with utmost paucity are rock's African American originators or their progeny allowed to the party—an archetype of colonist/colonized interaction: We don't want you per se, just control of you and your resources. Given the decades black rockers have vied for room underneath the rock 'n' roll umbrella, it's evident that the vast majority of whites—from top exec to average fan—feel no particular onus to share. As Reebee Garafalo opines in "Crossing Over: From Black Rhythm & Blues to White Rock 'N Roll":

> The history of popular music in this country—at least in the twentieth century—can be described in terms of a pattern of Black innovation and White popularization, which I have referred to as "Black roots, White fruits." The pattern is built not only on the wellspring of creativity that Black artists bring to popular music, but also the systematic exclusion of Black personnel from positions of power within the industry and on the artificial separation of Black and White audiences. Because of industry and audience racism, Black music has been relegated to a separate and unequal marketing structure. As a result, it is only on rare occasions that Black music "crosses over" into the mainstream market on its own terms.[4]

The purpose of this chapter is to illustrate how the music industry's racially charged policy and marketing strategy in reaction to America's historic biases have reinforced or exacerbated schisms the vexatious and erroneous tenet shared by both whites and blacks that rock is somehow "white music." While the industry is certainly not the sole arbiter—societal factors contribute mightily to this sophistry—its business practices serve only to buttress that position. This recognition is vital in grasping why black artists perennially suffer third-class status in musical genres they were at the nexus of originating.

# BIRTH OF AN ATTITUDE: BLACK EXPRESSION AS AN AMERICAN COMMODITY

As "subhumans"—three-fifths human, per the U.S. Constitution (Article 1, Section 2) and with no rights white men were bound to respect (Dred Scott decision, 1857)—slaves were human property. And all attendant effects of their "subhumanity" (i.e., their bodies, their labor and its bounty, their mates, their children, their creativity, their expressions) were deemed property of their masters as well.[5] It was common practice to outsource slave labor or sell any crafts and wares a slave may have created. So an owner or overseer didn't have a second thought before demanding vassals to sing a song, dance a jig, talk "gibberish," laugh like a loon, battle another slave, or be raped or cuckolded. Slaves were prime entertainment for their captors. Thus, since the first slave set chained foot on the sands of the so-called New World, the African Diaspora traded on its creative skills as a tactic to staying alive.[6]

Reciprocally, amusing "massah" imbued survival, to buy reprieve from the brutal alternatives to noncompliance. Former slave turned statesman Frederick Douglass wrote: "Slaves are generally expected to sing as well as work. [A] silent slave is not liked by masters or overseers. 'Make a noise, make a noise,' and 'Bear a hand,' are the words usually addressed to slaves when there is silence among them."[7] Sociologists W. D. Weatherford and Charles S. Johnson also noted, "No master could be thoroughly comfortable around a sullen slave; and, conversely, a master, unless he was utterly humorless, could overwork or brutally beat a jolly fellow, one who could make him laugh."[8]

Which is not to say that any talent a slave possessed bore any meaningful aesthetic currency with the white ruling class, certainly none equal to their own (an undercurrent that hampers black creative genius to this day). As Amiri Baraka (LeRoi Jones) points out in his landmark anthology, *Blues People*: "So-called 'non-literate' peoples (called by Western man 'primitive'), whose languages, and therefore whose cultural and traditional histories, are not written, are the antithesis of Western man and his highly industrialized civilization. But the idea of the 'primordial man,' or 'underdeveloped peoples,' becomes absurd if we dismiss for a change the assumption that the only ideas and attitudes which the West finds useful or analogous to concepts forwarded within its own system are of any value or profundity."[9]

To this end, the only "use" slaveholders had for black creativity, talent, or wit was as a natural resource for recreation and trade. American slave owners and traders dismissed any allusion to skill, acumen, and intelligence as genetic "queerness," a childish, savantlike product of inferior breeding.[10]

Acknowledging otherwise would contradict white American predisposition to black inferiority, what British historian Basil Davidson described as a "deep soil of arrogant contempt for African humanity."[11]

Ironically, the facade of subhumanity created a buffer of inscrutability, providing tools key to black subsistence. For example, the Diaspora's legendary "natural talent" for the arts has long been misconstrued. Historian Norman Coombs cites in his anthology, *The Black Experience in America*, that Africans conceived art as "integral part of the whole of life rather than as a beautiful object set apart from mundane experience. Song and dance, for example, were involved in the African's work, play, love and worship."[12]

Within the context of indenture, black creativity became a multitiered commodity. Obviously, it stayed the lash and curried favor with slaveholders. However, allowing Africans to foster their creativity—albeit under oppressive conditions—also enabled them to retain at least some of their cultural moors. It reconnected them with their humanity and provided a microscopic outlet for expression and release from the overwhelming trauma of inexorable cruelty and servitude. And it provided concealment for insubordinate or retaliatory behavior.[13]

# BIRTH OF A BUSINESS: MINSTRELSY PIMPING "BLACK" EXPRESSION FOR PROFIT

In a nation with as dubious a racial history as the United States, it would stand to reason that the first people to get paid for being black onstage would be white. This was evident in the first commercial venture exploiting black expression for entertainment, which manifested in a surreal phenomenon of the 1820s: minstrelsy. White actors coating their faces in burnt cork and beeswax, acting out coarse lampoons of black people and black life—or rather what they thought was black life— became a global rage, with several dozen troupes traversing the country and Europe at the genre's peak. Minstrels made the rounds at legitimate theaters, menageries, circuses, and traveling shows.[14]

In Constance Rourke's *American Humor: Study of National Character* (1931), she notes, "to the primitive comic sense, to be Black was to be funny, and many minstrels made the most of this simple circumstance."[15] Of course, even as minstrel shows began going out of vogue (albeit with an interminable hangover in vaudeville, film, radio, and early television), its impacts lingered: "Minstrelsy had established a fraudulent image of Negro behavior (in both the serious and the comic vein), to which all African Americans were forced to respond. And early Black entertainers—perhaps even more than Blacks in less visible occupations—bore the burden of working within the confines of that distorted standard. Indeed, they were expected not only to corroborate White minstrels' illusionary specter, but because they were authentic examples of the type, to heighten it."[16]

The arrival of the Industrial Revolution (which rendered human chattel expensive and obsolete) and crippling Confederate debt to European nations signaled the death knell of the "peculiar institution" of slavery.[17] However, white animosity only hardened from anxieties of having to mutually coexist with this newly liberated "mongrel" race. Meanwhile, former slaves found themselves "free" on paper, but with no means of infrastructure. Thousands of newly liberated black Americans were confined to subservient positions and punitive situations that posed little variance from bondage.[18]

# BIRTH OF AN INDUSTRY:
# BLACK MUSIC AS CONTENT PROVISION

Prior to rock's emergence, the music industry, for all practical purposes, was only about two and a half decades old. By 1919 Americans were buying more than 25 million 78-rpm records every year with reported annual sales of $150 million.[19] A year later radio exploded upon the national scene:

> The first broadcast had been made in 1920 and the public response had been quick and enthusiastic; by 1922 there were some 220 radio stations in the country. The sets themselves sold for ten dollars. Stores were not able to keep them in stock, manufacturers had to rush forward their orders. By 1923 there were already 2.5 million sets in the country. Millions of Americans made radio the focal point of their households, scheduling their day around their favorite programs. When "Amos 'n Andy" was on the air, the nation simply stopped all its other business and listened. When

Pepsodent sponsored "Amos 'n Andy," its sales tripled in just a few weeks. The way was clear.[20]

The turn of the twentieth century saw musical theater and musical-influenced pop ruling the taste of the day. The compositions of Sousa, Gilbert and Sullivan, Berlin, Porter, the Gershwins, Rodgers and Hart, and Cohan—from Broadway floorboards and Hollywood studios—made their way to people's homes.[21] In contrast, the black blues and jazz of the period was sneered at with acid derision. It was linked with depravity and criminality (especially against the puritan backdrop of Prohibition). In the December 1921 edition of *Ladies' Home Journal,* the headline screamed, "UNSPEAKABLE JAZZ MUST GO."[22] The antipathy for black music was perhaps best articulated by a sour editorial in the February 1924 edition of *Talking Machine Journal:* ". . . hundreds of 'race' singers have flooded the market with what is generally regarded as the worst contribution to the cause of good music ever inflicted on the public. The lyrics of many of these 'blues' are worse than the lowest form of doggerel and the melodies are lacking in originality, lilting rhythm, and any semblance to [sic] music worth."[23]

Despite this sentiment, black music still seeped in around the edges, either through culturally "sanctioned" movements like the Harlem Renaissance or filtered through white bandleaders like Glenn Miller, Paul Whiteman, Guy Lombardo, Al Goodman, Ozzie Nelson, Kay Kyser, Benny Goodman, and Tommy Dorsey.[24] The term "race music" was devised as a means of marketing black performers, irrespective of whether their genre was blues, jazz, gospel, or opera. Labels such as Black Swan, Pathé, Okeh, Paramount, Vocalion, Gennett, Victor, Emerson, and Columbia—often marketing their race product with updated imagery from the minstrel age—were launch pads for Bessie Smith, Louis Armstrong, Fletcher Henderson, Mamie Smith, King Oliver, Ethel Waters, Cab Calloway, "Blind" Lemon Jefferson, and Alberta Hunter.[25]

Although exact figures on race record sales are not readily available, they helped propel overall record sales to 100 million per year through the mid-1920s before the stock market crash of 1929 and the onset of the Great Depression.[26] Overall production of records was reduced drastically, and production of race, folk, and "hillbilly" records was stopped entirely for three years. Okeh, Gennett, and Paramount Records went out of business, and RCA Victor stopped making record players briefly and sold radios instead.[27] The industry did not recover until the mid-1930s. But from the flappers of the "Roaring '20s" to the zoot suit and bobby socks set of the Swing Era, the music of the black proletariat was permeating the nation's subconscious.

Unwitting co-conspirators furthered guided America's ears to black music. For example, the performance rights for the most eminent writers at the turn of the twentieth century were secured by the American Society of Composers, Authors and Publishers (ASCAP). According to music historian Eileen Southern, ASCAP held a "virtual monopoly on all copyrighted music" and maintained an impervious admissions structure black writers had no access to.[28] Even the great Duke Ellington had to fight to get a membership.[29]

In 1940 ASCAP announced plans to double the broadcast licensing fees with an eye on radio's lucrative income. (ASCAP's radio cash flow exploded from $757,450 in 1932 to $5.9 million in 1937, $3.8 million in 1938 and $4.3 million in 1939.)[30] Stations fought back with a boycott. The National Association of Broadcasters, representing 600 stations, created their own organization, Broadcast Music Incorporated (BMI). Not having access to the popular writers of the day, BMI relied on those disenfranchised by ASCAP—a large portion of whom, predictably, were black.

For the next ten months the United States was treated to an earful of its own root music. Authentic regional styles were broadcast to a mass public intact, not yet boiled down in the national pop melting pot; the Broadway-Hollywood monopoly on popular music was challenged publicly for the first time. Without this challenge, we might never have heard from composers like Huddie "Leadbelly" Ledbetter, Arthur "Big Boy" Crudup, Roy Brown, Ivory Joe Hunter, Johnny Otis, Antoine "Fats" Domino, and Wynonie Harris.

Black people would also be emissaries of their own music. Their mass exodus from the overtly hostile southern states would lead to the "birth of a demographic," if you will. In the 1940s, 1 million blacks emigrated to the North, three times the number during the depression. Southern GIs brought their music north and northern GIs were exposed to the music of the South. The influx of black audience, flush with newfound prosperity from the World War II economy, attracted programmers and black music found its way onto radio, usually during late night. Conversely, a growing audience of young white listeners would become enraptured with the new sounds filling the airwaves.

Content provision would be accelerated by new oxidized magnetic tape technology, which enabled low-cost recording devices, affordable and accessible studios, and several independent labels emerging in the late 1940s. The most notable of these were Atlantic, Vee Jay, Savoy, King, Chess, Sun, Peacock, Modern, Imperial, and Specialty because of their focus on black artists and black music.[31] Also at that time, Radio Corporation of America (RCA, owner of NBC radio and RCA Records) made television commercially available.[32] The conduits were now primed for the imminent revolution—the final component would be the evolution of black music's sound.

# BIRTH OF A PHENOMENON: THE ROOTS OF ROCK MUSIC

The Swing Era died out at the end of World War II, as it was no longer economically viable for venues to support huge orchestras. Ballrooms closed and most of the big bands broke up.[33] Smaller combos and more intimate clubs, notably on the jazz circuit where the "be-bop" sound was born, were on the rise. Other black artists found their niche by returning to the blues or, rather, "jumping the blues." Eliminating horn and string sections and emphasizing the rhythm section forged a new aggressive sound that swept over black communities across the nation.[34] By 1949 *Billboard* formally designated it as "rhythm and blues," a term devised by staffer-turned-legendary-record-man and R&B producer Jerry Wexler.[35]

Key figures would emerge in this movement—Louis Jordan, Wynonie Harris, John Lee Hooker, Bo Diddley, Fats Domino, Dave Bartholomew, T-Bone Walker, Johnny Otis, Big Mama Thornton, and Muddy Waters were but a few. Like the music, the singing and lyrical content was more bold, candid, uninhibited, and raw. Songs like "Open the Door, Richard," "Beans and Cornbread," "Caldonia," "Ain't Nobody Here But Us Chickens," "That's How You Got Killed Before," "Boogie Chillen," and "Good Rockin' Tonight" were becoming popular in major urban centers. And bands from Chicago, New Orleans, Los Angeles, Memphis, Kansas City, and New York each added their own hues to the rhythm and blues palette. Southern musicians in particular cross-bred the instrumentation and dynamics of folk and country, which for their part borrowed heavily from the blues.[36]

The new style of music gave birth to a new style of radio. As television took over the national programming and ad revenues, radio focused on local and regional interests. The informal structure in place at the time allowed local disc jockeys, or "personality jocks," to dictate the tastes of the times.[37] They were recruited from the community and had their fingers on the pulse of what records would be successful. They married the kinetic language of the streets with the energy of the records. Hal Jackson, Jack Gibson, Professor Bop, Sugar Daddy, Eddie O'Jay, and Jocko Henderson were some of black radio's pioneers.[38]

Later, white jocks copying black jock styles and play lists—most notably Arnie Ginsburg, Wolfman Jack, Stan Richard, Alan Freed, and Murray the K—came to national prominence.[39] Predictably, this was the talent pool for national shows, radio in big-market cities, and television, while black jocks made the most of local radio. Disc jockeys were the arbiters who made or broke records, and they wielded great power in rock's early days. (This was also a sticking point as the 1950s closed and radio's infamous payola scandals erupted.)[40]

But despite how the new sounds were winning fans, black artists were prevented from capitalizing on its growing popularity. It was standard practice for most record companies to flagrantly cheat talent of their publishing rights and record sales.[41] This spawned high artist turnover and fueled the industry's predisposition about breaking black performers through singles rather than albums.[42] Moreover, record companies began releasing records in 45-rpm and 33-rpm formats because of the higher fidelity (or "hi-fi") sound. But due to lack of money, most black households still had 78-rpm record players and it would be a few years before new ones became affordable.[43]

The primary encumbrance, however, was still the race question. Whereas brickbats over blues and jazz were confined to editorial pages, literary salons, and PTA meetings, this new rhythm and blues—this "race/devil music"—ignited the American-Christian-Anglicized equivalent of a jihad.[44] At the rabid height of the McCarthy era (the government-sanctioned witch hunt for communist activity during the Cold War) and apartheid rule of the Jim Crow South, rhythm and blues was an affront to aspirations of a white male homogeneous society.

The 1950s provided the right cultural, social, and political conditions for the emergence of a new musical form, a form rooted in rebellion and based on race. World War II veterans were returning from the war to start families en masse. This emphasis on family was to become a major theme of the decade. The family was the nexus for most activities in the culture at the time, or at least it was supposed to be. In the public sense, life was oriented around the family. Any sign of "dysfunction" was kept in private. Any deviation from the norm was identified and rooted out.[45]

Priests, politicians, pundits, and parents raised a deafening hue and cry, particularly in the southern states. Propaganda was disseminated through all available media. Town hall and committee meetings, even congressional hearings were held. Antidancing laws and curfews were enacted. Protests and boycotts were organized. Bonfires for records, books, and all other materials deemed "subversive" became community events.[46] Northern states for the most part went through no such histrionics. Most of the North's urban centers—experiencing the explosion of U.S. Afro-Americans from the South and Afro-Caribbean and Latin American populace from the islands—were deep in the throes of white flight to suburbia. But in the extremely repressed climes of the suburbs, the new music form

drew just as much enmity. During the payola scandal of 1960, Massachusetts State Representative Tip O'Neill demanded that the Federal Commu-
nications Commission investigate all stations whose employees were
involved in payola, convinced that the "captive audience" of American
youth must be safeguarded from the demoralizing effects of payola and
rock 'n' roll ("a type of sensuous music unfit for impressionable minds.")[47]
Rock was, in the minds of "right-thinking Christian Americans," a bona
fide threat to their way of life. And, for all intents and purposes, it was.

# BIRTH OF THE UNSEEN COLOR LINE: BLACK TALENT/WHITE FACES

Historically, in order for "race music" to be embraced by whites, it had to
be reinterpreted by white entertainers. Enterprising broadcasters, independent labels, and promoters had long recognized the commercial value
in putting out "race music." Still, their success was limited to regional singles. With hostile racial environs and limited resources, they could not
generate national hits based solely on the strength of their black talent.
While *Billboard* began its rhythm and blues chart in 1949 and Jackie
Brenston's "Rocket 88"—actually Ike Turner's band—would be the first
national rhythm and blues hit to make the pop chart, it would be years
before black artists achieved national recognition.[48]

Given the racial underpinnings of the rhythm and blues scene, it was
plain that white performers stood to gain little going that route. But they
could not call their music "pop" either—"pop" then was Bing Crosby,
Doris Day, Perry Como, Frankie Laine, Jo Stafford, and Frank Sinatra.[49]
The term "rock 'n' roll" (a euphemism for sexual intercourse) was lifted
from several rhythm and blues releases to lend nomenclature to the hot
new style. Alan Freed—anointed in mainstream circles as the "Father of
Rock 'n' Roll"—has been credited with coining the phrase in his broadcasts.[50] Thus yet another outlet was invented for white artists and entrepreneurs to exploit and profit from contemporary black music. "If only I
could find a White man who had the Negro sound and the Negro feel, I
could make a billion dollars."[51]

There is a reason why the words of Sam Phillips, owner of the legendary Sun Records label, resonate to this day. Because he did find his
white man with the "Negro sound" (several, in fact) and he did make millions, if not a billion, and in his innocuous quip, he laid out the blueprint
for rock success. It was imperative for every savvy record man to find

white artists who could give reasonable enough representation of "race music" without the attendant racial baggage. Bill Haley & His Comets would be the first white exposition of the "Negro sound" to spark the pop charts, and Elvis Presley later combusted them. Black artists took considerably longer to achieve such success (again, owing as much to limited indie resources as racially skewed marketing).

To illustrate, Bill Haley cracked *Billboard*'s year-end Top 50, landing at the number 26 spot in 1954 with "Shake, Rattle & Roll" (a cover of the Big Joe Turner classic). The following year he reached number 2 with his own classic "Rock Around the Clock," joined by Pat Boone at number 9 covering Fats Domino's "Ain't That a Shame." The first time black rock 'n' rollers—specifically Fats Domino, The Platters, Little Richard, and Frankie Lymon & The Teenagers—appear at all is in rock's watershed year of 1956—the year Presley began his chart reign. (He had five songs in the Top 50, including three in the Top 10.)[52]

But outside of The Platters, who scored number 4 with "My Prayer," no black artists would crack the Top 20. The first black nonballadeers to do so would be The Silhouettes in 1958 with "Get a Job" (number 14). The first black rock song to crack the Top 5—albeit with milquetoast vocal dubs and orchestra—was Lloyd Price's "Personality" in 1959. It would take until 1960, and Bobby Lewis with "Tossin' and Turnin'," for a black rock 'n' roll artist to reach number 1 on the year-end chart.[53] Presley, on the other hand, broke the Top 5 every year through the decade's end except for 1959 (when he was called up for a dubious two-year military hitch and could not record).

Throughout the modern rock era, black music has had to acquit itself with strong action on the rhythm and blues charts before it was deemed worthy of pop or rock promotion and airplay. Just because a song was a big hit on the R&B charts was no guarantee of mainstream or "crossover" success. And since there was no separate "rock" chart then, white artists did not go through the same preliminaries—their material was shipped straight to pop.[54]

Major labels dipped their toes into the rock/R&B pool, but only with white artists covering songs originally performed by black artists. Naturally, because of their advanced production and better distribution and promotion, the covers usually outsold the originals. Presley, Boone, Georgia Gibbs, The Crew Cuts, The McGuire Sisters, Ricky Nelson, and others had some of their biggest hits this way. Even long-established pop balladeers like Andy Williams, Perry Como, and Steve Lawrence got into the act.[55] By 1960 rock 'n' roll was officially out of the closet. Sadly, its black founding fathers and mothers were left inside.

# BIRTH OF SEPARATE AND UNEQUAL MARKETING: POST-ROCK REVOLUTION ENTRENCHMENT OF ARTIST/RACE DIVISION

As the 1950s were defined by conservative entrenchment of the status quo, the 1960s were defined by radical change. Various political movements (civil rights, antiwar, feminism, black power) faced off against defenders of the status quo and, though sociopolitical and economic barriers continue to plague American infrastructure, the awkward steps toward an integrated society were being taken. Rock music would be both soundtrack and sounding board for the shift of a nation's consciousness, and the industry transformed at a breakneck pace.

To say that television revolutionized media would be an understatement found wanting; it completely metamorphosed American life. While radio catapulted the music industry into another stratosphere, television would transport it to a different universe: In the 1950s, a gold record (500,000 units sold) was a profound benchmark; in the 1960s, television made million sellers a common occurrence. Shows like *Ed Sullivan, American Bandstand, Shindig,* and *Your Hit Parade* became premier showcases for rock talent.[56]

Radio underwent its own fundamental changes, though under acrimonious circumstances. In 1960 the Senate held hearings about "payola," the practice of bribery to get disc jockeys to put songs in rotation. To no one's real shock, payola was discovered to be the lay of the land. The laws were so weak and remedies so nominal that the payola bugaboo resurfaced in the 1970s and 1980s; some argue it still has a hand in the industry today.[57] Of greater import was the shift in the balance of power—jocks could no longer select records for air. That responsibility was transferred to the program director. This, in essence, was the beginning of the end of the personality jock and the beginning of specialized format radio. These formats proliferated as the technology for radio's frequency modulation band (FM) improved to the point where stereo broadcasts were possible, making it the ideal signal for music. FM became the standard and created new markets, multiplying revenues exponentially.[58]

Until the 1960s, most major record labels were still keeping black/rock music at arm's length—if they dealt with it at all, it would be through subsidiary labels or distribution/buyout deals. So several of the independents that came in on the ground floor became forces, specifically Atlantic, King, Chess and Roulette, Stax, and, of course, Motown.[59] These labels rewrote all the rules about black artists, black music, and black people's stature in the music industry—for better and for worse, as time would prove.

Against this backdrop black music was able to flourish; black people in the music, however, were a different matter. Granted, it was no longer inconceivable that a black person could get a job in the music industry and make a decent living. Creatively, it was a Golden Age as legends in black music were at the height of their powers: James Brown, Aretha Franklin, James Brown, Sly & the Family Stone, Jimi Hendrix, Curtis Mayfield, Aretha Franklin, Otis Redding, Ike & Tina Turner, Sam & Dave, the entire Motown roster, and many, many others. And black performers cracked markets once thought unassailable. But the devil, as ever, was in the details.

Race-neutral facades camouflaged the reality that the commercial music industry was founded, structured, and, indeed, profited along segregationist patterns. Excepting the rare odd birds like Hendrix, Stone, the Turners, or Richie Havens, rock music became the exclusive domain of white artists. Black artists were relegated to rhythm and blues, whether their sound had any discernable difference from rock or not.[60] In fact, rhythm and blues was further subdivided into yet another category: "soul music." While many a critic has burst many a synapse trying to parse together a plausible musical distinction, from a marketing standpoint it was not all that complicated.

Rhythm and blues was black music that could be crossed over and exploited in white markets; soul was black music that would go over only in the black community.[61] (This rationale proved specious in the 1970s as the purported "stylistic lines" between the genres blurred—plus, it turned out that white people also bought Otis Redding, Aretha Franklin, and James Brown records.)

The music business structure itself was (and is) segregated. Major labels established "black music divisions," in-house staff to implement all strategies whether it was with the label's own talent or to monitor and broker activity with a label subsidiary. These divisions, by and large, ran on a tight leash, had limited resources, and, if an act managed to become successful enough to cross over, the pop division took over.[62] Moreover, since labels labored under the notion that black artists' commercial value lay in singles rather than in albums, they mostly were shackled creatively. Songs had to be "marketable" (i.e., instant hits), whereas white rockers were more free to experiment. This often resulted in artists repeating formula or, even worse, jumping on the successful style of the moment, whether it suited them or not.[63]

Introducing artists and material to the market, the label seeks the most cost-effective forms of hit-making. Historical U.S. models of racism and racial polarization, while shunned in intellectual discourse, are pervasive in every aspect of American culture—including commerce. With few exceptions, the music of black pop artists is lumped into a category called "black music" within the industry and casually by consumers. For the purposes of marketing, the label often separates the stylistic offerings of nontraditional black artists from their ethnicity. While the corporate gatekeepers may be sold on the content produced by the artists, the historical model is one based on racial alignment unless a track record has proven otherwise. While the artists relegated to the term "black music" may offer works ranging from jazz vocals to thrash rock, the traditional model of R&B remains the traditional style associated with black artists. Industry and cultural investment in this concept prohibits proper marketing campaigns and anchors the potential of diversifying marginalized voices as well as creating new musical markets.[64]

And despite slight improvements in contract law, most black artists still got fleeced in onerous record deals.[65] In 1994 the Rhythm & Blues Foundation was established. It funded the Atlantic Foundation and other music industry organizations to aid destitute rhythm and blues performers of the early rock era whom the *New York Times* characterized as "victims of poor business practices, bad management and unscrupulous record companies."[66]

Media segregation took on farcical proportions. Radio's specialized formats—album-oriented rock (AOR), country, Top 40/contemporary hit radio (CHR), and urban (code language for black)—enabled advertisers to target specific audiences and demo groups. This has long been a source of great ire for black—or rather "urban"—stations because it gives ad buyers an escape hatch for not spending money with them or billing at lower rates than so-called general market (i.e., white audiences) stations without drawing accusations of overt racism.[67] This pattern was consistent in urban television, public relations, and print media as well.

Black audiences also contributed this schism. In *The Death of Rhythm & Blues,* critic Nelson George details the class and ideological rifts that shaped the black marketplace: privileged-class blacks who wanted no truck with the culture of their working class or poor brethren; conservative-minded folks repulsed by hippie and/or radical culture; embittered separatist elements within the black power movement who encouraged distance from white popular culture (even if it embraced, copied, or adopted theirs); cooler-than-thou hipsters who equated white with "corny."[68]

Frameworks of ethnic and national identity set up social boundaries. Even as memes migrate across these boundaries to serve people's emotional and physical needs, thereby reducing differences between groups, the need to maintain boundaries asserts itself. It also results in new musical styles, and black Americans continue to create music they can think of as specifically theirs. This is the mechanism that has been driving American culture through the twentieth century and into this one.[69]

It also bears repeating that the three largest major recording companies—CBS, RCA, Warner Brothers—did not bother with black rhythm and blues/rock performers in any significant way until some 20 years after the market for them had established itself and independents threatened to render them irrelevant. (Decca and EMI-Capitol beat the other majors by about two decades.)[70] When they finally penetrated the market, they did so with extreme prejudice—in every sense of the term. The majors, with near-monopoly control over the distribution network, kept the indies at bay up to a point. After all, they were getting a piece of whatever product was shipped.[71] What stuck in their craw was how much of the overall market share the baby labels commanded: As a genre, rock 'n' roll jumped from 15.7 percent of the market in 1955 to 42.7 percent in 1959. As a result of the popularity of rock 'n' roll, sales industry-wide grew from $213 million in 1954 to $603 million in 1959. From 1948 to 1955, the number of firms (as opposed to labels, since many labels can be owned by a single firm) that posted hits in the Top 10 ranged from four to seven. But from 1956 to 1959, this number rose to twenty-nine. For a brief time span, the majors lost half of their market share to independent labels.[72]

To "rectify" this disparity, majors consolidated with independent labels at furious pace, with the number of label-owning firms cut in half between 1960 (40) and 1971 (20).[73] (CBS was particularly noteworthy because it actually commissioned a university study—the now-infamous Harvard Report—on how to penetrate the marketplace.) Some labels folded by attrition. Others were bought outright or squeezed out. By the mid-1980s, even the two biggest players on the black music scene—Stax and Motown—were no longer factors. Stax was shuttered in 1975 by overwhelming debt and a rancorous legal battle with CBS.[74] Motown, after an uneven foray into the film business, was unable to keep its premier talent, keep pace with the music of the times, or handle the costs of running a major label. MCA bought it out in 1988.[75]

The 1980s and 1990s served as a time of entrenchment for major label formulas and continued consolidation. Majors merged with or bought out other majors, then multinational conglomerates bought them out. To date, there are only five major music distribution firms on the planet: EMI Distribution, Sony Music, Vivendi/Universal, Bertelsmann Music Group (BMG), and AOL Time Warner. In 2001 these companies posted about $40 billion in total sales.[76]

And while black music has gone through various permutations in the rock era—funk, disco, fusion, hip-hop, reggae, house, et al.—not one single black rock artist has cracked the *Billboard* year-end Top 50 since 1994, when Prince did with "The Most Beautiful Girl in the World," a middle-of-the-road R&B ballad.[77] Rock music in general has not enjoyed as active a presence on the charts in the last decade or so, but black rockers have been practically invisible, with sparse appearances by Prince (1983–1987, 1989, 1992, and 1994) and The Isley Brothers (1963, 1973).[78]

# BIRTH OF AN EPILOGUE

Rock 'n' roll adopted countless styles and spawned countless legends from its birth 60 years ago, but it is still the most popular form of music across the globe to this day. Sadly, there is also still a great deal of cultural apartheid in the music industry. Its originators—the great blues men of the 1920s, 1930s, and 1940s—have been all but forgotten. Its innovators—Little Richard, Chuck Berry, Fats Domino, LaVern Baker, The Isleys—while honored, have been largely relegated to footnote status within the context of their aggrandized white peers. Despite the obvious rock underpinnings of later artists like Sly and the Family Stone, Curtis Mayfield, Aretha Franklin, Otis Redding, Parliament-Funkadelic, Rufus & Chaka Khan, Stevie Wonder, Prince, and countless others—black artists continue to play second banana to white artists. It is a pattern that continues today with black rockers like Ben Harper, Fishbone, Living Colour, Me'Shell NdegeOcello, David Ryan Harris, Terence Trent D'Arby, Weapon of Choice, Kina, Martin Luther, Skunk Anansie, King's X, Seal, Tracy Chapman, and legions more.

The distribution of nontraditional black pop artists is challenging due to historical models built on segregation, black nationalism and racial politics, poor marketing campaigns, and the economics of niche marketing to the masses. In spite of the success of artists such as Lenny Kravitz, Living Colour, and Macy Gray, many nontraditional black acts will not find an audience due to the above-mentioned conditions. For the distribution of music to expand past a system predicated on race, more than talented artists with quality work must come to the marketplace. Our current system of marginalizing content based on race continues the historical model, even if cultural preservation is touted as a motivating factor. The demand does exist for quality work, regardless of ethnicity. What is needed is capital investment in the infrastructure of distribution that is sensitive to altering the color-coded system.[79]

Racist attitudes continue to hamper intelligent dialogue about rock's origins and black artists getting their due. While Presley, Haley, Carl Perkins, Jerry Lee Lewis, the Beatles, the Rolling Stones, Janis Joplin, and others have long acknowledged their debt to rock's black pioneers and visionaries, the music industry and mainstream media are unwavering in making them ride the back of the bus—as if everything Presley, Haley, Perkins, Lewis, et al. did manifested fortuitously. While rock's musical roots can be traced back to the days of slavery and sharecropping, it seems ironic that a genre that so symbolizes freedom and liberation is curated with attitudes that can be traced back to the same era.

# NOTES

1. Reebee Garafalo, *Rockin' Out: Popular Music in the USA* (Boston: Allyn and Bacon, 1997), p. 152.
2. Recording Industry Association of America (RIAA) press release, 2001 Consumer Profile, April 26, 2002.
3. RIAA press release, 2000 Consumer Profile, March 13, 2001.
4. Reebee Garafalo, "Crossing Over: From Black Rhythm & Blues to White Rock 'N Roll," from the anthology *Rhythm & Business: The Political Economy of Black Music,* Norman Kelley, ed. (Akashic Books, 2002), p. 112.
5. Norman Coombs, *The Black Experience in America* (New York: Hippocrene Books, 1972), p. 49.
6. Mel Watkins, *On the Real Side* (New York: Simon & Schuster, 1994), pp. 57–59.
7. Ibid. p. 58.
8. W. D. Weatherford and Charles S. Johnson, *Race Relations* (New York: Negro Universities Press, 1934), p. 284.
9. LeRoi Jones (Amiri Baraka), *Blues People* (New York: Perennial, 1963), p. 6.
10. Coombs, *The Black Experience in America,* pp. 48–49.
11. Basil Davidson, *Africa: History of a Continent* (London: Macmillan, 1972), p. 222.
12. Coombs, *Black Experience,* p. 160.
13. Watkins, *On the Real Side,* p. 85.
14. Ibid.
15. Constance Rourke, *American Humor: A Study of the National Character* (New York: Harcourt, 1971), p. 82.
16. Watkins, *On the Real Side,* p. 103.
17. Coombs, *Black Experience,* p.
18. Ibid., p. 89.
19. www.sonymusic.com, "History of Sony Music."
20. David Halberstam, *The Powers That Be* (Champaign: University of Illinois Press, 2000), pp. 14–15.
21. Eileen Southern, *The Music of Black Americans: A History* (New York: W. W. Norton, 1971), p. 353.
22. Ralph J. Gleason, *Celebrating The Duke & Louis, Bessie, Billie, Bird, Carmen, Miles, Dizzy & Other Heroes* (New York: Delta Books, 1975), p. 11.

23. Steven Calt, "The Anatomy of a 'Race' Music Label: Mayo Williams and Paramount Records," in Kelley ed., *Rhythm & Business*, p. 87.

24. Gleason, *Celebrating The Duke*, pp. 12–14; Watkins, *On the Real Side*, p. 270.

25. Watkins, *On the Real Side*, p. 270; Ken Burns' Jazz, Jazz Exchange webpage, "Race Records" page, www.pbs.org.

26. Ken Burns' Jazz.

27. Ibid.

28. Southern, *Music of Black Americans*, p. 353.

29. Gleason, *Celebrating The Duke*, pp. 157–158.

30. Russell Sanjek, *American Popular Music and Its Business: The First Four Hundred Years: Vol. III, From 1900 to 1984* (New York: Oxford University Press, 1988), p. 176.

31. Garafalo, "Crossing Over," pp. 113–118.

32. Ibid. pp. 119–120; Watkins, *On the Real Side*, pp. 293–294.

33. Garafalo, "Crossing Over," pp. 116–117.

34. Ibid. pp. 117–119; Watkins, *On the Real Side*, pp. 334–338.

35. Fredric Dannen, *Hit Men* (New York: Vintage, 1991), p. 87.

36. Garafalo, "Crossing Over," pp. 117–118; Watkins, *On the Real Side*, pp. 334–338.

37. Garafalo, "Crossing Over," p. 120.

38. Garofalo, "Crossing Over," pp. 120–121; Watkins, *On the Real Side*, pp. 294–297.

39. Garofalo, "Crossing Over," p. 121; Watkins, *On the Real Side*, pp. 295–296.

40. Garafalo, "Crossing Over," p. 120; Dannen, *Hit Men*, pp. 44–45.

41. Garafalo, "Crossing Over," pp. 122–123; Dannen, *Hit Men*, pp. 31 and 34.

42. Garafalo, "Crossing Over," pp. 122–123.

43. Garafalo, "Crossing Over," pp. 127–128.

44. Watkins, On the Real Side, pp. 338–339.

45. John Bulmer, *Devil Music: Race, Class, and Rock and Roll* (Russell Sage College Press, 1997).

46. Watkins, *On the Real Side*, pp. 338.

47. Charles William White III, "Payola Scandal Timeline," *The Beat* (1985).

48. Billboard, Top 50 Lists (1951–2001), pp.

49. Garafalo, "Crossing Over," p. 116.

50. Ibid., p. 121; Dannen, *Hit Men*, pp. 42–43.

51. Sam Philips quoted in Peter Guralnick, *Feel Like Going Home: Portraits In Blues and Rock 'n Roll* (New York: Outerbridge and Dienstfrey, 1971), p. 140.

52. Joel Whitburn, *Billboard Top 1000 Singles (1955–2000): 1000 Biggest Hits of the Rock Era* (Milwaukee: Hal Leonard, 1997), pp. 34–39.

53. Ibid.

54. Fred Goodman, *The Mansion on the Hill* (New York: Vintage 1998), p. 137; The National Association for the Advancement of Colored People

(NAACP) Economic Development Department, 1987 Report, "The Discordant Sound of Music: A Report on the Music Industry" from the anthology Rhythm & Business: The Political Economy of Black Music, pp. 46–47.

55. Garafalo, "Crossing Over," pp. 124–126.
56. Halberstam, The Powers That Be, p. 130; Garafalo, "Crossing Over," p. 120; Dannen, Hit Men, pp. 34,46–47; Museum of Broadcasting website archives: "American Bandstand" html, "Shindig" html, "Ed Sullivan" html, "Your Hit Parade" html.
57. Dannen, Hit Men, pp. 45–47, 109.
58. Goodman, Mansion on the Hill, pp. 36–40, 142.
59. Garafalo, "Crossing Over," p. 118.
60. Dannen, Hit Men, pp. 11, 87.
61. Samuel A. Floyd, The Power of Black Music (New York: Oxford University Press, 1995), pp. 203–206.
62. NAACP 1987 report in Kelley, Rhythm and Business, pp. 46–47; Garafalo, "Black Popular Music; Crossing Over or Going Under?" In Rock and Popular Music: Politics, Policies, Institutions (London Routledge, 1993).
63. Nelson George, The Death of Rhythm & Blues (Pantheon, 1988), pp. 150–153.
64. Kimberly Steger, "The Business of Stereotyping Black Music: The Stranglehold on Non-Traditional Black Artists in Pop Music," Fall 2001 report commissioned by Media Industry Perspectives, p. 4.
65. Garafalo, "Crossing Over," pp. 122–123; Dannen, Hit Men, pp. 31, 34.
66. Norman Kelley, "Notes on the Political Economy of Black Music," in Rhythm & Business: The Political Economy of Black Music (Akashic Books, 2002), p. 14.
67. George, Death of Rhythm and Blues, pp. 159–160;
68. Ibid., p. 68–69; Jones, Blues People, pp. 160–165, 233–236.
69. William Benzon, Beethoven's Anvil: Music In Mind and Culture (New York: Basic Books, 2001), p. 273.
70. Garafalo, "Crossing Over," p. 118; Dannen, Hit Men, p. 31; Michael Roberts, "Papa's Got Brand New Bag: Big Music's Post-Fordist Regime and the Role of Independent Music Labels," in Kelley, Rhythm & Business, p. 36.
71. Roberts, "Papa's Got Brand New Bag," pp. 31–32, 37–38; George, Death of Rhythm and Blues, pp. 147–149; Garafalo, "Crossing Over," p. 118.
72. Roberts, "Papa's Got Brand New Bag," p. 36.
73. Ibid.
74. David Sanjek, "Tell Me Something I Don't Already Know: The Harvard Report on Soul Music Revisited," in Kelley, Rhythm and Business, pp. 69–72; Rob Bowman, Soulsville. U.S.A: The Story of Stax Records (New York: Schirmer Books, 1997), pp. 277–371.
75. Berry Gordy, To Be Loved: The Music, The Magic, The Memories of Motown (Headline, 1994), pp. 389–398.

76. Roberts, "Papa's Got Brand New Bag" pp. 36–37; RIAA press release, 2001 Consumer Profile, April 26, 2002.
77. Whitburn, *Billboard Top 1000 Singles,* pp. 34–79.
78. Ibid.
79. Steger, "Business of Stereotyping Black Music," p. 15.

# KNOX ROBINSON

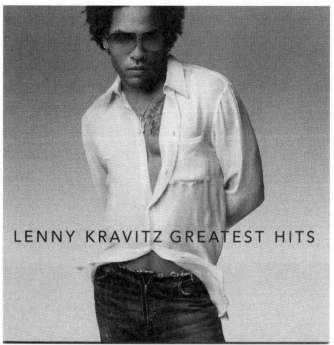

LENNY KRAVITZ GREATEST HITS

# INTERVIEW WITH
# L E N N Y
# KRAVITZ

KNOX ROBINSON: I'd like to ask about your childhood. I guess people know that you kind of grew up in between Los Angeles and New York, and that your parents were both involved in the entertainment industry. But briefly, what was it like growing up in that sort of environment?

LENNY KRAVITZ: Well, you know that I grew up in New York, right? And I grew up in a really cool time. I had interracial parents, and it was, I think the combination of the time that it was, and the fact that I had mixed parents . . .and that all their friends were artists, musicians, actors, writers, etc. I had a really colorful childhood. I was exposed to a lot of different things. There were always musicians around. We were always going to the theater, and there was always some creativity going around. I was with my mom at her theater rehearsals, and it was really great. When I look back, my life set me up to be a musician; I really didn't have a choice. Or to be some type of artist rather. Because I also did acting, etc.

KR: Why didn't you become an actor?

LK: Well, music really was my passion from the time I was five years old. I don't want to say that I knew that I was going to be a musician, but I knew that music was the thing that turned me on. I was very aware of that. I did other things as well, but the reason that I acted was that my mother was an actress, and I had an agent, and I used to go out for commercial auditions, and I did a few commercials.

KR:  Weren't you in a Burger King commercial?

LK: Yeah, that and a few other things.

KR: That was a long time ago. [laughs]

LK: Yeah, in VH1. [laughs] I ended up doing theater, but music was it. I listen to music all the time,you know.

KR: What were you listening to in those early years?

LK: I was listening to Motown. The Jackson Five was the first thing that blew my head off. And you know—Stevie Wonder, Marvin Gaye, Gladys Knight and the Pips, the Temptations, the Supremes—you know, it was basically Motown. And also Curtis Mayfield. And also the Stax sound . . .and Al Green. And then I was also listening to Jazz— Miles Davis, Coltrane, and so forth.

KR: You say that you had been into music really since age five. But at what point did you say, "Ok, I'm listening to the Temptations, or Al Green, or the Jackson Five. This is something that I can do, or that I'm going to do?"

LK: Well I guess around that same time, maybe closer to when I was like six, seven years old. I would put on the Jackson Five record, and I would have this pen in my hand, and you know that would be like the microphone. And I had those rain galoshes—but they were the ones that went up your leg a little bit—and those were my funky boots. [laughs]

KR:  Right, of course, the funk boots. [laughs]

LK: My funk boots. Because I had seen the Jackson Five, and they had these like really funky boots. So, I would put those on, and I had my little pen, and I would be mimicking . . . so that is where it all started.

KR: When did you start making music/recording music?

LK: I didn't really start making music . . . well, technically I started making music/performing music when I was about eleven years old. We moved out to California. My mom got a TV show out there, so we had to move. I joined this boy's choir when I was in L.A. They were called the California Boy's Choir. At that time they were rated the second best boy's choir in the world next to the Vienna Boy's Choir, which is like the number one choir on the planet.

And so I joined this choir, because my mom was trying to like . . . you know we had moved to L.A., and she was trying to keep me off the street, and have something for me to do, and she knew I loved music. But classical, I was never expecting to go into classical—even though I was exposed to it and I had gone to classical concerts.

But, I joined this choir. You had to audition, and then you had to go thorough a training program, and then after you've graduated from [the] training program, you graduate into the concert choir. And so I graduated into the concert choir, and I was with them for about three years. And through singing with them, I sang with the New York City Opera company, the Joffrey Ballet, and the American Ballet Theater. And I sang with all these great conductors like Zubin Mehta and Erich Leinsdorf, and I was like in the middle of this whole classical career. I wasn't writing my own music yet, but I was performing. I did about ten, eleven operas. I remember my first concert was the opening of the Hollywood Bowl for that season, and it was the Mahler's Third Symphony. It was just "this is crazy!"

But when I graduated from that choir, I went into high school. And that's when I really started to jam and play with musicians, and I started to learn how to play different instruments. I was playing guitar, I was playing bass, I was playing keyboard, and I was playing drums. And that is when the multi-instrumental thing started for me.

KR: Were you in a high school band program?

LK: I was in more music classes than academic. I was in the jazz band, I was in the marching band, I was in the orchestra, I was in the choir . . . I was doing a lot of music.

KR: Were you aware of the LA underground scene at that time?

LK: I wasn't so much in the scene. I wasn't in a band. Our whole thing was that we used ditch class and go to whoever's house had guitars and amps. We would go jam. That is when I started listening to

Hendrix and Zeppelin. Well actually, the end of junior high is when I started that.

The whole California experience for me was the whole rock 'n' roll thing. When I was in New York, I listened to R&B, jazz . . . and then when I moved to LA, we moved to Santa Monica. This is actually before I joined the choir, when we first moved there. I moved to Santa Monica, and it was that time when it was that whole *Dog Town and Z Boys* thing. I was in the middle of all that. I knew a bunch of those guys. Actually, you know the guy who started with the Dog Town thing—Wes Humpston? I knew his brother Mike. We were in class together. He used to bring the skateboards to school and show us what his brother was starting. It was like in the beginning, man.

KR: Wow.

LK: I met a bunch of guys that were surfers, and of course stoners, and the whole smoking pot thing, and listening to Zeppelin . . . and that whole thing started in California. That was *all* new to me you know. I remember listening to "Black Dog" for the first time on *Zeppelin Four.* You know gettin' high, ditching class . . . it was like a whole new world. That whole Santa Monica skate culture turned me onto that whole thing.

KR: You knew Slash in high school?

LK: Yeah, Slash went to Beverly. We never jammed then, but I knew him from hanging out in the hallway.

KR: Okay.

LK: He kind of had the same persona that he's got now. [*both laugh*]

KR: Well, how did the Romeo Blue persona come about?

LK: That was toward the end of high school, when I really started thinking about putting my own thing together. It was that time when you're searching for yourself, and trying to find out who you are. I was heavily into Prince at the time, Rick James, and what was the alternative black music at that time. These guys were all doing their own thing, it was left of center, it wasn't typical. I thought, "Lenny Kravitz" what kind of name is that? You know I can't use that name. And these friends of mine actually gave me the name Romeo—I guess because of my whole thing with the girls in high school—and then I stuck the Blue on the end of it. And it just kind of was born; it was pretty funny.

I actually found some pictures. There's this guy who's making this book on me right now, and we were digging through all the old archives you know, and the other day I found a bunch of Romeo Blue pictures of myself, and it was pretty funny.

KR: [*laughs*] You never released anything under Romeo though?

LK: Thank god, no!

KR: [laughs] I remember seeing you in the Jet magazines and the Ebonys when you first got together with Lisa Bonet . . .

LK: Yeah, that was my name . . .And I just finally realized, like, "what am I doing?" And I went back to being my self. But it was a good way to find myself—by going full circle.

KR: So your first album came out in '89?

LK: Yes.

KR: Let Love Rule is obviously a classic rock album. But I was thinking about it today and . . .

LK: Thank you. I feel the same actually.

KR: Yeah! Of course, man. But at that point in time there were already other classics of rock music being produced, I guess you could say. But that album, in retrospect, stands out . . .

LK: Well that album stuck out, and it stuck out for a few reasons. First of all, it was the end of the eighties. And production at that point was really vaulted at the big eighties sound—the big triggered drums, the big gated drums, the big guitar sounds—and all these effects. That is when technology really started to take off.

KR: Why didn't you want to make it happen like that?

LK: It didn't sound like the records I grew up with. I wanted to go back, and strip it back, and turn the reverb off, everything dry, everything natural—no synthesizers. Because I thought it sounded dated, even at that time. Even though there's cool stuff that was done in the eighties, but a lot of it, you put on the eighties stuff now, and you go "Yeah it's the eighties." It just sounds dated. And it's funny that even at that time I thought that way, but never wanted my records to sound dated. I wanted them to sound classic. And I didn't want you to be able to know when they were recorded. And the thing about my records to me is that with all of them, you don't know when they were recorded.

KR: Right.

LK: It could have been in the '60s, '70s, '80s, '90s, now. And so that's what I did. Also, I was trying to write. People around me at the time tended to start with the production side of music. It didn't start with the songwriting. It started with "Let's try it on the drum machine, let's find a keyboard sound, and let's put this thing together." It was production first. And to me that was really uncomfortable, and I wasn't flowing that way. So I had this equipment . . . I had a bunch of stuff—sequencers, and keyboards, and drum machines. One day I tossed it out. I gave it away. I was like, "you want this thing? Take it. And you want this? Take it."

Out of everything I [only] kept a guitar. Then I went and got a Fender Deluxe amp from Voltage Guitar up in Hollywood, and I bought a couple more guitars, a bass, an acoustic. . . . And then I just started writing from my heart, and letting the production follow the writing. That's how it all started. I was just tired of it—you know, having to turn on all these machines. And so I just stripped it back.

KR: How do you feel about the reception of that album when it came out, back then? A lot of people had the attitude of, "What are you doing?" including a lot of people in the business. Because first of all it was like, "What is it"?

LK: I loved hip-hop from when I first heard "Rapper's Delight" on the radio as a kid in L.A. That was the first rap thing that I'd ever heard . . . but you know, I think I just got tired of that question. and I was like, "Look man, you know, nothing against these hip-hop artists, but I'm doing my thing. I like playing music. I'm an instrumentalist, you know? I sing; that's what I do."

KR: Have you ever been angry at any point in your career, along the lines of a Public Enemy or any group like that?

LK: My whole thing has been about being positive. I've always sung about love, and God, and unity, and different you know social situations, and so . . . yeah, you have anger. I've had to fight a lot to do my own thing. But I used that to motivate me, in a positive way.

KR: Has it been lonely being Lenny Kravitz?

LK: I've had fun with it. I enjoy being different. I had no problem with it.

KR: It is interesting also to think about what happened during your next two albums, in 1991 and in 1993. At that time, the American musical landscape had shifted really quickly into a sort of Grunge direction. What was it like to be coming out with your second and third albums sort of as an already seasoned musician and yet not getting swept up in that mainstream?

LK: No, the cool thing was that I never followed any trend. And yeah, when I think back to it you're right, you know—this came in, that went out, this came in, that went out—I just kept doing my thing. Which is really a blessing to be a . . . I mean that's sort of a difficult thing you know. But it didn't affect me.

KR: How do you think you've been able to achieve that sort of longevity, or that sort of consistency?

LK: I think just by the fact that I've always done what's honest, what's real to me. I've never tried to follow something to have success. And I guess that can be tempting you know. With artists sometimes being forced to think, "Well this is happening right now, I better kind of go that way." But no, I guess I've always done what I felt. I've never wanted to follow anything; I just wanted to express myself. And I just had so much different music inside of me that occupied my attention.

KR: Right. What you believe is real?

LK: Real to me? Just whatever comes out of me. I mean like if you listen to my records you'll hear rock, you'll hear soul, you'll hear funk, you'll hear folk, you'll hear reggae, you'll hear blues and gospel. I mean all that stuff, whatever comes to me. There's a whole lot of different genres within my albums. Because I grew up around all that you know. What's real is what just comes out. And that's what I do. That's how the albums are so schizophrenic—because whatever comes out I'll do.

KR: Do you have a favorite album of yours?

LK: No. They're all a part of me. And whether one did better than the next, or sold more, or whatever, they are all a part of me. And when I listen to them I remember that time, because the records are all very honest, and they represent a piece of my life. So, it's kind of like looking back on photo albums. You know it's hard to say what your favorite period of your life was. But you look back and you go, "Wow look at that, I remember that, and I looked like that, and you know I did this then, I was doing that." And so, they all sort of stand for their own thing.

KR: Wasn't there an unreleased sort of blues-based album that you recorded down in New Orleans over a year ago?

LK: A funk record. Yeah, that's coming out next, man.

KR: What were the circumstances for recording that? I just read a report of it one day.

LK: That album was sort of . . . you could almost call it the other side of *Circus*. Because it was during that time, and I just got tired of making that. I was working really hard, and that album was really intense, and I was in the studio, and so I took off to New Orleans for a week. I was like, "You know what, I'm running [to] New Orleans, I'm going to take a break." And I went down to New Orleans, because I wanted to go to Jazz Fest, and I always loved New Orleans, and Aretha Franklin was playing, and I've never seen her play live. So, I went down to do that. And while I was down there—you know, I'm really into architecture and design, and so the French Quarter is a beautiful place, you know, with the buildings. And so, I wanted to see what the inside of homes looked like, but I didn't know people there. So I got a realtor, and I was like, "You know what? I want to buy a house." [*laughs*] So, and I just did it so that I could go look at houses. I was like, "Show me around, show me the different houses." I was already known then and so they were like, "Oh yeah, let's go."

KR: "Now." [*laughs*]

LK: Yeah, but I had no intention of buying anything. And so I went into my first house and I was like, "Oh this is cool." And then this lady took me to the second place. And I walked in, and I felt really comfortable. And it had this atmosphere, and it was just this little Creole cottage. And it was all brick and whatnot on the inside, and you could see the two hundred years of age in the house. It was beautiful, the decay. And I just looked at the woman and I said, "I'll buy it." And I thought to myself, "What am I doing?" but I just bought it. And that was the first house I'd ever bought.

So I'd bought this house—and next thing was, you know . . . I was with this girl I'd been seeing, and was really into her, and my guitarist Craig Ross was with me. And so I said, you know, "Craig, you know what? We should go find a studio. Just to fuck around for a few days while we're down here." Well, we went and found Allen Toussaint's studio, which is called Sea Saint where all those great recordings have been made . . . "Lady Marmalade" was done there . . . And "Yes We Can Can" by the Pointer Sisters. And this great Allen Toussaint music—the Meters, and you know blah blah blah. And so [we] went in there and just started making music. And next thing I knew man, we were in that studio for like a couple of months. And we would stay in there for like 24 hours straight, never come out. Ordering food, just eating in there, and it was just great. People delivering weed to us and food. We would just never come out. And we started making this music. And then I just put it away, and never did anything with it. And it was just a mess. It was really raw. I just pulled it out several months ago and started putting it together. And started writing new material that was inspired from that, and finishing a lot of that material. And so that's the record that I'm working on right now.

KR: Do you have a title for that yet?

LK: No, I mean everybody calls it "the Funk" [album].

I feel like I'm really in the zone right now. Like I've said, I've been in the studio and the creativity is really flowing in a beautiful way. So, more records for myself, more production, working with other artist, really working on my instruments—becoming a better drummer, bass player, keyboard player, guitarist, singer. I'm traveling down that road. I'm just working to become more expressive on each instrument.

KR: Is that what drives you to keep making music?

LK: Yeah. It's still a fever. It's amazing to be thirteen years in the game and to still be passionate about it. You know I see a lot of guys get kind of fat. After they have been in it and they have had a lot of success, they get kind of complacent you know. I'm not saying everybody. I've seen only some people do that. A lot of people don't, and a lot of people are still passionate about it. I just happen to be one of those people.

KR: Do you think today that you are more conscious of being a black musician, or earlier when people were telling you "Oh, you can't sing this kind of [rock] music."

LK: No, it's always a trip, bro, to be an African-American. I mean I'm mixed, but you know I'm a, you know . . . and to look out every night in front of twenty-five thousand people, and to see it's basically all white folks. Nothing wrong with it! I appreciate anybody, I don't care what color people are out there! But it's just a trip.

You know what I'm saying. You see a handful of black people, and it's like, wow. And then I look around in the business, and it's like you know, "Where are the other black rock 'n' roll artists that are out right now"? Or that have been out since I've been out, or since Living Colour stopped, or you know—not that they have stopped . . . I heard that they are making new records. But I mean, you don't see that. It's always very limited. It's just very strange to me. So I'm very aware of the place that I'm in.

KR: How is it now? Do you think more black people are hip to your music? I mean I remember walking into a club in the hood a couple of years ago, in Bed Stuy, like some grimy shit at like 3A.M., and . . .

LK: I'm from Bed Stuy man . . .

KR: Right, I know . . . but [in this club] people are slow dancing to your music.

LK: That's a trip. I've heard stories like that. [For example] people started telling me—hip-hop artists are telling me—"Man, you don't know how we love you man . . . you don't know how we listen to you." It started slowly, but I started realizing it. And in the last few years a lot of hip-hop artists have become close to me. They are always telling me, "Man, you don't know how much I listen to your shit." Then Jay-Z asked me to do that thing with him, and more people have started getting in touch with me. It's been a trip.

KR: What's next for Lenny Kravitz?

LK: Just you know to keep making records man. To keep experimenting, and to keep coming up with fresh stuff.

# "AIN'T NOTHIN' LIKE REAL GHETTO MUSIC": PHARRELL WILLIAMS, MOS DEF, AND ANDRE 3000 FORGE A RAP-ROCK POETICS

The name of the song is "Rock Star," and the guy fronting the video fits the bill perfectly: stylishly dressed, covered in a splash of tattoos, effortlessly controlling the movements of a gymnasium full of thrashing and moshing kids. And he's grinning widely, because he knows that he's pulling off a masterly stunt. Addressing his song to "you fuckin' poseurs," he eases into a rant notable for its arrogance, its vitriol, and, mostly, its presumptuousness: "You think the way you live's ok / You think posing will save your day / You think we don't see that you're running / Better call your boys cause I'm coming / You can't be me / I'm a rock star!"

Here's the joke: The man orchestrating the scene, the one pushing the buttons on the boards and the one oh-so-snidely crooning this tale of antirockist rocking is one of hip-hop's most talented producers, Pharrell Williams, a black man. Known in the mainstream mostly as a guest fixture in videos for rap heavyweights like Jay-Z, P. Diddy, and Busta Rhymes—on songs that he coproduced with Chad Hugo, his partner in the Neptunes—Williams has nevertheless cultivated his own cult of personality, becoming something of a celebrity himself, one of the first producers to do so. In 2000, after years of churning out a signature brand of aggressively musical hip-hop, the Neptunes parlayed their pop success into a record deal for their side project, N.E.R.D. (No one Ever Really Dies). Instead of shoring up their already considerable fan base with a set of crunk-happy industrial hip-hop, the Neptunes made a left turn somewhere around Steely Dan, another by Johnny Cash, and then headed straight for the Beach Boys. The result, an album titled *In Search Of* confused far more people than it sated. Hip-hop magazines panned it. The songs from the record that did get radio spin were played more on K-Rock than Hot 97. Instead of the expected cavalcade of bling-happy guests, Williams and Co. collaborated with Trent Reznor of Nine Inch Nails (on a remix) and skateboard legend Tony Hawk (on a video). In short, Williams made a rock album and, in the process, expanded the range of what exactly that might mean in a postrap era.

"As a black artist, I'm expected to do a certain type of music all the time," he said. "People hear me on the radio talking one way and making hot beats, and they think that's all I want to do. They're wrong. I'm not trying to reclaim [black rock], but hopefully my music will pave the way for people to be different and not think that because we're black that we wear a lot of Jacob jewelry and we all hold our balls and drink a lot. There's so much more to us."

Why isn't hip-hop rock and roll, anyhow? Plenty of critics, in their broad brush strokes, have felt free to relegate rap to virtual sub-genre status, as much a tool of smear as convenience. To do so is hardly any fairer than placing the two worlds at direct odds with each other. The truth lies somewhere in between. Both hip-hop and rock emerged from the same womb and have faced similar obstacles on their journeys to respectability. And while contemporary rock, for the most part, is but a shadow of its former self, its bloodline still can be traced back to a more potent era, in sound *and* attitude.

Both hip-hop and rock emerged as music of transgression, and both, to different degrees, have been neutered by their encounters with the mainstream. Black music in the Americas has traditionally had a strain of strategic rebellion woven into it. As form after form was co-opted by white performers, black music mutated, shape-shifted, and evolved into something new and progressive, only to have the cycle repeated every couple of decades. In the latter part of the twentieth century, these changes happened at a frighteningly rapid pace. By the time rock had gone to the dogs, in the 1960s, black music had rearranged itself, first around soul music and, later, around funk. Funk eventually gave way to a sort of orchestral rhythm and blues, with groups that relied on full bands to back their ballads of love and politics. Eventually, by the mid-1970s, the much-maligned disco took the baton and ran with it, eventually clearing the way for hip-hop, a dancefloor music that prized physicality as well as orality, a direct descendant of the soul movement.

By the 1990s, no one was talking about black rock anymore. The critical mass that had developed around the movement to resuscitate the scene in the 1980s—and it was always more of a movement and an idea than an actual unified sound—had largely dissipated, and hip-hop, already a force for over a decade, finally began to trump rock at the retail counter and in the imagination of America's teens. All of a sudden there wasn't a need for black rock; the oppositional statements were being made—loudly—and in an entirely new arena that hardly gave a whit what was happening back in the old country.

But as rap became commodity pop, a handful of the genre's visionaries began to chafe at the notion that they had indeed reached the promised land. Moreover, the sudden cultural capital afforded them by the success of rap music gave them license for a whole range of innovations and eccentricities. As rock struggled to dig itself out of its post-grunge grave, hip-hop artists were making the most edgy music in the country, and many of its leading figures were taking their blinders off, seeing what other spaces, and sounds, they could colonize. It should have come as little surprise, then, that some of these artists made their way back around to rock. For some it came in the form of sample choices—M.O.P., borrowing a phrase from Foreigner—or unlikely collaborations—Jay-Z's partnering with Lenny Kravitz. However, no matter how organic the final results of these one-offs sounded, they never truly achieved a distinctive sound. For many artists, dabbling became a *de rigueur* stylistic move, but when stacked up against the rest of their body of work, its flimsiness as a strategy was revealed. Instead, the artists who found the greatest success with their attempts at fusion were those who chose to make studying and synthesizing the past a vital part of their music-making present. Rather than drizzle a bit of rock onto their traditional hip-hop, a new class of artists—Mos Def, Pharrell Williams, and Andre 3000 of OutKast most notable among them—began slowly carving a niche for themselves outside the reach of categorization. And in so doing, they made vital steps toward saving the genre they were learning how to leave behind.

For all his rhetoric, Pharrell Williams wasn't the first artist of the hip-hop generation to plant a flag in rock's white sands on behalf of its African American heritage. As far back as the late 1970s, when Afrika Bambaataa would cut up Rolling Stones' songs in between "Apache" breaks, rock was never more than a stone's throw away from hip-hop's core. In fact, 15 years before Pharrell became an MTV staple, rap's first global superstars, Run-DMC, were finding that all it took to grow an audience beyond the usual circle of hip-hop listeners was to sprinkle a little rock into their mix. On the group's first album, coproducer Larry Smith brought a guitar-playing friend of his into the studio to get loose on "Rock Box," a song that achieved something no other hip-hop song yet had: steady MTV rotation. Noting the formula's success, they repeated it almost verbatim on their second album, *King of Rock,* using the same guitar player and the same song structure for the title track. When DMC booms at the song's opening "I'm the king of rock / There is none higher / Sucker MCs / Should call me 'sire,'" it's clear that no one told him rappers couldn't rock, and if they did, he surely wasn't listening. Once again, the video for "King of Rock" proved even more telling than the song. Shot in a mock rock and roll museum, it shows the three members of Run DMC overrunning the joint, stomping on rock ephemera and colonizing the space for themselves. So successful were they in making their mark on the rock mainstream than when it came to making their third album, they opted to tread on sacred ground. Aerosmith's "Walk This Way" was a staple of rock radio in the late 1970s and early '80s, one of the songs that kept the group famous and admired even as their personal demons were threatening to unseat them from rock stardom. Run-DMC's DJ, the late Jam Master Jay, had made a habit of cutting "Walk This Way" into his DJ set and having the guys rap over it. Its drum pattern, when isolated from the rest of the song, was decidedly funky. The idea to remake the song came from Rick Rubin, a young white college student cum record producer who had teamed with Russell Simmons (brother of Run) to found Def Jam Records. Rubin, whose affinity for hard rock was almost as pronounced as his love of the nascent hip-hop culture, had replaced Larry Smith as the group's coproducer. Rubin enjoyed music that titillated, and putting a couple of rappers from Queens in the same room with the grizzled rock icons Aerosmith certainly qualified.

The result, to say the least, shook the music world off its axes of comfort. Not only was the video, which showed the two bands in musical union and collegial embrace, in seeming permanent rotation on MTV, but the song itself was receiving the adulation of hip-hop and rock fans alike. For a moment, it seemed like the two communities, which heretofore had very little to talk about, might be collapsing the schism between them.

And then, nothing. For the next decade "Walk This Way" remained the rap-rock collaboration of note, a striking fact. Perhaps other artists realized that to do it better, they would have had to do it bigger (R.E.M. and

KRS-ONE tried, and failed, with 1991's "Radio Song," as did the producers of the 1993 *Judgment Night* soundtrack, which paired rappers and rockers to generally disastrous effect. Don't even ask about Puffy's soundclash with Jimmy Page for the *Godzilla* soundtrack.). Or maybe the song was so elegant in its synthesis that any other attempts to replicate its success were immediately dismissed as frauds. Whatever the reason, "Walk This Way" was, for a time, both the beginning and the end of the rap-rock movement.

By the late 1990s, both Run-DMC and Aerosmith had retreated to self-parodic forms of their earlier glory and their legendary collaboration, while still a touchstone event, had become part of the historical fabric. But then a funny thing happened. Rock music, which hadn't fully recovered from its postgrunge fallout, found a new source of angst and grit: hip-hop. Artists like Kid Rock, Limp Bizkit, Linkin Park, and Korn were part of the first generation of musicians who didn't know a time without hip-hop music. When they were making their own music, it was only natural for cross-pollination to be the order of the day (though not always fruitfully).

Even though the very idea of rap-rock had been all but abandoned, certainly no one expected that the artists looking to revive the template and bridge hip-hop into the mainstream would be almost uniformly white. (Special mention goes to Zach De La Rocha, the rapping Chicano frontman of agit-rock band Rage Against the Machine, who showed his hip-hop stripes on RATM's covers album, Renegades—produced by Rick Rubin, not surprisingly—on which he covered Rakim, Cypress Hill, and Volume 10.) Though these artists were almost universally reviled by the media, they became the face of rock at the turn of the millennium: snarling, steroidal, inauthentic.

A handful of rap heavyweights did get in on the act while it was hot. Method Man collaborated with Limp Bizkit's Fred Durst. Timbaland expressed his affection for Linkin Park, a band that, in a shocking move of solidarity with the hip-hop underground, released *Reanimation*, a remix album that featured such below-the-horizon stars as Pharoahe Monch (from Organized Konfusion), Zion I, and sometime Kool Keith producer Kutmasta Kurt.

At the dawn of the millennium, though, the much-maligned rap-metal movement had its leave thrust upon it. Its farewell moment may well have been the collective performance, on the 1999 MTV Music Awards, of Aerosmith, Run DMC, and Kid Rock, who gathered for a holy-rolling, roof-raising rendition of "Walk This Way." By the time this same troika hit the road a year later for a national tour, the steam behind the movement they'd helped pioneer, perpetuate, and popularize was all but gone. In

2002, when it was announced that Metallica had joined forces with synth-happy hip-hop producer Swizz Beatz, a hard rock shock jock locked himself in the on-air booth until someone from Metallica called to explain themselves. So much for a hand-holding tomorrow.


Ask Mos Def about the Great Rap-Rock Movement of the late 1990s, and he can hardly contain a sneer, and his anger: "I just got tired of people saying rap-rock, hip-hop-rock-and-roll. I wasn't hearing it. It wasn't real to me, as a rock and roll fan *and* a hip-hop fan. The stuff that I've heard that's hip-hop-rock-and-roll is hip-hop records. 'Bad Boy for Life' is a hip-hop-rock-and-roll record. M.O.P. is hip-hop-rock-and-roll. Noreaga doing 'Superthug.' 'Let's Get Dirty' from Redman. 'The Takeover' from Jay-Z. That's real to me. That's hip-hop and rock and roll fused in a way that is sonically ready for both audiences. It's not rock and roll peppered with hip-hop, or hip-hop garnished with rock and roll. It's the whole attitude. A lot of that stuff seems so co-opted. 'Oh, you're gonna use a DJ to scratch over the guitar solo.' It's everybody's right to do that, but it don't make you hip-hop. Wearing your Yankees hat to the back don't make you hip-hop. You can't just go buy a starter kit and be hip-hop. It's like me getting a Rolling Stones T-shirt, cutting off the sleeves, and picking up a guitar. Does that make me a rock and roll star?"

Certainly not, but that's not to say Mos was going to give up without a fight. Born and raised in Brooklyn, Mos—born Dante Beze Smith—quickly found that his ears were tuned to a slightly different frequency than those of his peers. Raised on a steady diet of hip-hop, Mos also found solace in the alternative-rock of the late 1980s and early 1990s: the Sugarcubes, the Sundays, the Cure, the Pogues. As Mos began to find his own voice as an artist, he found the most kinship not in Brooklyn's ruff-neck hip-hop scene, but in downtown Manhattan's burgeoning spoken-word scene. Before long he was a fixture at events like Bobbito Garcia's "All That" gatherings at the Nuyorican Poets Café, sharing the stage with poets and progressive rappers alike, a set that included Talib Kweli, Mos's future partner in Black Star, and Saul Williams, later the star of *Slam* and a black rock revivalist himself.

By 1999, when Mos released his first solo album, *Black on Both Sides,* he'd enjoyed enough success with the Black Star project to feel comfortable taking some risks. Accordingly, his first take-back-the-rock salvo came on that record. Simply titled "Rock N Roll," it had all the enthusiasm, idealism, and naivete of a kid's first manifesto. For the first four minutes, over a hypnotic, near-ambient hip-hop loop (produced by Psycho Les of the Beatnuts), Mos coolly runs down a litany of black rock icons, identifying a sonic diaspora that counts John Lee Hooker, Otis Redding, John Coltrane, and Fishbone among its children, and kicks pretenders like Elvis, the Rolling Stones, and Limp Bizkit to the side. Then, as if sensing that the gently throbbing sound of the song wasn't enough to deliver the point, the song slips into fifth gear, switching almost without warning to a traditional hardcore punk blast of focused energy. Over spitfire guitar work, Mos shouts himself hoarse asserting genre entitlement: "Who am I?" "Rock and roll!" "Who am I?" "Rock and roll!"

At the time of its release, "Rock N Roll" was treated politely. No one was willing to quibble about the black origins of rock, and certainly no one was going to argue in favor of mook-hop when faced with such literate and accurate criticism. "It would seem to me that the natural progression would be for my generation to be making rock and roll music anyway, from a historical point of view," Mos argued. "That don't mean no white folks, Latinos, etc. But if y'all is invited, I'm certainly invited. If y'all is invited, I'm throwing the fucking party, and you're not gonna card me at the door at my fucking party. It's my party. I got every right to be doing this, and why not? I certainly don't think that Chuck Berry or Bo Diddley or John Lee Hooker who started this rock and roll shit in America would have foreseen a day where their grandsons and granddaughters wouldn't be making rock and roll music. I think they had it in their mind when they were old that young black people would be making rock and roll music."

Nevertheless, response to the song was somewhat patronizing: One minute of clunky hardcore in the middle of an otherwise excellent hip-hop album sent up red flags. Instead of heeding the criticism and, having made his point, backing away from the debate, Mos took the high road less traveled. Within a year he was touting the imminent return of black rock, thanks to his band of "X-Men": Dr. Know of Bad Brains on guitar, Bernie Worrell of Parliament-Funkadelic on keyboards, and from Living Colour, bassist Doug Wimbish and drummer Will Calhoun. He called the supergroup Jack Johnson, after the first black world heavyweight boxing champion. (It was later changed to Black Jack Johnson, because of a half-Hawaiian ex-surfer folk-pop singer of the same name.) A telling choice, considering the fight that lay ahead. "The thing that they all have in common," Mos says, "is that they got stopped at the same checkpoints that I'm getting stopped at. They all revolutionized some shit. They stepped out and expanded on a sound, an idea, in a big way. Bad Brains is just straight gnash-your-teeth-type business. Living Colour is hard, with a great sense of melody, that raw shit with that lushness. And you got Funkadelic which is like if you was black and wanted to be a hippie but it was a little too white for you, you could go to Funkadelic. You could be in the P-Funk army and you straight, you about peace and love but you was a lowdown dirty muthafucka too."

In December 2000 Mos unveiled his monster lineup on hostile territory: the release party for Rawkus Records' Lyricist Lounge 2 compilation, a magnet for hip-hop puritanism if ever there was one. (Both Mos Def's solo album and the Black Star project were released on Rawkus). Mos and his band were slated to headline after a series of serious-minded MCs, an awkward enough slot for a visionary who hoped to turn the whole underground on its ear. By the time Black Jack Johnson hit the stage, the crowd was antsy and unforgiving. Worse still, the band sounded unfocused, its performance more like a long jam session than a coherent set of songs. Still relatively young as a collective unit, BJJ failed to sway the fickle crowd. Even Mos's ample charisma wasn't enough to carry the day.

Again, though, instead of giving up, Mos tried harder. Soon the band was woodshedding regularly and writing a bevy of original material. They embarked on a minitour and, in late 2001, retreated to Massachusetts for their first recording session. Even though disputes with his label have prevented the release of any of the Black Jack Johnson material, Mos remains sanguine: "This project has been a lot of fun. I been real happy doing it, but it's been painful, man. It's sweet, it's dark, it's heavy. Everything is real intense on this record, and I'm a catch 'em sleeping, 'cause they think I'm crazy."

Crazy seems to be the appellation of choice when discussing these sound pioneers. When their albums are reviewed in mainstream hip-hop magazines, their unique amalgamations of sound are dismissed as "weird" and "different." As black music has become ever more financially successful, the risks of yesteryear seem anachronistic. Resting on laurels became the default mode for hip-hop and R&B. Accordingly, the 1990s didn't birth a Prince, a George Clinton, or even an Afrika Bambaataa. And the sartorial choices of the 1990s were tame too (outsized jewelry notwithstanding) compared to the space cowboy looks of the '70s. It's as if the slightest disruption would stunt the money flow.

No contemporary rapper has received more flack for his aspirations— for himself and for the genre—than Andre 3000, the more eclectic half of Atlanta's OutKast. When the duo debuted in 1995 with *Southernplayalisticadillacmuzik,* they offered a much-needed alternative to hip-hop's preoccupation with coastal dominance. While California offered gangsters and pimps to balance out New York's hustlers and politicos, OutKast suggested a different approach: the organic hustler. Dirt was being done, for sure, but the folksiness with which Andre and his partner Big Boi delivered their tales gave them an earthy, unaffected feel that was as close to pretense-free as hip-hop got at the time.

As they got older, though, the two MCs began to let their minds and their sounds run free. On their second album, they dubbed themselves ATLiens, and by their fifth album, they'd completely abandoned the conventional understanding of what a hip-hop album should sound like. Unlike Pharrell Williams's N.E.R.D. project, OutKast's *Stankonia* wasn't meant to be a negation of the hip-hop tradition but an extension of it.

That might not be clear from the opening track, "Gasoline Dreams," a gritty rock scorcher that instantly places OutKast on uncommon ground. And truth be told, it's not clear throughout most of the album, from the Afro-rock of "Humble Mumble" to the psychedelic soul of "Slum Beautiful" to the anarchy-on-wax that is "B.O.B. (Bombs Over Baghdad)," the most incendiary five minutes in hip-hop since the heyday of [Public Enemy production team] the Bomb Squad. On "Gangsta Shit," Andre offers a more musical solution than the usual thuggery: "We'll pull your whole deck, fuck pulling your card / And still take my guitar and take a walk in the park / And play the sweetest melody the street ever heard."

Not surprisingly, the soundtrack to the making of *Stankonia* was a black rock cornucopia: "a lot of Hendrix, a lot of Chuck Berry, and believe it or not, a lot of Little Richard. A lot of Prince. A lot of early Funkadelic when they were more rock, more of a rock band," Andre recalled. But *Stankonia* is undeniably hip-hop. Not because, for years, hip-hop has been making play dates with other sounds, but rather because each of these tracks is infused with a certain edge—vicious bass lines, machine-gun percussion, undeniable cocksureness—that, when coupled with the most nimble rapping in the game today, leaves no doubt as to its point of origin. "I think *Stankonia* is our best effort of getting the best of both worlds," Andre said at the time. "But I hope I'm not being too fast with it. I don't know if people want to blend it like that. Perfect example: a lot of black people didn't get into Hendrix, because they couldn't dance to it like James Brown. It was totally different. Hendrix had elements of James Brown in it but it was like it was too far-going for people to appreciate at the time. But I guess you gotta take that stand, like as an artist, what do you want to do?"

So the chasm between hip-hop and rock isn't so vast as previously thought, as has been proved both by white artists looking for street cred on loan and by a new vanguard of black artists who stopped worrying about other people's opinions a long time ago. Indeed, the easy presumption that there are indeed essential differences between hip-hop and rock turns brittle under closer inspection. Rock purists dismiss hip-hop as predominantly digital, a genre for drum machine manipulators and "producers" who can't read music. There's certainly truth in those allegations, but dismissing the genre outright as a result is just shortsighted. "I think cats are inclined to do instrumental music," Mos Def argues, "but the instruments have changed. I don't think they're using traditional instruments per se, but the Neptunes, Swizz Beatz, Rockwilder, their music is very musical to me. So dudes are making fantastic instrumental music, it's just that their gear is different. People think it's simple, but it's not."

And in case the point needs further proving, these artists are taking the creation of their unique sounds into their own hands, literally. Mos Def is learning to play the bass guitar, and Andre from OutKast is looking to become a musical polymath. "I play guitar, piano. I just started upright bass. It's real exciting. [Playing instruments] is a good songwriting tool for me. I can get my ideas out and get the melodies out. When my parents went to school, everyone had to take music comprehension. Everyone knew how to read music a little bit. Everybody knew how to play some kind of instrument. But now it's not even required. It was required back then. And I think if you put it back in people's face, you'll get a whole different type of music." For his part, Pharrell is studying up on his guitar playing, but instead of using it to court validation from doubters, he's just following his muse: "I can't waste my time trying to prove shit to people all day. Fuck 'em. We're musicians, and were not afraid to learn new things."

# AMY LINDEN

# THE LAST MAVERICK: ME'SHELL NDEGEOCELLO AND THE BURDEN OF VISION

**W**hen it comes to music, categories can be a real bitch. You know the way labels, and radio, and retailers and whomever subdivide and segment artists. Alt-country. Neo-soul. Ambient-trance. Fusion-polka. Black rock. Sure, some sort of description is clearly needed; you just can't have a section in the store that simply says Music (or can you?), but most of the labeling is a cheat, and the end result is that the category serves to isolate and alienate artists not only from each other but sometimes even from prospective listeners.

From the moment she stepped in the arena, with her potent debut *Plantation Lullabies,* and continuing through her latest release *Cookie: The Anthropological Mixtape,* Me'Shell NdegeOcello has defied categorization and sent any number of critics and industry executives scrambling to dig deep into their respective trick bags to find a neat, simplistic description that would suit her. Or maybe just suit them. She's been lumped in with progressive artists, both black and white, female musicians, gay musicians, gay single mother musicians, pop, jazz, funk, rock, R&B, hip-hop, and any possible netherland that manages to bridge all of those and anything else that might slip between the cracks. She carries the double-edged sword of not only being a female musician but a black one who is not traditionally R&B or hip-hop—the two entry-level positions most accessible to woman of color. Defiantly, Me'Shell answers to no one except for what she instinctively senses sounds good and feels right. She's recorded with a disparate array of musicians from Scritti Politti, to Roy Hargrove, Citizen Cope, and John Mellencamp and seems as at ease being the focus of the record as she does keeping it rock steady in the background. She is that most odd of birds: a star who behaves like a session player and a session player with the undeniable charisma and chops to become a star. Me'Shell's ability—hell, one might even declare it a mission—to make music that does what it needs to do regardless of what it happens to sound like has been instrumental (no pun intended) in sealing her position as one of the most consistently inconsistent artists of the past ten years. That is a good thing, unless, of course, you have the unenviable task of creeping over to the studio to let someone know that, "Wow, you know, I'm not really sure if I hear a single."

The one-two punch of iffy sales, critical acclaim, and a fervent fan base harkens back to a now almost ancient concept, that of the prestige artist. Someone who the suits decided to keep on the roster not because of the money he or she generated but because having such an artist made the label look good. Look smart. Look like they weren't just in it for the pay-off. What exactly the relationship is between Me'Shell and her label, the optimistically named Maverick, owned by Madonna, isn't the point. Yet Craig Street has a theory based on little more than intuition. Street, who produced Me'Shell's stark, soulful opus *Bitter* and has worked with gifted loss leaders like Joe Henry, Chocolate Genius, and Toshi Reagon (as well as relative hitmaker Cassandra Wilson), offers: "I don't know any of this. All I can say is that whatever conflicts exist between Me'Shell and [Maverick] there's an incredible amount of respect for her, 'cause they keep her there. Maybe they keep her there because they keep hoping she's going to put something really commercial and huge out. Or maybe they keep her because there's one or two people there who understand that she's an artist. Maybe what's really scary on a lot of levels is that it's really possible to maintain ethnicity and self-awareness and be a human being at the same time. I think it's great that Me'Shell makes people nervous. That's what great art does."

I had the opportunity to interview Me'Shell early on. *Plantation Lullabies* was on the verge of being released, and the buzz that spun around the tiny bassist/singer/songwriter's shaved head was hard to ignore. The then twenty-something D.C. native was being hailed as a savior of all things R&B, the heir apparent to the smart soul throne (the term neo-soul hadn't been cooked up yet) and a Next Big Thing. She and I met for lunch, publicist in tow, at the then trendy downtown New York City restaurant the Time Café, which back in 1993 was where you went to spend the money that the labels still had. In that way that women do, Me'Shell and I exchanged small talk about a variety of subjects, chief among them our kids and I Ching tattoos. She was animated, intense, outgoing, and friendly, and I recall that as we were talking she'd shift her chair so that she could face me head on, leaning in close as if sharing a secret. I liked her. I also liked the album, which possessed a fluid, fierce funkiness that had been absent from black music and from anything that might actually get on the radio. The irony is that is for all of the talk about Me'Shell not being a commercial artist, she hit the charts with the single "If That's Your Boyfriend (He Wasn't Last Night)," which peaked at number 23 R&B. The success and the accompanying media splash probably did the wildly idiosyncratic Me'Shell more harm than good because it raised expectations and appeared to fit her into a slot where she clearly didn't belong. "I think what happened to Me'Shell is that the label, from the beginning, got attached to one particular thing that she does," opines Street. "Because they thought that would generate money. So they heard "If That's Your Boyfriend" and their immediate thing from that point on is we want more of this."

Yet more of "that" the labels and the public did not get. In 1994, Me'Shell followed up the moderate success of *Plantation Lullabies* by dueting with mainstream roots rocker Mellencamp on Van Morrison's "Wild Night," which must have confused the sistas in the coffeehouse to no end but that helped her land on Top 40 radio (the single went number 3 pop) and VH1. As odd as the pairing might have been and as much as it confused and disturbed some of the faithful (myself included), no doubt Me'Shell joined John because the song rocked and she got to play. She is, after all, a musician.

The mass appeal that "Wild Night" brought would fade fast. Me'Shell's next solo album was the funky and lyrically uncompromising (if not a tad heavy-handed) *Peace Beyond Passion* (1996). With its searing views of sexuality and spirituality, the album actually charted higher than her debut but never quite connected with the almighty overseers at radio. Likewise 1999's *Bitter,* which was recorded, as Street jokes, for "Puffy's water budget" and received little if any support from the suits. Lush with orchestrations, *Bitter* muted Me'Shell's "trademark" funk in favor of a moody elegiac hushed tone that was mesmerizing. Longtime fan and friend Street notes, "Out of the forty-fifty odd records I've worked on, *Bitter* is one of the ones I really feel great about."

If the folks thought *Bitter* marked a new shift in direction, they were proven wrong when, in 2002, Me'Shell dropped the guttural and eclectic *Cookie,* a CD deeply personal and unflinching. Again, sporting not much support from the executives along with the lack of a discernible (and marketable) single, *Cookie* was relegated to best-of lists and press acclaim. By all indications the lack of overt, consistent success doesn't seem to have slowed Me'Shell's mustang down. As this book went to press, she was in the studio preparing for two projects, among them a jazz record, which in a perverse fashion might end up a hit if only because then the label would have a definite way of categorizing her. Of course this means that there will just be a new script for Me'Shell to flip gleefully.

# KNOX ROBINSON

# if I can get into it,
## it's commercial enough for me

In early 2003 Apollo Heights had a big party to celebrate the release of its single "Disco Lights," a pulsating psych-funk exercise that captures the band's unique sound but is not necessarily indicative of its best work. No actual-factual single was released at the party, and months later one has yet to appear, but this fact seemed to go unnoticed by the hundreds of scenemakers who rammed Pianos (a new and well-executed club in the Lower East Side that is the very hallmark of gentrification—the hip hang that takes its name from the old-timey preexisting signage of the unassuming business before it), perhaps because only a handful of people at the party had actually seen Apollo Heights play before. That's no one's fault, really; the band members themselves are also mainly known scenemakers, having become part of the fabric of New York City's emergent downtown elite through a constant party-crashing regimen. For their part, Apollo Heights took full advantage of the moment to do what they do best, plying the smoky atmosphere at Pianos with trippy power pop vocals, elliptical riffs, and the occasional angular sax solo until the air inside the venue was charged with an element of the surreal.

Surreal: more or less real. Borges touched on this. Someone once told me, he wrote, "You have not woken in to wakefulness but into another dream. That dream is within another and so on 'til the infinite, which is the number of grains of sand." And so as the flawed idea of a hip-hop nation loses its grip on the imagination of many who previously bought into such an idea, the entertainment-industrial complex that sprung up to propagate hip-hop's soulless, remorseless ubiquity scrambles around for another dream to blow up. The machine has many eyes, all of them lazy, and it might be suggested that one has fallen on what Digable Planets described a decade ago as "niggas with guitars, common sense and puffy afros." Hip-hop ain't dying a natural death, but the alternatives are already popping up; what started as a steady trickle of newish music has given way to an onslaught of stylized videos, E-mail blitzes, half-hour showcases, and breathy press releases trumpeting "black rock stars" are the new shit, the hot shit, that next shit: the next chapter in the eternal quest for the elusive manifestation of cool.

How did we get here? Cultural shifts happen every day, of course, but the first time you witness one firsthand it kinda takes your breath away. Three or four years ago, Apollo Heights and other black rockers in New York City usually gigged on off nights, like Mondays, playing downtown in dank, near-empty back rooms and basements of clubs in front of a handful of other musicians and a couple bored lesbians at the bar, all for a couple free drinks and the chance of meeting sidetracked groupies from Japan, northern Europe, or the American Midwest. There were no flyers, no lines, no lists, and no buzz.

There was only the music—and the seemingly insane fuckers who made it, of course. Incomprehensible lyrics, genuflected guitar solos, spirals of musical chaos, and moments stunningly inspired composition from brothers and sisters who wore leather in the morning and sunglasses at night. Nowadays armchair musicology hacks and strident message-board posters would suggest black rock stars are interesting or new or next or hot or worthy of hyped-up showcases, record deals, magazine articles, and appreciative anthologies because as black musicians addressing the rock tradition they are fighting to be recognized in an art that black folks had a large part in creating, even as their constant presence in the music was erased as the music evolved—their validity, in this scheme, derived from or defined by a position of lack. But this type of thinking is as banal as the term "black rock" is redundant. Many musicians on the scene—the ones that for better or for worse gave their whole lives up to the muse—never seemed too caught up in the idea that their blackness might be ignored by a blanched-out rock establishment. Rather than the brief gloss of "black people playing white music" this was something different and more nuanced: black people playing an outlaw music outside the rigid, conformist, conservative mainstream of their own black culture. (It took years for this fact to settle in my brain; I'm not embarrassed to admit that as a raw-boned newcomer in the city, I often sought for signs of a nationalist agenda in the music I found myself discovering. In an overwrought explanation, I felt myself exiled from the hip-hop nation and ended up in a state of rock; I had brought some baggage with me, however, and it took a while to realize that the reason why a few musicians seemed to lift off the stage when they played was because they had attained a certain freedom. Freedom: more or less free.)

The fissure of the late 1990s cultural monolith provided me with a space and an opportunity to write about some of these observations and experiences. In a magazine article I worked on last year, I used some ideas from social critic Todd Gitlin pondering what might happen to the black rock underground. In his book *Media Unlimited,* Gitlin reported that the average American child lives in a home with 2.9 TV sets, 1.8 VCRs, 3.1 radios, 2.6 tape players, 2.1 CD players, 1.4 video game players, and 1 computer, before making the point that in the last few decades, media has grown from an aspect of how information is received to its totality. Furthermore, media isn't solely the newspapers and magazines and TV shows it has become convention to deride—it's the record industry and cable TV networks and promotional outfits and carpetbagging show promoters and overactive ectomorphic publicists and journalist harpies and the slick magazines that enable them. It's the entire entertainment industry, which has subsumed news, art, and culture, rendered them all "product," all equally grist for the mill. It was me writing the article, and it's me now rehashing parts of it for this chapter. It's the machine, and we are utterly and completely plugged in to it and turned on by it.

But the hazy demographic once described as the "hip-hop generation" is growing less and less satisfied by commercial music offerings. The machine knows this. Pop/urban acts will continue to sell, but the post–hip-hop listener isn't going to be buying the same old bullshit; we need new bullshit to consume, and the machine knows that, too.

The media fascination with Cody ChesnuTT brought all this to a head. It would be a mistake to think that the media made ChesnuTT; the Atlanta-born singer/songwriter had already had two nonstarter careers as a syrupy R&B singer and a Britpop sound-alike when MTV showed up at the Los Angeles area house he was sharing with his sartorial cousin/manager Donray Von and four other people along with a wolfish-looking dog, a sickly green fish tank, and a fifteen-foot python. It was spring 2002 and the MTV crew was filming ChesnuTT for the network's "You Hear It First" segment because a few weeks earlier ChesnuTT had crashed a taping of a Strokes concert, ending up onstage and holding aloft a Rasta-colored scarf during the Strokes' hit "Last Night." It took several weeks for the network to track down "Scarf Man," but once they did they were quick to check his star potential.

ChesnuTT had been living in L.A. since moving there from Atlanta in 1996. He earned money writing songs for pop groups that never appeared until his band the Crosswalk scored a deal with Hollywood Records in late 1997. The label funneled $420,000 into the project before dropping it six months later, at which point a devastated ChesnuTT locked himself in the Sonic Promiseland—the tiny bedroom recording setup where he would spend the next several months creating *The Headphone Masterpiece*. The 36-song double album of lo-fi, overdubbed, and underproduced disto-synth charm ChesnuTT recorded almost entirely by himself with $10,000 worth of equipment and a pair of Sony MDR-7506 headphones. Thirty-six tracks is a lot of . . . music, even when some of the best songs last less than a minute, but ChesnuTT used the space to detail the full complexity of what he's "been through"—namely falling in love with rock and roll, falling in love with his wife and the dysfunctional reconciliation of this latter love with the trappings of the rock lifestyle, even those accrued by a musician down and out on the edge of Beverly Hills with no record deal to speak of.

If everything that happened in the year that followed—the magazine mentions and newspaper features, the rounds of parties in L.A. and New York, the high-profile gigs at Central Park Summerstage and on late-night TV shows, the recording of one of his songs with the Roots and the video and tour that followed, the tour bus wrapped with his image, the independent release of *The Headphone Masterpiece* (Von says he and ChesnuTT turned down various offers including $1.5 to $3 million from Universal, electing instead to put it out through Ready Set Go!, the "artistic content company"), the eighteen hits of his name on eBay this morning—none of it seemed to be a surprise to ChesnuTT and Von. The two still follow a meticulously detailed fifty-two-page blueprint mapping their success, written when both men were still living the broke life. Of course, anyone who has sat through a Cody ChesnuTT show will also tell you that as a man, a musician, and a minor test case for artistic independence he receives most of his validation from his lord and savior Jesus Christ rather than record company offers or fans, famous or not.

It remains to be seen what will become of Cody ChesnuTT. He spent what seemed like most of his first year in the spotlight and the beginning of the next criss-crossing the country and making occasional jumps to Europe, gigging and jamming where he could and getting his photo taken when he wasn't. His live show was a competent, feel-good classic rock and soul revival that pleased the latest crop of post–hip-hop heads but confounded those seeking onstage interpretations of the beautiful and often bizarre moments of intimacy and self-revelation that was the essence of *The Headphone Masterpiece*—to say nothing of those who had heard only the hype and somehow thought he was going to drop to his knees and light his ax on fire. This might be only a question of more chops and more resources; more curious is that at times ChesnuTT allowed himself to be surrounded with lesser talents, poseurs and pretenders, the immediate effect of which is to diffuse his own modest gifts of emotive songwriting and deft, raw lyrics. Throughout his unlikely rise, ChesnuTT has shown a preternatural penchant for confounding expectations, usually rocking an earnest try-anything-on-any-given-night approach when a situation might have called for a slick commercialized professionalism.

In this way, ChesnuTT could have happened only in L.A. It was there that he learned to blend underground credibility and an ambition that went beyond the desire for mainstream acceptance, since to hear him tell it, the music was all about the message—the DIY/WWJD Cody ChesnuTT message.


Maintaining a critical public interest is hard, though. Apollo Heights had already released three major-label albums as the Veldt, a band associated with the college rock scene in Chapel Hill, North Carolina, for a brief spell in the 1990s. Five years before the meta-release of "Disco Lights," the band was done with all that, done with touring with the Cocteau Twins and getting thrown out of hotels in London. That's five years of shit jobs and failed relationships and near evictions—five years on the downside of the rock-and-roll lifestyle—and five years building a new sound, wondering all the while who might hear it or even give a fuck. At the high point of their show in January (2003) a good amount of the audience stood transfixed, some A&R hacks took notes in the back while up front a few thugged-out cats swung fists to the beats though careful not to spill the drink in the other hand. It's unclear what ended the show—whether the DAT stopped and the band kept going, or the other way around. The moment reverberated with the zeitgeist masterfully captured by the Strokes, who at this writing have also yet to release a follow-up to their 2001 debut: *Is This It?* Apollo Heights ambled offstage and some party-goers stayed around for the DJs who started to spin. The rest walked out into the cold and sooty night in search of the next next big thing.

JESSICA WILLIS

# INTERVIEW WITH
# S L A S H
# (SAUL HUDSON)

**B**orn in Stoke-on-Trent, Staffordshire, England in 1965, Slash (né Saul Hudson) spent his formative years listening to classical music, blues, folk, and British pop. In the mid-70s he moved to

Los Angeles with his family. Although he was raised among entertainment industry insiders (his white English father is an album art director and his black American mother is a clothing designer), little could have prepared Slash for his role as guitarist in Guns N' Roses, inarguably the greatest band to emerge from (and transcend) the white, middle-class detritus of the '80s L.A. metal scene.

Guns N' Roses eventually foundered in a shitstorm of artistic differences, drug problems, controversy, and superstardom, and Slash officially left the band in 1996. Slash's Snakepit and Blues Ball kept him fairly busy throughout the '90s, and he is currently working on a project with other ex-members of Guns N' Roses. Slash still lives in Los Angeles.

JESSICA WILLIS: What is your heritage actually?

SLASH: I was born in England. My mom is black American and my dad is British.

JW: Did you ever define yourself as a black musician? Was that ever an issue?

SLASH: No, it wasn't really an issue. I never really defined myself as anything when it comes down to it. I was raised around all kinds of different music. Guess it's kind of important on my mom's side of my family—my grandmother was a classical pianist, you know. She was born in like 1918 and she was raised in a black family but it was a well-to-do black family, so they had a lot of strict rules, like my grandmother hated honky-tonk music because she was trained not to like it when she was little. So when I was coming up my mom was in the music business and she listened to all kinds of stuff. So I was raised on anything from classical to a lot of blues and a lot of folk music and a lot of rock music on my mom's side. Then on my dad's side it was all British rock 'n' roll. So, that's sort of the beginnings of whatever it is I came from—so I never really differentiated between black music and white music, or what kind of musician I was.

JW: Did anyone ever try to define you that way?

SLASH: No, I've never been put into any kind of category. In "rock guitarist," yeah, but that's about it. Eventually I've been recognized over the years as having a little more "something" than just one-dimensional rock guitar player.

JW: You feel that being called a black musician is an epithet or a putdown or a way to make things one-dimensional?

SLASH: I don't know, I think it's sort of cool, you know. All the black artists I grew up loving are considered black artists, and I think that they're very proud of it. I'm very proud of my black heritage and what it is, and who I am. If someone was to say, you know, Jimi Hendrix—black rock guitarist—all things considered, I see that as sort of being cool. He might not appreciate it too much because it's sort of an eclectic style he's gotten. . . . I don't know if that would make anyone one-dimensional. You think of Muddy Waters being a black guitarist, does that sound one-dimensional to you?

JW: Unh-uh, no, but I'm thinking of people from our generation, not from generations past.

SLASH: Let's see, that's a good question. I never really thought about it, and I'm thinking about that now and I couldn't really tell you.

JW: It just seems maybe for people like Muddy Waters, that they . . .

SLASH: Think of say Whitney Houston as a black soul singer. That's a stretch with her, I think she's more commercial, don't think anyone calls her that. But she'd be considered a black artist. I'd think that would be something that one would be proud of.

JW: For a long time I thought you were Jewish. Do you hear that?

SLASH: You know, I'm in a Jewish book of celebrities. I think 'cause my first name is Saul, that's why.

JW: Is that common? Do a lot of people think that?

SLASH: A lot of people in the industry think it. As far as fans and stuff are concerned, I've never been pulled aside by an overzealous Jewish fan who said, Hey, glad you're around . . .

JW: Overzealous Jewish fan. . . . Respond to this, this is more of a statement than a question—in the band Guns N' Roses you certainly played as a foil to a very white guy. Do you sense that?

SLASH: I sense looking back on it. I felt, you know, all throughout my growing up there were little points here and there where it was sort of awkward being half black and half white. [Axl is] a very white bread, middle-America kind of guy.

JW: That's interesting. Expand on that, Slash, if you would. Why was it awkward?

SLASH: There would be moments where the depth of where I come from really . . . It's not something I walk around trying to express or trying to convey anything. . . . But sometimes I felt sort of short-changed in that environment. I didn't want to try and be something I wasn't. But I was also in a situation where being alongside him, if he would say certain things, I'd feel very uncomfortable. There were songs that he wrote . . . he insisted upon conveying certain messages I didn't agree with.

JW: Can I go so far to say the song "One in a Million?"

SLASH: That was definitely one of them. Obviously, that was the big one. I got approached by a lot of black people about that. I didn't necessarily allow him to do it, you know, but . . . The guy was so insensitive about anybody else, and at the same time wanting to get his own feelings about a certain subject across. It just sort of happened and the repercussions afterward spread out to more than just him. The rest of us had to deal with it, as well.

JW: Uh-huh.

SLASH: But other than that, being on stage, 'cause I never thought about it, it never intimidated me, I never thought about it in the sense of, "Oh I feel uncomfortable because I'm this." I was actually very proud of [my heritage]. I never really made an issue out of it. When it all first started I didn't aspire to become the rock star–lead guitar player––frontman that I ended up turning out to be. And because I didn't have any ambitions to be that, it just happened naturally, there wasn't a lot of conscious effort, and there wasn't a lot of inhibitions and so on, about where I come from.

JW: How has your pride about your culture, about your race changed over the years, from when you were young?

SLASH: No, it's a long story. When I was little, being born in a very middle-class neighborhood in England, in Brighton, in the middle 1960s, my parents, the only reason that they met in the first place was there was this sort of cultural revolution going on anyway. And so my grandparents were probably quite shocked when my dad and mom hooked up. And then I was born, you know, trying to explain it to the neighbors. But I never felt any of that. And then when I came to America . . . You know, there was like, to put me in a school, is he black or is he white? And there was part of that shit going around, I'll never forget that. Every time I enrolled in a new school, which was all the time because we never stayed in one place for long. But my parents were so cool, and 'cause I was raised in such a wide variety of cultural—I'm trying to think of the right way to put it. My Mom was very open, my Dad was very open, all my friends were open, everyone was hippies, it was a melting pot. So I never really felt weird. You know, my Mom worked with a lot of white people, she worked with a lot of black people; I never thought of my Mom as really being black. I had all my cousins, my aunt and uncle, my cousins all from South Central L.A. On my dad's side—he was in the music business as well—he was surrounded by lots of different kinds of people. So I never really felt a big segregation thing going on. The only times I ever did feel in certain places, in school, a couple weird comments from some of my colleagues over the years. One guy, I won't name his name, you know, said black people shouldn't have tattoos. I was like, what?!

JW: Wow.

SLASH: At the same time, I was raised in such a rich musical thing, with people and all that, I never really got hit too hard with anything. So much cool shit. I was influenced by all different races. I just sort of did my thing. The fact that I chose rock guitar as my main means of expression wasn't a thought out thing. I was turned on to a certain kind of guitar playing. I was turned on to a lot of different things. But when I picked up the guitar and played it I went for one thing. But I had tons of different musical influences.

JW: Can you name some of them?

SLASH: As far as musical influences? A lot of the music I was turned on to when I was little was, especially on the English side, was the [Rolling] Stones and the Beatles, the Eagles and the Kinks, Eric Clapton, you know, Cream, stuff like that. Then there was all the background that they came from, Muddy Waters, Willie Dixon, that kind of thing, Chuck Berry, so on. Lots of rock 'n' roll going on. My mom's side, there was a lot of Bob Dylan, Sly and the Family Stone, Joni Mitchell, Neil Young, Minnie Riperton, Carly Simon. There was a lot of different kinds things going on. I got off on, say, B.B. King, then the Who. Aerosmith and Funkadelic. A lot of different stuff going on. Zeppelin and then Charlie Christian. Know what I mean, lots of . . .

JW: What was first record you bought?

SLASH: First record? I can't remember the first record I bought. The first one I ever stole was I think [Led] *Zeppelin 2,* which doesn't make sense 'cause my mom had that record anyway. When I played guitar I started picking out records that were mine. But yeah, *Zeppelin 2, Zeppelin 1,* sorry.

JW: So what's life like now?

SLASH: What's it like now? Pertaining to what?

JW: To anything. An open question: What've you been doing?

SLASH: Playing all the time. I quit my band a while back, 'cause of differences between my old lead singer and—

JW: Which band are we talking about?

SLASH: GNR. That was like six years ago. I'm still pretty much recognized for being in that band. And then at this point I've hooked up with a couple of the guys from the original GNR, some of my teammates I guess you'd call it. Duff [McKagan], bass player, Izzy [Stradlin], also the drummer I hired in the middle of the band's career. So we've been writing and looking for a good singer to lead this thing, and it sounds amazing, so that's what I'm working on. The rest is just jamming. I'm just playing all the time. I have a kid . . .

JW: Who's drumming?

SLASH: Matt Sorum. He's the guy who I hired for Guns in the middle of its career. He's playing with us now.

JW: You have a baby, a kid?

SLASH: I have a little boy, named London—three and a half, almost four months ago.

JW: Wow. Your first baby?

SLASH: My first.

JW: Yeah, you're married now?

SLASH: Yeah, actually my second marriage.

JW: Your wife, if I could be so bold, a white lady, black lady? I couldn't tell on the phone.

SLASH: She's Cuban. Yeah, that's a whole other trip . . .

JW: Wow, I know.

SLASH: Let me ask you, what's the crux of everything you're trying to establish here? I'm just answering questions . . .

JW: You know what, there is no crux, this is for a book about black rock 'n' rollers. So the questions primarily pertain to your heritage, how you feel about your bloodline.

SLASH: I'm trying to see what I wanna express about it. I just, it's really cool for me, because I have a lot of stuff that's natural in me that a lot of cats don't have, at least in my peer group. And it has to be from where I come from. So even though one might not hear it upon first listening, because you know rock 'n' roll, especially the kind of rock 'n' roll I'm recognized for, seems sort of loud and in your face. But at the same time underneath all that there's a lot of subtlety, stuff that goes on all throughout. I think that's the only reason I haven't been pigeonholed as an Eddie Van Halen type. There's a lot of blues and stuff in my playing than really meets the eye, at least the face value. So that's really cool. I'm very proud of all the craziness in my upbringing, it's taught me about a lot about a lot of stuff.

JW: It must have been . . . looking back on it now, on what was going on in L.A. when you were coming up? It must have been peculiar. There must have not been a lot of black faces out there.

SLASH: Well, yeah, it was really exciting. I left England in the 1970s.

JW: How old are you now?

SLASH: I'm thirty-seven.

JW: Oh! Okay.

SLASH: So, my parents both being so entrenched in the music business, I think, contrary to what John Lennon might have said, the '70s was a pretty exciting time. It was great to be born in the '60s because I was part of that generation, that's where I come from. But the '70s was exciting, there was such a musical explosion going on. A lot of cultural crossing over, and this and that and the other. It seemed a lot funner to me, being a little guy, watching everything go on around me, as compared to say like the '80s. But I thought the music was pretty exciting.

JW: Isn't it funny how in the 1980s, we had Prince and Michael Jackson, that's basically the only icons we were left with. It crossed over, black and white people like them. Seemed like it was really segregated back then.

SLASH: In the '70s?

JW: In the '80s.

SLASH: I'm definitely the product of lashing out. I was a teenager, I was a little past my teens in the '80s. GNR, the band I ended up being in, was definitely sort of against whatever the '80s was about. Still, to this day we never get called an '80s band, which is sorta nice. Before that, what was really cool, what I remember the most is just lots of really really talented people putting out records on regular basis. Very stuck in a groove, in the '80s. It hasn't really gotten that exciting. There's an artist that comes out here and there . . . peppers each decade. But you know it just seemed a little more exciting when I was really young. There's a lot of that music I still listen to, the majority of music I listen to comes from the mid-'70s, early '70s. Every so often something cool comes out. Prince was great, Prince is great. Michael was great, [he] had his moment. He actually . . . I worked with him enough times, as fucked up as he is, he's one of the most amazing performers I've ever worked with.

JW: Sure. He's so so bright.

SLASH: People forget he's such a pop star . . . that's his own problem.

JW: Pop stardom seems like an affliction.

SLASH: An affliction/addiction kind of thing. People get a taste of a certain aspect of it, they just get lost.

JW: Those are really my only questions, Slash. Is there anything you feel I haven't asked?

SLASH: I'm trying to think. What else would be really interesting about all that? Interesting phone call. First time I haven't been asked anything at length having to do with, you know, my . . .

JW: Really? It must be sort of weird to talk, to talk about the very nature of what you are. Not really something you put into words.

SLASH: I'm very happy about the whole thing. Much as I don't like to stop and recognize it as such, every so often I do appreciate the fact that I have a little bit more texture, something in my soul point of view, than some of those people. I guess colleagues or whatever.

JW: You think that sort of aspect of you, not having it in your band mates—you think that's responsible for the dissolution of GNR, for that implosion?

SLASH: No, no. The guys in my band were very cool. Even Axl, he's a brilliant guy. Certain things about the band's image he sort of made.

JW: He wanted to go completely techno . . .

SLASH: When it started losing its earthiness, and I couldn't grab the reins at all, you know what, while it's still cool, I'm gonna bail out. Everyone thought I was crazy or stupid for doing it, but six years later I'm vindicated. I knew what I was talking about but absolutely no one would listen to me. That has to do with the bureaucratic fuckin' kind of way this business works. They see things a certain way and they can only see what's directly in their faces, they have no fucking depth whatsoever in terms of seeing where things will go, planning ahead and this that and the other. That's why it's such a stiff business. Why the art that comes out of it, the stuff that does come across these days, it's hard to get into . . . They keep following some sort of pattern that worked in the past, they don't realize [it] was a spontaneous thing in the first place.

JW: Sure. Here's a question, in terms of black musicians in the industry. You think black artists are still getting ripped off, you think a lot of them are?

SLASH: I think everyone in the industry is getting ripped off.

JW: It's not a racial thing anymore?

SLASH: Although, man, I do know a lot of old black musicians who will never ever stop being bitter.

JW: It gives me chills just thinking of how people were used back then.

SLASH: The great thing about music is, people never really want to know. People didn't really want to know about the business aspect. That's great in one way, the freedom to create, to express yourself. But there's a money thing attached. People just get screwed, they just don't see it, people who handle your cash, they can see that you're naive to it and they take advantage. It's really very evil in a way. Now that's coming around. People are getting hip to their rights as musicians, as professional recording artists, or whatever you want to call it. At least someone's wised up to it.

# BLACK ROCK GLOSSARY

**AD** 1990s black punk/hardcore act led by Anthony De More. Noted for two albums, *AD* (1993) and the follow-up, 1995's *Dead Will Rise.*

**ALLMAN BROTHERS BAND** Early multiracial blues-rock outfit from Jacksonville, Florida, founded in 1969. Viewed as the first southern rock band, the ABB has featured three black members: Otis Redding's former drummer Jaimoe (drums), the late Lamar Williams (bass), and current bassist Oteil Burbridge. The band is noted for its extended modal jams heavily influenced by jazz mavericks such as John Coltrane and for blues covers like Willie McTell's "Statesboro Blues." They also had a black woman, the legendary "Mama" Louise Hudson, owner of Macon, Georgia's H&H restaurant, as a patron in their salad days.

**JOAN ARMATRADING** West Indian–born, Birmingham, England-bred introspective and well-regarded female singer-songwriter. Had huge U.K. hit with "Drop the Pilot" in 1983.

**BASEMENT 5** Prototypical black British punk group formed by noted music photographer Dennis Morris and molded by producer Martin "Joy Division" Hannett.

**THE BELL RAYS** Like the Stooges, only with Tina Turner instead of Iggy Pop, this Los Angeles soul-punk band features vocalist Lisa Kelaula.

**EDWIN BIRDSONG** Noted Roy Ayers collaborator and primary composer of black rock classic *Supernatural,* which showcases the talents of guitarist and Hendrix idolater Ronnie Drayton.

**THE BLACKBERRIES** (see Venetta Fields interview by Kandia Crazy Horse) Female vocal group featuring ex-Ikette Venetta Fields and renowned session singers Sherlie Matthews, Clydie King, and Billie Barnum. After an aborted deal with Motown Records, the group went on to briefly join second wave British Invasion rockers Humble Pie and individually do session work for everyone from the Rolling Stones, to Bob Dylan, Steely Dan and Barbra Streisand. They often worked with other ubiquitous sisters from the era, including Merry Clayton, Emmaretta Marks, and Julia and Maxine Waters.

**BLACK JACK JOHNSON** (see chapter by Jon Caramanica) Conscious rapper Mos Def's rock project with Dr. Know, Will Calhoun, Doug Wimbish, and Bernie Worrell.

**BODY COUNT** Rapper Ice-T's heavy metal side project that pissed off a lot of tight-ass crackers in 1992 with the infamous song "Cop Killer." The debut album was removed from shelves and then re-released without the volatile song.

Guitarist Ernie C. produced the 1995 Black Sabbath album *Forbidden,* which also featured Ice-T on the cut "Illusions of Power." Ice also collaborated with Mötorhead on their 1994 classic track "Born to Raise Hell."

**BRONX STYLE BOB** Former member of Ice-T's rhyme syndicate, he released a critically acclaimed solo album in 1992 (featuring guest vocals by Bad Brains' HR). He continued to redefine himself as a performer, first in hard rock group Super 8, and then the pop rock group Khaleel (his last name).

**BUS BOYS** Lumped into the New Wave category, they were actually a straightforward rock unit that found moderate success with "The Boys Are Back in Town" (not the Thin Lizzy song), which they performed in the Eddie Murphy film *48 Hours.* Despite that exposure, the Bus Boys were never able to build on the momentum and became little more than a one-hit wonder. Some members would go on to form Total Eclipse along with former members of Sound Barrier.

**JON BUTCHER** Boston guitar hero who recorded several albums during the 1980s. Opening for the Scorpions on part of their 1984 Love at First Sting tour would be the highest profile for his band, Jon Butcher Axis. Two of the singles from his 1986 album *Wishes* would get minor rotation on MTV. Ignorant rock critics inevitably compared him to Jimi Hendrix. Though Butcher himself took great pains to acknowledge Jeff Beck as his primary inspiration, it seems many people could not make the distinction between two black guys playing guitar.

**CEE-LO** Scratchy-voiced, speed-rapping former member of Dungeon Family/Dirty South group Goodie Mob. Went solo in 2002 with often-brilliant Arista release *Cee-Lo Green and His Perfect Imperfections,* a recording equally influenced by Earth, Wind & Fire and the Doors.

**THE CHAMBERS BROTHERS** 1960s rock/gospel/soul/psychedelic hybrid act that had biggest hit in 1968 with the flower power/metal classic "Time Has Come Today."

**NENEH CHERRY** As the daughter of an artist and stepkid of the late jazz legend Don Cherry, Neneh was to bohemia born. Yet her artfulness was anchored by a sturdy pop/dance/hip-hop craft, and her blending of genres helped usher in the trip-hop era of British music. Cherry's eclecticism and exuberance was evident on her 3 solo albums, 1989's *Raw Like Sushi,* 1992's *Home Brew,* and 1996's *Man,* on which she blissfully threw down in every conceivable musical language.

**CODY CHESNUTT** (see chapter by Knox Robinson) Alternative rock and soul phenomenon from Los Angeles via Atlanta who recorded thirty-six eclectic tracks invoking every musical idea from power pop and bling-bling rap to Love and the British Invasion in his bedroom and defiantly released them as *The Headphone Masterpiece.* As of this printing, the double album remains in the hip consciousness without benefit of major label distribution, available solely through ChesnuTT's cousin Don Ray Von's Ready Set Go! Through late 2002 and early 2003, ChesnuTT enjoyed a popular tour with Philly alternative hip-hop outfit the Roots.

**CHOCOLATE GENIUS** The boastful alter ego of avant-garde funk/bluesman Marc Anthony Thompson is a black rock avatar via collaborations with musicians like

Marc Ribot and Me'Shell NdegeOcello. Known for his mournful intensity and wry rage on *Black Music* and *Godmusic.*

**SAM CLAYTON** Brother of Merry Clayton (leader of her own much in demand Merry Clayton Singers, immortalized by vocal on the Rolling Stones' "Gimme Shelter"). Clayton is the longtime percussionist and vocalist for Los Angeles boogie outfit Little Feat.

**CLARENCE CLEMMONS** Saxophonist and most recognizable member of Bruce Springsteen & the E-Street Band (aside from Springsteen, of course), he's also done solo work, including the big 1980s hit "You're a Friend of Mine," a duet with Jackson Browne.

**BILLY COBHAM** Black drummer for rock/jazz fusion act of early 1970s Mahavishnu Orchestra centered around founder John McLaughlin's guitar histrionics. Mahavishnu's mid-70s fusion landmark *Spectrum* is highly regarded.

**PAPA JOHN CREACH** Senior citizen Chicago-born fiddle legend, discovered in a Windy City hotel by Jefferson Airplane's Jack Cassady and Jorma Kaukonen, who utilized him in their Hot Tuna solo project. Also recorded and toured with Jefferson Airplane/Starship from 1970 to 1975 and released solo albums.

**THE DAN REED NETWORK** A hard rock outfit that emerged during the 1980s under the shadow of Bon Jovi, DRN was perhaps the most racially diverse band of all time, featuring a white guy, a Hawaiian, a Japanese American and two blacks (Melvin Brannon on bass and Brian James on guitar). The band released several albums and toured with Bon Jovi and the Rolling Stones before breaking up. James went on to play with Body Count for a time, and Brannon played with 68 (formerly known as Dreadneck).

**TERENCE TRENT D'ARBY** British-based soul rocker who released a magnificent debut album, *Introducing the Hardline According to . . .* in 1987. He began alienating fans with his press statements proclaiming himself a "genius" and posing on the cover of U.K. music weekly *NME* as a crucified Christ. Weaker follow-up album *Neither Fish nor Flesh* failed to deliver on his early promise, yet the subsequent release, *Symphony Or Damn,* was undeservedly slept on, being a power pop masterpiece that would be deemed one of the top albums of the 1990s if some whiteboy like Beck had recorded it. *Vibrator* too possessed a few cuts that ably honored D'Arby's black rock antecedents but was undermined by the unfortunate track "Supermodel Sandwich w/Cheese."

**BETTY DAVIS** (see chapter by Vivien Goldman) As the young model turned wife of jazz legend Miles Davis, the once (and again) Betty Mabry performed the legendary introduction between her husband and Jimi Hendrix, whom she'd gotten to know via friend/supergroupie Devon Wilson (for whom Hendrix wrote "Dolly Dagger"). Post-Miles, Betty launched a solo career, which saw her record with members of Sly Stone's and Janis Joplin's bands as well as featuring Leon Russell associate Kathi McDonald, the Pointer Sisters and Sylvester on backing vocals. The wild, freakish persona crafted by Mabry/Davis continues to inspire a new generation of mack divas, especially Joi Gilliam-Gipp.

**BO DIDDLEY** Seminal and influential first-generation rocker whose "Bo Diddley" beat influenced countless to follow, most notably Buddy Holly.

**ELECTRIC FLAG** Blues rock mainstays of late 1960s scene led by late guitar hero Michael Bloomfield. Drummer Buddy Miles went on to form his own band, the Buddy Miles Express, who hit with "Them Changes." Miles was also famously a member of Hendrix's Band of Gypsys and has played often with P-Funk in addition to his solo work.

**EQUALS** First black British pop band, which gave Eddie Grant his start. Grant later enjoyed big hits with "Walking on Sunshine" and "Electric Avenue." He continues to record today at his own studio in Barbados, which is often frequented by friend Mick Jagger.

**FAMILY STAND** (see chapter by Mark Anthony Neal) This Black Rock Coalition member band consisting of Peter Lord, Sandra St. Victor, and V. Jeffrey Smith based their style of singing harmonies and arrangements on obvious primary influence Sly and the Family Stone. Their "Ghetto Heaven" was a black radio hit but "Plantation Radio" from their second album, *Moon In Scorpio*—perhaps the second most satisfying of the latter-day black rock era, kicking off as it does with the incendiary "New World Order" featuring Ronnie Drayton on guitar—was more revolutionary in taking mainstream radio and the rock business to task for its apartheid practices. Production team Lord and Smith went on (unfortunately but lucratively) to work with Paula Abdul, while St. Victor enjoys a solo career and had a minor hit with "Chocolate."

**FISHBONE** Combining equal parts of deep funk, high-energy punk, and frantic ska, the Los Angeles–based Fishbone was one of the most distinctive and eclectic alternative rock bands of the late 1980s. With its hyperactive, self-conscious diversity, goofy sense of humor, and sharp social commentary, the group gained a sizable cult following but were never able to earn a mainstream audience.

**FOLLOW FOR NOW** This Atlanta-based group was one of the black rock acts to be signed after the success of Living Colour. Their self-titled debut, which featured a blistering cover of Public Enemy's "She Watch Channel Zero," managed to find only a cult following. A second album was rumored to have been recorded but was never released. The band broke up, and leader David Ryan Harris went on to become the bandleader for Dionne Farris. In 1997 Harris released a sublime self-titled album, and in 2001, he formed Brand New Immortals with members of the Black Crowes.

**FUNKADELIC** (see chapter by Michael C. Ladd) The granddaddy of all black rock bands as George Clinton a.k.a. the Funky President a.k.a. Dr. Funkenstein successfully fused the R&B rhythms and church-derived singing of his doo-wop past with the Parliaments to the heavy metal innovations of Jimi Hendrix in a way more accessible to the black masses. After the early 1970s spent recording a series of brilliant acid rock manifestos at United Sound in Detroit, legal and aesthetic issues as well as the influx of James Brown's junior band featuring brothers William "Bootsy" and Phelps "Catfish" Collins determined that Clinton's mob should be split into two bands: the head's Funkadelic ("[Not Just] Knee Deep") and the booty-shaking Parliament ("Flashlight"). Other offshoots, such as Bootsy's Rubber Band, Parlet, and the Brides of Funkenstein, followed with a revolving door of rock and soul greats, including Buddy Miles, Sly Stone, Cynthia Robinson, and the late Phillippe Wynne, putting in appearances. As a solo artist in the 1980s, Clinton hit big with "Atomic Dog." Today, having gained a vast New Wave hippie audience in the wake of Jerry Garcia's death, he continues to tour frequently in the company of his P-Funk All-star mainstays Belita Woods, Gary Shider, Michael Hampton and son Trey Lewd.

**JEFFREY GAINES** One of life's biggest mysteries is why this outstanding singer/songwriter is not one of the biggest stars in rock. Philly-born and bred, Gaines cut his teeth in Rush-type hard rock bands but found an outlet for more acoustic-based introspective and philosophical material reminiscent of some of John Lennon's best solo stuff.

**ROCKY GEORGE** Longtime guitarist for Los Angeles punk band Suicidal Tendencies.

**MELVIN GIBBS** Former member of the New York black rock group Eye & I, which covered Lou Reed's "Venus in Furs," he went on to play bass for the Rollins Band.

**SCREAMIN' JAY HAWKINS** Before Rob Zombie and Marilyn Manson—even before Alice Cooper—New Orleans–born pianist/vocalist Screamin' Jay Hawkins invented theatrical shock rock by popping out of coffins and dressing like a witch doctor to wail his biggest hit, "I Put a Spell on You." Also made album with immortal title *Black Music for White People*.

**RICHIE HAVENS** The high-energy acoustic folkie (there's an oxymoron for ya) who's best known for his 1960s and 1970s work such as "Handsome Johnny" and "Freedom," which was improvised on the spot at Woodstock to pad time. Although in many ways the "acoustic Hendrix," Havens is never rightly recognized in the pantheon of rock guitar gods (or as an able thespian: he wrote music and costarred in the 1977 Richard Pryor vehicle *Greased Lightning*). The Woodstock myth overshadows his brilliant readings of Dylan, the Beatles, and Marvin Gaye material as well as his own complex, experimental compositions ("Woman," "Missing Train") on the Stormy Forest label. His concept album *Richard P. Havens 1983* with its eerie infrared cover and both *Mixed Bag* and *Alarm Clock* should be considered staples of the *rock* canon. For every commercial for Amtrak, Havens can count another year into the new century of ecstatic capacity audiences across the nation.

**(HED) PLANET EARTH** Rap-metal outfit from Huntington Beach, California, led by charismatic and tortured brother front man Jahred.

**JIMI HENDRIX** (see chapter by Paul Gilroy) Universal guitar hero from Seattle, Washington, who never garnered any real success among blacks and subsequently has been claimed by the white rock establishment in a manner similar to the art world's fetishization of Jean-Michel Basquiat. In the wake of his "death" (some say murder at the hands of former girlfriend/fiancée Monika Danneman), Hendrixology fills the coffers of many warring parties and sees the annual release of as much product as Tupac Shakur. Still, Hendrix, who overshadowed former bosses Little Richard, Ron Isley, and

Arthur Lee, is viewed as the greatest guitarist in history and *the* black rock star *par excellence.*

**MARSHA HUNT** Rock singer, once Mick Jagger's girlfriend, *Hair* costar, and all-around hottie.

**RANDY "THE EMPEROR" JACKSON** As detailed in VH1's *Behind the Music,* in 1987, before Journey recorded the heaping slab of AOR crap called *Raised on Radio,* Steve Perry had a hissy-fit and fired the bassist and drummer. Jackson took over on bass for the album and subsequent tour.

**GARLAND JEFFRIES** Singer-songwriter who has remained virtually unknown, despite having recorded several excellent albums.

**JAI "JAIMOE" JOHANNY JOHNSON** Longtime drummer for the southern rock group the All-man Brothers Band.

**JESSE JOHNSON** Guitar virtuoso who first made a name for himself slinging ax for The Time. He recorded three solo albums in the 1980s (one featured a track with guest vocalist Sly Stone) that were very dance-oriented. He also produced the obscure band Da Krash, a rock/soul ensemble that got minor rotation on Black Entertainment Television's music video programs. In 1996, after a series of personal problems, Johnson released *Bare My Naked Soul*— one of the best (black) rock albums of all time.

**JOI (GILLIAM-GIPP)** Wife of Goodie Mob's Big Gipp and daughter of black NFL hero Jeff Gilliam. A native of Nashville, Tennessee, Joi came into her freaky-deke own when recording a series of eroto-funk solo albums in her adopted home of Atlanta, Georgia. A.K.A. the Star Kitty, Joi's *Amoeba Cleansing Syndrome* remains the great lost treasure of late modern black rock.

**IVAN JULIAN** Julian started out as a teenager in the Foundations, of "Build Me Up Buttercup" fame, and later reemerged in the New York punk scene as a key member of Richard Hell and the Voidoids. Artists as diverse as the Clash and Matthew Sweet have sought out his writing and production services. Julian now largely devotes himself to scoring films and television, his contribution to Sandra Bernhard's *Without You I'm Nothing* being of particular note.

**B. B. KING** Highly influential blues legend whose career dates back to 1949, when he was signed by none other than Ike Turner. Has also recorded with Carole King, Leon Russell, Eric Clapton, U2, Ringo Starr, and myriad others. The "B. B." stands for "Blues Boy."

**KING'S X** Christian rock power trio from Texas led by black gay frontman Doug Pinnock.

**LENNY KRAVITZ** (see interview by Knox Robinson) The former Romeo Blue and son of the late Roxie Roker ("Helen Willis" from TV's *The Jeffersons*) is today's most enduring and successful black rocker. Dismissed throughout the 1990s as a retro fan of giants such as the Beatles, Hendrix, Zeppelin, Bob Marley, and Curtis Mayfield without an original voice of his own, Kravitz has withstood the vicissitudes of the rock biz, marrying Afro-hippie idol Lisa Bonet, recording with then–Guns N' Roses member Slash, and getting the seal of approval from Beatle widow Yoko Ono and Bob Marley's mother Cedella. While his work has moved from flower power sentiments and psychedelia to more closely resembling modern rock, Kravitz remains a mainstream favorite.

**LAFAYETTE AFRO ROCK BAND** Formed in Long Island, the group split for Paris when it seemed like there were too many funk groups already in the 1970s. Source of samples and breaks for everyone from Public Enemy to Janet Jackson.

**CLAUDIA LENNEAR** Rhode Island–born Ikette and 1970s session singer. Lennear came to fame as a member of Joe Cocker's legendary Mad Dogs and Englishmen tour, after being introduced to bandleader Leon Russell by her friend Gram Parsons. One of the two women given solo spots during the show (Rita Coolidge was the other), Lennear was signed to Warner Brothers for whom she recorded her sole release, *Phew!* in 1973. Produced by Brit Ian Samwell and New Orleans funk master Allen Toussaint, as well as overseen by producer Jim Dickinson, the record was a failure—despite such great work as her own composition "Not at All" (about her romance with Mick Jagger)—that vainly attempted to serve the white "rock" and black "soul" audiences and wound up luring neither. Before retiring from the rock business, Lennear went on to do sessions for such luminaries as Russell, Harry Nilsson, Stephen Stills, and David Bowie, who wrote "Lady Grinning Soul" for her. Her hope of having a bluegrass trio with fellow Mad Dog singers Donna Weiss and Donna Washburn never came to fruition. Today she lives quietly in California.

**LINDA LEWIS** With a high, multi-octave voice to rival Minnie Riperton's, 1970s British folk artist Lewis was a queen of lovelorn poetry, her music fitting into neither the folk or soul-R&B categories. An incredibly unique vocalist who recorded for both Reprise and Arista, Lewis remains one of the prime grails for rare groove collectors.

**LIVING COLOUR** The group (singer Corey Glover, guitarist Vernon Reid [see interview by Harry Allen], bassist Muzz Skillings, and drummer Will Calhoun) first formed in the mid-1980s, with Reid being the only member with real prior band experience. They honed their act at New York's famed CBGB's, finding an unlikely supporter in Mick Jagger, who took the band under his wing, produced a demo for the quartet, and helped them secure a record deal with Epic. They opened for the Stones' 1989 stadium tour, hit the big time with "Cult of Personality," and later disbanded in '95. Their scathingly satirical "Elvis Is Dead" questioned Presley's position as "King of Rock," and featured a rap by self-styled "Architect of Rock 'n' Roll" Little Richard.

**LOVE** (see chapter by Barney Hoskyns) Seminal psychedelic-rock band led by "first black hippie," Arthur Lee, and featuring fellow brothers Johnny Echols (guitar) and Tjay Cantrelli (saxophone). Their masterpiece, 1967's *Forever Changes,* was viewed as the L.A. version of *Sgt. Pepper* and voted as the greatest album of all time in the early 1970s (beating out rock classics like *Blonde on Blonde*). Drugs, interpersonal problems, and Lee's insularity are said to have contributed to the demise of Love's original lineup featuring the late Bryan MacLean, yet Lee's new incarnation of the band (comprising members of young multiracial band Baby Lemonade) continues to tour in this 35th anniversary year of *FC*. Lee deserves his nods as godfather of punk.

**PHIL LYNOTT** Vocally influenced by Jimi Hendrix, the black Irishman also embraced punk when his guest Sid Vicious turned him on to the Ramones' debut.

Thin Lizzy not only covered the Sex Pistols' "Pretty Vacant," but Lynott recorded with that band's Steve Jones and Paul Cook as well as with Johnny Thunders. Lynott is the author of at least one rock classic: "The Boys Are Back in Town."

**MAGGIE'S DREAM** The former bandmates of Lenny Kravitz (when he was going by the name Romeo Blue). Ex-Menudo singer Robi Rosa replaced Kravitz, and the multi-ethnic band released an excellent self-titled album.

**MAXAYN** 1970s Capricorn signees from California featuring husband and wife team Andre and Maxayn Lewis. The band started out as rock 'n' soulers covering Rolling Stones' tunes then morphed into a "space funk" outfit when on the Motown label in the late 1970s as Mandre. Their early song "Tryin' for Days" is a classic of gospel-influenced blues rock.

**TONY MCALPINE** Barely known outside of heavy metal circles, guitarist (and sometimes keyboardist) McAlpine is considered a god among hardcore headbangers. A contemporary of such 1980s metal axmen as Yngwie Malmsteen, Joe Satriani, and George Lynch, he began building his reputation in the early part of the decade in bands like Lodestar, before eventually going solo. He frequently plays with other musicians, including Steve Vai.

**BUDDY MILES** One of the unsung players of classic rock, the portly bassist/drummer was a founding member of the multiracial 1960s cult band the Electric Flag and had a big hit with his own Buddy Miles Express. He is best known for his participation in Band of Gypsys, Jimi Hendrix's short-lived all black unit that debuted on New Year's Eve in 1969.

**MOTHER'S FINEST** Talented rock band that recorded throughout the 1970s and '80s, maintaining a cult status but never achieving mainstream success. Their last album was the aptly titled *Black Radio Won't Play This,* referring to the lack of support given by black radio. White radio wasn't any better. Each format played conservatively, afraid to alienate its respective audiences, and in doing so kept Mother's Finest from being discovered.

**ME'SHELL NDEGEOCELLO** (see chapter by Amy Linden) D.C. native and eclectic bass player signed to Madonna's label who came up playing with such local go-go outfits as Trouble Funk. After moving to New York in the early 1990s, NdegeOcello hit twice with her own "If That's Your Boyfriend (He Wasn't Last Night)" and a duet with John Mellencamp on Van Morrison's "Wild Night," which took VH1 by storm. Her work since debut *Plantation Lullabies* has been increasingly strong and complex, from the pointed critiques of black homophobia on *Peace Beyond Passion*'s "Leviticus: Faggot," to her brilliant cover of Hendrix's "May This Be Love" on her masterpiece of love lost *Bitter,* never resting easy in the mainstream, to almost everyone's dismay. Despite rumors of NdegeOcello renouncing the rock biz, she returned in 2002 with the magnificent *Cookie: The Anthropological Mixtape,* to the joy of her cult.

**NEON LEON** A New York punk scenester and habitué of Max's Kansas City from its earliest days, Neon Leon was known to the readers of *Rock Scene* via Paul Zone images and Jayne County's columns. He was also immortalized on celluloid in the 1978 porn film *Punk Rock* featured in a club scene as a guitarist in the Stilettos, a band that spawned Debbie Harry and Chris Stein of Blondie.

**ODYSSEY** Boogie-ish rock band featuring the divine guitarist/vocalist Donnie Dacus, who released a self-titled album in 1972. Not the purveyors of "Native New Yorker."

**THE OHIO PLAYERS** Midwestern, high-energy funk outfit led by the gravelly voiced Sugarfoot whose horn-happy string of extended jams ("I Want to Be Free," "Skin Tight") and borderline pornographic album covers made them virtual gods for a fair chunk of the 1970s. Even Northwestern Grunge gave them the nod in the early 1990s when Soundgarden covered "F.O.P.P."

**OSIBISA** This 1970s unit is, to our knowledge, the only black rock group from Africa. One of the first rock bands to incorporate African sounds in a rock format, they emigrated from Ghana to Britain before disbanding in 1976.

**SHUGGIE OTIS** Son of R&B legend Johnny Otis. Once tapped to replace Mick Taylor as guitarist for the Rolling Stones, Otis the Younger adhered to his own vision, sharing the same A&R as Sly Stone. Years of misfortune and apparent mental illness kept Otis's sublime psychedelic rock a cult secret until the 2002 reissue of *Inspiration Information* on David Byrne's Luaka Bop label made him an indie star.

**PIPE** Early 1990s Chapel Hill garage rock.

**POLY STYRENE OF X-RAY SPEX** The seminal English punk group that proved their worth with one great album: 1978's *Germ Free Adolescents*. Half-black lead singer Poly Styrene (Marion Elliot) wrote the lyrics, provided the band's worldview, and also led it into the fray via the UK's late 1970s "Rock Against Racism" movement.

**BILLY PRESTON** Master of the Hammond B-3 Organ who has the distinction of many "firsts." One of the first artists signed to the Beatles' Apple label; the only artist to get co-billing on a Beatles' single ("Get Back" in 1969); and he also performed his biggest hit "Will It Go Round in Circles" as the first musical guest on *Saturday Night Live* in 1975. Oh, yeah—had the greatest Afro in the history of the world!!!

**PRINCE** (see chapter by Barry Walters) Minneapolis' own miniature maestro of funk 'n' roll, Prince Rogers Nelson has been one of the twentieth century's most provocative acts, from his precocious late 1970s debut as a triple threat (performer, writer, producer) through his '90s appearances on music television in pants revealing his ass cheeks. His classic compositions include *1999, Sign O' the Times,* and some would debate *Lovesexy,* in addition to his chart- and consciousness-dominating soundtrack for his rock biopic *Purple Rain.* Prince is also responsible for launching the varying talents of Sheila E., Morris Day and Jerome Benton, Rosie Gaines, Vanity, and Apollonia into the mainstream.

**PURE HELL** 1970s black metal act; also the first black punk band.

**ROACHFORD** 1980s rock 'n' soulers; their one classic is "Cuddly Toy."

**NILE ROGERS** Guitarist (and cofounder, with Bernard Edwards, of Chic), songwriter, and producer. His long résumé includes penning Sister Sledge's "We Are Family" (with Edwards) as well as producing the likes of David Bowie ("Let's

Dance"), Madonna (first three albums), and Mick Jagger (*She's the Boss*). Was member of Apollo Theater House Orchestra and the Black Panthers.

**ANNIE SAMPSON** 1970s session singer and member of Stoneground.

**SANTANA** Many great black players have passed through guitar legend Carlos Santana's fraternity of Latin hard rock, including percussionists Michael Carabello, Ndugu Chanticleer, Armando Peraza, Coke Escovedo (Sheila E.'s father), singer/keyboardist Chester Thompson (ex–Tower Of Power), and original bassist Dave Brown.

**SEVENDUST** Atlanta hard rock outfit featuring black lead singer Lajon Witherspoon.

**SKUNK ANANSIE** British super–hard rock ensemble includes bassist Cass and female vocalist Skin. Easily the most intense woman in contemporary rock, Skin has a dynamic vocal range and an unbridled, live stage energy that surpasses everyone in rock—male or female. Several songs from their debut album appeared in the film *Strange Days.*

**SLASH** (see interview by Jessica Willis) Although almost never mentioned in the media, the original guitarist for 1980s poster children of bad-boy rock, Guns 'N Roses, is actually black. His songwriting and guitar playing made *Appetite for Destruction* the most successful debut rock album ever. Now doing his thing with Slash's Snakepit, he has also done session work for both Lenny Kravitz and Michael Jackson.

**FRED SMITH** A.K.A. the Freak (not to be confused with the MC5's late Fred "Sonic" Smith), this D.C. guitar hero was a member of the punk-funk Dischord band Beefeater and later postpunk Gothic bands Madhouse and Strange Boutique. He was also employed at the venerable 9:30 Club.

**SLY STONE** (see chapter by Dalton Anthony) Né Sylvester Stewart, this former child gospel star from Texas turned resident of Vallejo, California, matured musically quite early and earned his stripes both as a producer at Autumn Records of the embryonic Jefferson Airplane and a popular Bay Area DJ mentored by big daddy jock Tom Donahue. Stone's debut, *A Whole New Thing,* introduced the world to black rock's baddest sister, horn player Cynthia Robinson, and a rough template of how his fusion of holy-roller gospel conventions with James Brown and San Francisco's acid rock sounds would soon take over the airwaves for about five years and almost single-handedly revolutionize pop music. For a brief shining moment at Woodstock, the Family Stone's communal, polyrhythmic vibe lifted the flower power ideal to dizzying heights. And then there was the comedown of Sly's brilliant but increasingly dark post-*Stand!* albums: *There's a Riot Goin' On, Fresh* and *Small Talk.* Still, the quickening of Motown as the 1960s waned can be attributed to the house producers assimilating Stone's innovations (in the Jackson Five, the Detroit Spinners, the Temptations, Eddie Kendricks, and even Stevie Wonder). And the stunning strength of his vision persists in work as varied as that of The Family Stand, Beck, D'Angelo, the Red Hot Chili Peppers, and World Party.

**SPACEY-T** A shredder on a par with current peers like Steve Vai, Spacey-T was in the 1980s metal band Sound Barrier. After they broke up, T played in a band called Gangland with future members of 24–7 Spyz for three years until 1991.

**STIFFED** Philly-based neo-punk outfit featuring Santi White, who cowrote the debut record for rock chanteuse Res.

**CREE SUMMER** Raised on the Cree Indian reservation in Canada on the likes of Frank Zappa, Lotti Golden, Dinah Washington, and traditional pow-wow music, Cree Summer joined her first band at thirteen. From 1986 on, she gigged locally in Toronto with acts such as the Maxx, Mystique, and Deborah Cox. During her famed stint as a cast member of NBC's Cosby spinoff *A Different World,* she sang backgrounds on costar Jasmine Guy's 1990 eponymous debut and gained a persona as a dizzy Afro-hippie in the vein of her best friend Lisa Bonet. As lead singer and songwriter, Summer led the band Subject To Change in the early 1990s, touring with Fishbone and the Gin Blossoms. Their 1994 album for Capitol, *Womb Amnesia,* was unfortunately never released. In 1999, with a deal at Sony's Work label and Bonet's ex-husband Lenny Kravitz as her producer, Summer released her solo debut *Street Faërie,* a largely hippie-ambient outing notable for its hardcore "Curious White Boy," a fitting sista rock anthem for the age.

**SWAMP DOGG** Cult icon who's often compared to Frank Zappa because of his keen balance of satire and social commentary (usually on black culture). The first black artist signed to Elektra in 1969 after reinventing himself from a derivative R&B singer named Jerry Williams to a Sly Stone-inspired rocker. Still records periodically on indie labels.

**SKEETER THOMPSON** Thompson was the great bass player for Scream, one of the longest-lasting D.C. punk bands. A full-energy, rock-embracing band, Scream was one of the few acts that still presided over genuinely fun shows even after Emo took the piss and vinegar out of D.C. punk in the mid 1980s. Though the band became a little too RAWK in the later stages, when Dave Grohl (future Nirvana) joined the band, Thompson always delivered, and when he wasn't on the wrong end of the drugs he could be the best. One of his more memorable moments was his turning some tables by singing Minor Threat's "Guilty of Being White" at a show. Even in Scream's late 1990s reunion tour (capitalizing on Grohl's newfound superstar status), he was on the top of his game. Sadly, recurring cocaine problems have left him M.I.A. too often over the course of what should have been a more active career. He currently lives in Little Rock.

**THE TIME** Primarily a funk and R&B group, this talented ensemble rose to prominence as part of the creative force from Minneapolis, led by Prince. Band members included vocalist Morris Day, guitarist Jesse Johnson, and Jimmy Jam and Terry Lewis, who went on to become powerful producers. Among the other performers who rose up from the Minneapolis scene during the 1980s were André Cymone, Colonel Abrahams, Alexander O'Neal, and members of Prince's band The Revolution.

**TRULLIO DISGRACIOUS** Legendary band out of Los Angeles that's always rotating its lineup of musicians. Includes members of Fishbone, P-Funk, and the Red Hot Chili Peppers, Spearhead, Weapon of Choice, and others. Although they've never recorded, they occasionally tour, usually opening for Blow Fly.

**TINA TURNER** Regarded by many as the queen of rock 'n' roll, she rose to prominence as the bombastic vocalist for the Ike and Tina Turner Revue in the 1960s. Although the band is more often considered a dance/soul act, there are no two ways about it—they were a rock band (the much-reviled Ike actually authored what is considered the first rock song: Jackie Brenston's "Rocket 88"). Tina's powerful performances and charisma made her the female counterpoint to Mick Jagger and garnered her film parts in Ken Russell's *Tommy* and *Mad Max Beyond Thunderdome*. After many personal setbacks, she reemerged in the 1980s to reclaim her crown with *Private Dancer.*

**24–7 SPYZ** Bronx-based hard rockers that fused metal, funk, rap, and punk into a glorious auditory assault. Lead by guitar wizard Jimi Hazel (who took his first name from Hendrix and his last name from P-Funk's Eddie), the Spyz came along in the wake of Living Colour but never found the same level of success. Best known for their hardcore cover of Kool & the Gang's "Jungle Boogie," as well as an appearance on a beer commercial, the band went through several lineup changes. Original drummer Anthony Johnson left, as did frontman Peter Fluid, who was replaced with Jeff Boardnax (who also left). Eventually only bassist Rick Skatore and guitarist Hazel (now on vocals) remained.

**UGH UGH UGH** Self-billed as "hardcorereggaeskafunkdamagetypeshit," Ugh Ugh Ugh was a local New York band that gigged at CBGB's, the now-defunct Garage, and similar-sized venues. Its fans were known as "Ugh Thugs" and danced like mad people to Ugh Ugh Ugh's unique kick-ass beat and tight guitar riffs. The band, fronted by bald, Minneapolis native Dave Deal, was influenced by Living Colour, Bad Brains, and Fishbone but were more primal: young and fun in a Ramones-like way. It produced one tape, the centerpiece of which was its signature song "Will Science (Is a Mean Mother-Fucker)," before disappearing into California.

**THE UNTOUCHABLES** A multiracial ska/rock band that enjoyed minor success during the 1980s.

**WAR** Originally formed in 1962 as the Creators by guitarist Howard Scott and drummer Harold Brown, later morphing into War, which became known for its time as backup band for ex-Animal Eric Burdon. War hit with "Spill the Wine" in 1969. Burdon left, and this L.A. based Afro-Latin band had a string of hit albums and singles in the 1970s including "Why Can't We Be Friends?" and everyone's favorite "Low Rider." Before joining with Burdon, War also played backup for saxophonist Tjay Cantrelli, formerly of the psychedelic band Love.

**BERNIE WORRELL** (see chapter by Michael C. Ladd) P-Funk keyboard player, played on two Talking Heads albums, worked with Keith Richards, and the rhythm section of Cream. "I was a child prodigy at three-and-a-half years old. I had my first classical concert at four. At eight, I wrote my first piano concerto, and at ten, I played three piano concertos with part of the Washington Symphony Orchestra and Plainfield Symphony." On Jimi Hendrix: "We play with each other every day. You know, he's still here."

**WEAPON OF CHOICE** Quirky L.A.-based band heavily influenced by P-Funk.

# ABOUT THE CONTRIBUTORS

**HARRY ALLEN** Hip-Hop Activist & Media Assassin, writes about race, politics, and popular culture for several national publications. Currently developing a book on architecture, he lives in Harlem.

**DALTON ANTHONY** is a writer, father, friend, and activist. He dedicates this piece to all victims of the prison industrial complex and the U.S. government's war on drugs.

Legendary rock critic **LESTER BANGS** died in 1982. His collected essays, *Psychotic Reactions and Carburetor Dung*, is published by Random House.

**JON CARAMANICA** has written about music and popular culture for *Rolling Stone, GQ*, the *New York Times, Spin, Vibe, XXL,* the *Village Voice*, and a host of other publications.

**ANDY GILL** has written for *NME, Q, Mojo, The Independent*, and numerous other publications. He is the author of *Don't Think Twice, It's Alright: Bob Dylan, the Early Years* (Carlton).

**PAUL GILROY** is Professor of Sociology and African American Studies at Yale University. He is the author of *The Black Atlantic Modernity and Double Consciousness* (Harvard University Press).

**VIVIEN GOLDMAN** is a London-born writer living in New York who has written extensively on Fela. She is the author of Bob Marley's first biography, *Bob Marley: Soul Rebel, Natural Mystic* (St. Martins Press, 1981), and is currently writing her fifth book, *The Book of 'Exodus': The Making and Meaning of Bob Marley's Album of the Century*. She was also a founding member of 1980's combo, the Flying Lizards.

Editorial Director of Rocksbackpages.com, Londoner **BARNEY HOSKYNS** was a major feature writer for *NME* in the '80s, as well for *Vogue, Mojo,* and other publications in the '90s. His books include *Across The Great Divide*, about The Band, and *Waiting For The Sun*, about L.A.

**DARRYL JENIFER**—multi-instrumentalist–producer–composer–arranger–founding member of the original roots rock rebels, the bad brains.

**SACHA JENKINS** is a musician and former graffiti writer turned "writer" who lives in Brooklyn.

**MICHAEL C. LADD** is a poet and a producer. He has been published in several anthologies, including *Everything but the Burden*. He is also the writer and producer of six albums, "Easy Listening for Armageddon," "Welcome to the Afterfuture," "Vernacular Homicide," The Infesticons: "Gun Hill Road," The Majesticons: "Beauty Party" and "Mike Ladd, Live from Paris." He is currently collaborating with pianist Vijay Iyer on a performance and CD titled "In What Language?"

**AMY LINDEN** is a senior writer for *XXL* and a frequent contributor to *Honey, Savoy,* and others. She lives in Brooklyn.

**DARRELL MCNEILL** is a journalist, musician, and producer based in Brooklyn, NY. He is the director of operations for the Black Rock Coalition and has written for the *Village Voice, Vibe, Oneworld, SPIN, BRE, Demographix online, Audio Gliphix,* and WBAI-FM (99.5).

The author of books on the Drifters and the Coasters, **BILL MILLAR** was also Consultant Editor on Panther's *Encyclopedia of Rock* (1976) and Orbis's *History Of Rock* (1981). His "Echoes" column was a feature of *Record Mirror, Let It Rock,* and *Melody Maker.* Bill, who was awarded the MBE in 1996, lives in Dartford, Kent.

**MARK ANTHONY NEAL** is the author of three books including *Songs in the Key of Black Life: A Rhythm and Blues Nation.* He is Associate Professor of American Studies at the University of Texas at Austin.

**JENNY LEE RICE** likes country fried steak, Los Angeles freeways and Al Green. She is lily white.

**KNOX ROBINSON** is Editor at Large at *The Fader.*

**GREG TATE** is a cultural critic and writer for the *Village Voice.* He is editor most recently of *Everything But the Burden* (Broadway Books, 2003).

**BARRY WALTERS** is a Senior Critic for *Rolling Stone.* He was the pop music critic for the *San Francisco Examiner* for eight years, has written for magazines like *Spin,* the *Village Voice,* and *Out* since the mid-'80s, and has worked as a disco consultant for the Experience Music Project in Seattle.

**JESSICA WILLIS** lives in Paradise City.

# PERMISSIONS

The cover image from Funkadelic's album "Maggot Brain" appears courtesy Westbound Records, Inc.

Lenny Kravitz's "Lenny Kravitz Greatest Hits" album cover image reprinted by permission of Virgin Records America, Inc.

The cover image from Guns N' Roses' album "Appetite For Destruction" appears courtesy of Geffen Records.

The cover image from Sly and the Family Stone's album "Anthology" appears courtesy of Epic Records.

The cover image from Living Colour's album "Time's Up" appears courtesy of Epic Records.

Ike and Tina Turner's "Absolutely the Best" album cover images reprinted by permission of Virgin Records America, Inc.

N.E.R.D.'s "Rock Star" album cover images reprinted by permission of Virgin Records America, Inc.

From Cody ChestnuTT's album "The Headphone Masterpiece," cover art: Sy Acosta (R.I.P.)

The cover image from Betty Davis' album "Nasty Gal" appears courtesy of Universal Music Special Markets.

The cover image from Bad Brains' album "God of Love" appears courtesy of Warner Strategic Marketing, Warner Music Group, an AOL Time Warner Company. P 1995 Maverick Recording Company. Used by Permission. All Rights Reserved.

The use of the cover image from "Arthur Lee: A Live Performance at the Academy, Liverpool, May 1992" appears courtesy of the Viper Label. / Design: Nonconform Ltd, Liverpool, UK.

The album cover artwork of Family Stand's "Moon In Scorpio" appears courtesy of Elektra Entertainment Group Inc.

The photograph of Lorraine O'Grady appears courtesy of Lorraine O'Grady. Photographer unknown.

The photograph of Venetta Fields appears courtesy of © Jill Furmanovsky/Starfile.

The photograph of Jimi Hendrix: ©1968–2003, Eddie Kramer, courtesy of ARIAPHOTOS.COM.

"Free Your Mind And Your Ass Will Follow" Writers: George Clinton, Jr./Lucious Ross/Eddie Hazel Publishers: Copyright © 1971 by Bridgeport Music Inc.

# INDEX

Abdul, Paula, 206
Abrahams, Colonel, 213
Absolution, 99
Aerosmith, 178, 179, 199
Afrika Bambaataa, 116, 177, 182
Allen, Lee, 2
Allison, Mose, 14
Allman Brothers Band, 65, 66, 86, 88, 89, 203, 208
American Four, 11, 12
Anderle, David, 9, 11, 16, 18, 23
Andre 3000, 175–184
Angel, David, 19
The Animals, 214
Anthony, Dee, 62
Anthony, Marc, 204
Apollo Heights, 189, 190, 193, 194
Apollonia, 118, 119, 211
Armatrading, Joan, 203
Armstrong, Louis, 150
Asheton, Ron, 106
The Association, 17
Aswad, 55
ATLiens, 183
Audio Two, 97
Austin, Joan, 60
Ayler, Albert, 109, 110

B-52's, 136
Baby Lemonade, 22, 209
Bacharach, Burt, 14, 16
The Bad Brains, 93, 94, 97–101, 122, 181, 214
Baker, LaVern, 160
Band of Gypsys, 206, 210

Banks, Hamp "Bubba," 46
Barnum, Billie, 62, 203
Bartholomew, Dave, 2, 152
Basement 5, 203
Beach Boys, 176
The Beatles, 12, 20, 45, 46, 87, 160, 199, 207, 208, 211
Beatnuts, 180
The Beau Brummels, 45
Beck, 205, 212
Beck, Jeff, 204
Beefeater, 212
The Bell Rays, 203
Benson, George, 131
Benton, Jerome, 211
Berlin, Irving, 150
Bernhard, Sandra, 208
Berry, Chuck, 87, 92, 109, 160, 181, 183, 199
Big Boi, 182
Big Gipp, 208
Bill Haley and the Comets, 87, 155
Bill Monroe and His Blue Grass Boys, 1
Billy Ward and the Dominoes, 1
Bingenheimer, Rodney, 13
Birdsong, Cindy, 203
Birdsong, Edwin, 203
Black Box, 126
Black Crowes, 206
Black Flag, 94
Black Jack Johnson, 145, 181, 182, 203
Black Rock Coalition, 68, 122, 129, 138, 139, 142, 206
Black Sabbath, 204

Black Star, 180, 182
Blackberries, 59, 61, 64, 66, 67, 203
Blaine, Hal, 18, 19
Blake, William, 29
Blige, Mary J., 138
Blondie, 211
Bloomfield, Michael, 206
The Blossoms, 61
Blow Fly, 213
Blue, Leon, 5
Blue, Romeo, 168, 208, 210. *See also* Kravitz, Lenny
Blue Thumb, 21
Blues Ball, 196
Boardnax, Jeff, 214
Bobby Womack and the Valentinos, 12, 51, 107
Bobby Z, 118
Body Count, 203, 205
Bomb Squad, 183
Bon Jovi, 205
Bonet, Lisa, 208, 213
Booker T, 12
Boone, Pat, 2, 155
Bootsy's Rubber Band, 206
Botnick, Bruce, 18, 19
Bowie, David, 4, 107, 116, 209, 211
Bramlett, Delaney, 66
Brand New Immortals, 206
Brannon, Melvin, 205
Brass Ring, 20
Brenston, Jackie, 154, 214
Brides of Funkenstein, 207
Bronx Style Bob, 204
Brooks, Rosa Lee, 10
Brown, Bobby, 117
Brown, Dave, 212
Brown, Djinji, 99
Brown, H. Rap, 46
Brown, Harold, 214
Brown, James, 2, 6, 46, 47, 49, 62, 75, 76, 88, 109, 117, 157, 183, 206, 212
Brown, Roy, 151
Brown, William Wells, 73
Browne, Jackson, 205

Bruce, Denny, 14
Bruce, Jack, 131
Bruce, Lenny, 107, 108
Buckley, Lord, 46
Buckley, Tim, 17, 66
Buddy Miles Express, 206, 207, 210
Buffalo Springfield, 14
Bugout Society, 99
Burbridge, Oteil, 203
Burdon, Eric, 214
Burk, Eddie, 5
Burn, 100
Burning Spear, 55
Burrell, Kenny, 37
Bus Boys, 204
Busey, Gary, 11
Butcher, Jon, 204
Buzzcocks, 92
Byrd, Donald, 129
The Byrds, 11, 12, 13, 14, 21
Byrne, David, 211

C & C Music Factory, 126
Caesar, Shirley, 3
Cage, John, 109
Calhoun, Will, 132, 181, 203, 209
California Boy's Choir, 167
Calloway, Cab, 150
Cantrelli, Tjay, 209, 214
Captain Beefheart, 10
Carabello, Michael, 57, 212
Caravans, 3
Carlisle, Belinda, 117
Carmichael, Stokley, 46
Carnegie, Andrew, 93
Cash, Johnny, 176
Cass, 212
Cassady, Jack, 205
Cavett, Dick, 36
Chambers Brothers, 53, 204
Chance, James, 110
Chanticleer, Ndugu, 212
Chapman, Tracy, 160
Charles, Ray, 46, 47
Checker, Chubby, 44
Cherry, Don, 204

Cherry, Neneh, 204
Cherrybusters, 44
ChesnuTT, Cody, 192, 193, 204
Chic, 211
Chocolate Genius, 186, 204
Christgau, Robert, 111
Christian, Charlie, 33, 34, 36, 131, 199
Churchill, Savannah, 86
Citizen Cope, 186
Clapton, Eric, 131, 199, 208
Clara Ward Singers, 3
Clark, Dick, 116
Clark, Gene, 66
Clark, Roy, 42
Clash, 109, 208
Clayton, Merry, 61, 62, 67, 203, 205
Clayton, Sam, 205
Clemmons, Clarence, 205
Clinton, George, 75, 81, 131, 138,
    182, 206, 207
The Coasters, 43
Cobham, Billy, 205
Cocker, Joe, 209
Cocteau Twins, 193
Cohan, George M., 150
Cole, Nat "King," 12
Coleman, Lisa, 118
Coleman, Ornette, 109
Collins, Phelps "Catfish," 206
Collins, William "Bootsy," 206
Coltrane, John, 76, 139, 166, 181,
    203
Commodores, 116
Como, Perry, 154, 155
Conka, Don, 14
The Continentals, 44
The Contortions, 109, 110
Cooder, Ry, 12
Cook, Paul, 210
Cooke, Sam, 3
Coolidge, Rita, 66, 67, 209
Coombs, Norman, 148
Cooper, Alice, 109, 207
Copland, Aaron, 16
Coppola, Francis Ford, 74
Corinthian Gospel singers, 60

Cosby, Bill, 213
County, Jayne, 210
Coup, 52
Cox, Deborah, 213
Cramps Nervus Rex, 109
Creach, Papa John, 205
Cream, 20, 199, 214
Creation, 20
The Crew Cuts, 155
Crocker, Frankie, 136
Cropper, Steve, 37
Crosby, Bing, 13, 14, 154
Crosby, David, 9, 13
The Crosswalk, 192
Crudup, Arthur "Big Boy," 151
The Crystals, 15
Cuicoland Express, 131
Culture Club, 116
The Cure, 180
Curtis, King, 5
Cymone, Andre, 213
Cypress Hill, 179

Da Krash, 208
Dacus, Donnie, 211
The Dan Reed Network, 205
D'Angelo, 212
Danneman, Monika, 207
D'Arby, Terence Trent, 160, 205
Daryl Douglas Workshop Choir, 125
David, Hal, 14
Davidson, Basil, 148
Davis, Betty, 53–58, 205
Davis, Jesse Ed, 66
Davis, Miles, 53, 54, 55, 166, 205
Day, Doris, 154
Day, Morris, 211, 213
Dead Boys, 113
Dead Prez, 52
Deal, Dave, 214
Decoding Society, 129
Delaney and Bonnie, 66
De La Rocha, Zach, 179
De More, Anthony, 203
De Veaux, Masani Alexis, 122
Dickinson, Jim, 209

The Dictators, 110
Diddley, Bo, 152, 181, 205
Digable Planets, 190
Dirty South, 205
Dixon, Willie, 199
Dr. John, 66
Dr. Know, 181, 203
Domino, Antoine "Fats," 151, 152, 155, 160
Donahue, Tom, 44, 45, 212
Donnellan, Jay, 21
Donovan, 89
The Doors, 17, 18, 19, 22, 204
Dorsey, Tommy, 150
Douglass, Frederick, 147
Drayton, Ronnie, 203, 206
Dreadneck, 205
Dreamboy, 118
Du Bois, W. E. B., 33–36, 124
Dunbar, Paul Laurence, 122
Dungeon Family, 205
Durst, Fred, 179
Dylan, Bob, 46, 199, 203, 207

E-Street Band, 205
The Eagles, 199
Earth, Wind & Fire, 204
Eater, 92
Echols, Johnny, 12, 14, 18, 20, 209
Edwards, Bernard, 211
Electric Flag, 206, 210
Elektra, 9, 10, 14, 17, 18, 21, 213
Ellington, Duke, 139, 151
Elliot, Marion, 211
Ellis, Trey, 121, 122
Ellison, Ralph, 34–36
Emerson Lake and Palmer, 138
Equals, 206
Ernie C., 204
Errico, Gregg, 39, 46, 47, 57
Ertegun, Ahmet, 14
Escovedo, Coke, 212
Eshun, Kodwo, 75, 80
Eye & I, 207

Fagen, Donald, 63

The Family, 118
Family Stand, 121–127, 206, 212
Fanon, Frantz, 25, 28, 37
Farrell, Perry, 101
Farris, Dionne, 126, 206
Fayad, Frank, 20, 21
Felix Da Housecat, 119
Fields, Danny, 110
Fields, Venetta, 59–70, 203
Fields, W. C., 108
Fifth Dimension, 47
Fischer, Claire, 125
Fishbone, 134, 160, 181, 206, 213, 214
Fitzgerald, Ella, 67
Flavor Flav, 134
Flea, 101
Fluid, Peter, 214
Follow for Now, 206
Foreigner, 177
Forssi, Ken, 14, 18–20
The Foundations, 208
4 Hero, 80
Frankie Lymon & The Teenagers, 155
Franklin, Aretha, 57, 61, 70, 91, 157, 160, 171
Freed, Alan, 152, 154
Freeman, Bobby, 44, 45
Fugazi, 94
Funkadelic, 72, 73, 74, 76, 78, 80, 81, 122, 160, 181–183, 199, 206, 207, 213, 214
Furay, Richie, 66
Furious Five, 72, 116

Gaines, Jeffrey, 207
Gaines, Rosie, 211
Gangland, 212
Garafalo, Reebee, 146
Garcia, Bobbito, 180
Garcia, Jerry, 207
Gaye, Marvin, 166, 207
George, Nelson, 158
George, Rocky, 207
Gershwin, George and Ira, 150
Gibbs, Georgia, 155

Gibbs, Melvin, 207
Gibson, Jack, 152
Gilbert and Sullivan, 150
Gilliam, Jeff, 208
Gilliam-Gipp, Joi, 205, 208
Gilmour, Dave, 62, 63, 69
Gin Blossoms, 213
Ginsburg, Arnie, 152
Gitlin, Todd, 191
Gladys Knight and the Pips, 166
Glover, Corey, 100, 132, 136, 209
Golden, Lotti, 213
Golden, Thelma, 121, 122
Goodie Mob, 204, 208
Goodman, Al, 150
Goodman, Benny, 150
Gordy, Berry, 61, 88
Gottehrer, Richard, 105
Goude, Jean-Paul, 56
Gradney, Kenny, 207
Graham, Larry, 39, 46, 47, 57
Grandmaster Flash, 72, 116
Grant, Eddie, 206
The Grass Roots, 11, 192
Grateful Dead, 17
Gray, Gerald, 5
Gray, Macy, 54, 160
Green, Al, 166
Green, Cee-Lo, 204
Green, Grant, 37
Greenspoon, Jimmy, 14
Grier, Pam, 47
Grohl, Dave, 213
Gruber, Mike, 20
Guns N' Roses, 196, 199–202, 208, 212
Guthrie, Arlo, 66
Guy, Jasmine, 213

Haley, Bill, 87, 155
Haley, Jack, 160, 161
Hamilton, Chico, 23
Hammerstein, Oscar, 13, 16
Hampton, Fred, 40
Hampton, Michael, 168, 207
Hancock, Herbie, 131

Hannett, Martin "Joy Division," 203
Hargrove, Roy, 186
Harper, Ben, 160
Harris, David Ryan, 160, 206
Harris, Thomas Allen, 143
Harris, Wynonie, 86, 151, 152
Harron, Mary, 110
Harry, Debbie, 211
Hart, Lorenz, 150
Hathaway, Donny, 135
Havens, Richie, 157, 207
Hawk, Tony, 176
Hawkins, Screamin' Jay, 207
Hayes, Isaac, 48
Hazel, Eddie, 76, 77, 81
Hazel, Jimi, 214
(HED) Planet Earth, 207
Hell, Richard, 104, 110, 208
Henderson, Fletcher, 150
Henderson, Jocko, 152
Hendrix, Jimi, 2, 10, 11, 20, 21, 25–38, 47, 49, 53, 54, 67, 92, 94, 95, 98, 116, 136, 138, 140, 157, 168, 183, 196, 204, 206, 209, 210, 214
Hendryx, Nona, 57
Henry, Joe, 186
Herman's Hermits, 45
Holdsworth, Alan, 37
Holiday, Billie, 57
Holloway, Patrice, 61, 62
Holly, Buddy, 205
Holzman, Jac, 10, 14, 17, 18, 23
Hooker, John Lee, 152, 181
Hopkins, Lightnin', 28
Hot, 97, 176
Hot Tuna, 205
Howell, Portier, 5
Howlin' Wolf, 1
H. R. See Hudson, Paul "H. R."
Hudson, Earl, 100, 101
Hudson, "Mama" Louise, 203
Hudson, Paul "H. R.," 94, 100, 101, 204
Hudson, Saul. See Slash
Hugo, Chad, 175

Human League, 116
Humble Pie, 59, 62, 68, 70, 203
Humpston, Wes, 168
Hunt, Marsha, 208
Hunter, Alberta, 150
Hunter, Ivory Joe, 151

Ice-T, 203, 204
Iggy Pop, 106, 107, 109, 203
Ike and Tina Turner Revue, 5–7, 214
The Ikettes, 6, 59, 61, 203, 209
Iron Maiden, 138
Isley, Ron, 207
Isley Brothers, 45, 122, 137, 138, 160

Jackson, Hal, 152
Jackson, Janet, 118, 209
Jackson, Mahalia, 3
Jackson, Michael, 75, 116, 118, 201, 212
Jackson, Randy "The Emperor," 208
The Jackson Five, 61, 166, 167, 212
Jacobson, Mark, 108
Jagger, Mick, 12, 13, 14, 16, 65, 89, 109, 126, 206, 208, 209, 212, 214
Jahred, 207
Jaimoe, 203, 208
Jam, Jimmy, 118, 213
Jam Master Jay, 98, 178
James, Brian, 205
James, Elmore, 1
James, Etta, 43, 61
James, Rick, 168
Jane's Addiction, 100
Jay-Z, 173, 175, 177, 180
Jefferson, "Blind" Lemon, 150
Jefferson Airplane, 17, 47, 205, 212
Jeffrey, Michael, 30
Jeffries, Garland, 208
Jenifer, Darryl, 91–95, 100, 101
Jerden, Dave, 100
Joey Piazza and the Continentals, 44
Joffrey Ballet, 167
John, Elton, 4
Johnson, Anthony, 214
Johnson, Charles S., 147

Johnson, Jack, 181
Johnson, Jai "Jaimoe" Johanny, 203, 208
Johnson, Jesse, 118, 208, 213
Johnson, Robert, 33, 34
Joi (Gilliam-Gipp), 205, 208
Jon Butcher Axis, 204
Jones, Bill T., 129
Jones, Brian, 11
Jones, Gloria, 62
Jones, Grace, 56
Jones, Jill, 118
Jones, LeRoi, 147
Jones, Quincy, 118
Jones, Steve, 15, 210
Joplin, Janis, 160, 205
Jordan, Louis, 86, 152
Jordan, June, 123
Journey, 208
Julian, Ivan, 104, 106–108, 208

Kapralik, David, 46, 51
Karp, Charlie, 21
Kashif, 117
Kaukonen, Jorma, 205
Kaye, Lenny, 16, 17, 20
Kaye, Swingin' Sammy, 1
Keita, Salif, 129
Kelaula, Lisa, 203
Kelley, Norman, 126
Kelly, R., 125
Kendricks, Eddie, 212
Khaleel, 204
Khan, Chaka, 160
Kid Rock, 179
Kina, 160
Kines, David, 5
King, Albert, 27, 32, 37
King, B. B., 37, 199, 208
King, Carole, 208
King, Clydie, 61, 62, 64, 203
King, Evelyn "Champagne," 116, 117
King, Rodney, 23
Kings of Rhythm, 5
King's X, 160, 208
The Kinks, 199

Kiss, 110
Knight, Etheridge, 123
Knight, Gladys, 166
Kool & the Gang, 72, 116, 214
Kool Keith, 179
Korn, 179
Kraftwerk, 117
Kravitz, Lenny, 126, 160, 165–173,
    177, 208, 210, 212, 213
Kristal, Hilly, 136
Kristofferson, Kris, 65, 69
Kubernik, Harvey, 17
Kurt, Kutmasta, 179
Kuti, Fela, 123
Kweli, Talib, 180
Kyser, Kay, 150

Labelle, 54, 57
LaBostrie, Dorothy, 2
Ladysmith Black Mambazo, 126
Lafayette Afro Rock Band, 209
The LAGs, 11, 12
Laine, Frankie, 154
Lauper, Cyndi, 117
Lawrence, Steve, 155
Leadbelly, 58, 151
The Leaves, 15
Led Zeppelin, 20, 21, 168, 199, 208
Ledbetter, Huddie "Leadbelly," 58, 151
Lee, Arthur, 9–23, 67, 137, 208, 209
The Left Banke, 17
Leinsdorf, Erich, 167
Lennear, Claudia, 209
Lennon, John, 200, 207
Levine, Susan, 22, 23
Lewd, Trey, 207
Lewis, Andre, 210
Lewis, Jerry Lee, 160, 161
Lewis, Linda, 209
Lewis, Maxayn, 210
Lewis, Terry, 118, 213
Lichtenstein, Brad, 143
Li'l Kim, 58
Limp Bizkit, 179, 181
Linkin Park, 179
Linna, Miriam, 109

Little Eva, 45
Little Feat, 205, 207
Little Richard, 1–4, 87, 92, 155, 160,
    183, 207, 209
Little Walter, 1
Living Colour, 100, 122, 126,
    130–137, 141, 143, 160, 173,
    181, 206, 209, 214
Locke, Alain, 35
Lodestar, 210
Lollipop Shoppe, 15
Lombardo, Guy, 150
Lone Justice, 21
Lopez, Jennifer, 119
Lord, Peter, 124, 127, 206
Lorde, Audre, 122
Love, 9, 11, 13, 14, 15, 16, 17, 18, 19,
    20, 21, 22, 23, 67, 137, 204, 209
Love, Courtney, 126
Love Mk. 1, 20
Love Mk. 2, 21
Lovecraft, H. P., 141
Loveless, Patty, 21
Luther, Martin, 160
Lyman, Mel, 107
Lymon, Frankie, 155
Lynch, George, 210
Lynn, Cheryl, 118
Lynott, Phil, 209, 210

Mabry, Betty. See Davis, Betty
McAdams, Janine, 126, 127
McAlpine, Tony, 210
McDonald, Kathi, 205
McGee, Alan, 20
McGhee, Jacci, 127
McGuinn, Roger, 13
The McGuire Sisters, 155
McGuire, Wayne, 106
Mack, Bruce, 142
McKagan, Duff, 199
McKay, Claude, 123
McKaye, Ian, 94
McKee, Maria, 21
McLachlan, Sarah, 145
McLaughlin, John, 205

Maclean, Bryan, 9–20, 21, 23, 209
McNeil, Legs, 108, 110, 111
McTell, Willie, 203
Madhouse, 118, 212
Madonna, 116, 186, 210, 212
Maggie's Dream, 210
Mahavishnu Orchestra, 205
Mahler, Gustav, 167
Malcolm X, 40, 124
Malik, Chaka, 98–100
Malmsteen, Yngwie, 210
Mandela, Nelson, 123
Mandre, 210
Manfred Mann, 14
Manson, Marilyn, 19, 207
Marcuse, Herbert, 31
Marks, Emeretta, 203
Marley, Bob, 55, 110, 208
Marley, Cedella, 208
Marriott, Steve, 62, 64, 65, 70
Martha and The Vandellas, 61
Martini, Jerry, 39, 44, 47, 49, 50
Mathis, Johnny, 16
Matthews, Sherlie, 61, 62, 203
Maxx, 213
May, Brother Joe, 3
Maycock, James, 54
Mayfield, Curtis, 37, 157, 160, 166, 208
Mazarati, 118
MC5, 110, 212
Mehta, Zubin, 167
Melvoin, Wendy, 118
Mellencamp, John, 186, 210
Meltzer, Richard, 16
Menudo, 210
Merry Clayton Singers, 67, 205
Metallica, 180
The Meters, 172
Method Man, 179
Miles, Buddy, 206, 207, 210
Miles, Lee, 5
Miller, Gary "Dr. Know," 100, 101
Miller, Glenn, 150
Milli Vanilli, 126
Mingus, Charlie, 105

Minnelli, Liza, 13
Minogue, Kylie, 119
Minor Threat, 94, 213
Mitchell, Bob, 44, 45
Mitchell, Joni, 199
Monch, Pharoahe, 179
Monk, Thelonius, 139
Monroe, Bill, 1
Monroe, Marilyn, 119
Montgomery, Wes, 92
Moore, Melba, 117
M.O.P., 177, 180
Morris, Dennis, 203
Morrison, Jim, 17, 18
Morrison, Toni, 86
Morrison, Van, 187, 210
Morton, Jelly Roll, 131
Mos Def, 145, 175–184, 203
Mother's Finest, 122, 210
Motley Crüe, 95
Mötorhead, 204
Murphy, Eddie, 204
Murray, Arthur, 89
Murray the K, 152
Music Machine, 15
The MVPs, 100
Mystique, 213

NdegéOcello, Me'Shell, 122, 127, 145–146, 160, 185–188, 205, 210
Nelly, 119
Nelson, Ozzie, 150
Nelson, Prince Rogers. See Prince
Nelson, Ricky, 155
Neon Leon, 210
Neptunes, 119, 126, 175, 176, 184
N.E.R.D., 126, 176, 183
New Kids On the Block, 117
New York City Opera, 167
Newton, Huey, 39–41, 50, 52
Nico, 110
Nilsson, Harry, 209
Nine Inch Nails, 176
Nirvana, 213
Noreaga, 180

Oberman, Ron, 86, 87, 88
Odyssey, 211
O'Grady, Lorraine, 85–90
The Ohio Players, 211
O'Jay, Eddie, 60, 61, 152
Oliver, Joe "King," 150
O'Neal, Alexander, 213
O'Neill, Tip, 154
Ono, Yoko, 208
Orange 9mm, 100
Organized Konfusion, 179
Osibisa, 211
Otis, Johnny, 43, 151, 152, 211
Outkast, 52, 177, 182, 183, 184

P. Diddy, 175. *See also* Puff Daddy
P-Funk. *See* Parliament-Funkadelic
Page, Jimmy, 179
Palmer, Earl, 2
Parker, Charlie, 110
Parker, Colonel Tom, 3
Parker, Paulette, 6
Parlet, 206
Parliament-Funkadelic, 72, 78, 79,
    160, 181, 182, 206, 207, 213, 214
Parsons, Gram, 209
Paulekas, Vito, 15
Pearlman, Sandy, 16
Peraza, Armando, 212
Pere Ubu, 109
Perkins, Carl, 160, 161
Perry, Steve, 208
Pfisterer, Alban "Snoopy," 14
Phillips, Esther, 43
Phillips, Sam, 154
Piazza, Joey, 44
Pickett, Wilson, 46
Pink Floyd, 62, 63, 68, 70
Pinkston, Richard, 104, 109, 112
Pinnock, Doug, 208
Pipe, 211
Plant, Robert, 20
The Platters, 155
Poco, 66
The Pogues, 180
The Pointer Sisters, 57, 172, 205

The Police, 109
Poly Styrene, 211
Porter, Cole, 150
Pratt, Awadagan, 140
Presley, Elvis, 3, 87, 155, 160, 161,
    181, 209
Preston, Billy, 2, 45, 64, 211
Price, Lloyd, 155
Prince, 57, 115–119, 131, 160, 168,
    182, 201, 211, 213
Professor Bop, 152
Pryor, Richard, 207
Psycho Les, 180
Public Enemy, 99, 134, 183, 206, 209
Public Image Ltd, 109
Puff Daddy, 119, 175, 179, 187
Pure Hell, 211
Pyramid, 98

Queens of the Stone Age, 143
Quidd, Jimmi, 99
Quincy Troupe, 54
Quine, Bob, 106, 110

Rachmaninoff, Sergei, 140
Rage Against the Machine, 179
Raitt, Bonnie, 66
Rakim, 179
Ramone, Joey, 109
Ramones, 104, 106, 109, 209, 214
Randi, Don, 18
Rappaport, Neil, 18
Ray, Man, 86
Ready For the World, 118
Ready Set Go!, 192, 204
Reagon, Toshi, 186
Red Hot Chili Peppers, 212, 213
Redding, Otis, 47, 48, 108, 157, 160,
    181, 203
Reece, 126
Reed, Jimmy, 5
Reed, Lou, 109, 207
Reed, Rochelle, 15
Reid, Vernon, 129–143, 209
R.E.M., 178
Reo, 126, 213

Return to Forever, 92
The Revolution, 118, 119, 213
Reznor, Trent, 176
Rhymes, Busta, 175
Rhythm Dukes, 110
Ribot, Marc, 204
Richard Hell and the Voidoids, 104
Richard, Stan, 152
Richards, Deke, 61
Richards, Keith, 13, 214
Richie, Lionel, 118
Ricketts, Noony, 20, 21
Righteous Brothers, 89, 90
Riley, Teddy, 117
Riperton, Minnie, 199, 209
Rising Sons, 12
Roachford, 211
Rob Zombie, 207
Robinson, Cynthia, 39, 44, 47, 49,
    207, 212
Rockwilder, 184
Rodgers, Richard, 13, 16, 150
Rogers, Nile, 211
Roker, Roxie, 208
Rolling Stones, 5, 14, 16, 20, 45, 65,
    89, 130, 138, 160, 178, 180, 181,
    199, 203, 205, 209, 210, 211
Rollins, Henry, 94
Rollins Band, 207
Rosa, Robi, 210
Ross, Craig, 172
Ross, Diana, 116
Rosskam, Edwin, 32, 33
Rotten, Johnny, 15
Rourke, Constance, 149
Rowles, Gary, 20
Roxanne Shanté, 97
Rubin, Rick, 99, 178, 179
Ruffin, David, 107
Rufus, 160
Run-DMC, 98, 117, 178, 179
Rush, 98
Russell, Ken, 214
Russell, Leon, 205, 208, 209

St. Victor, Sandra, 125, 127, 206

Sainte-Marie, Buffy, 66
Sam & Dave, 157
Sampson, Annie, 212
Samwell, Ian, 209
Sanneh, Kelefa, 79
Santana, 57, 130, 129, 212
Santi White & Stiffed, 213
Satriani, Joe, 210
Savelle, Taja, 118
Scaggs, Boz, 64, 69
Scorpions, 204
Scott, Howard, 214
Scott, Ronnie, 55
Scott-Heron, Gil, 123
Scream, 213
Scritti Politti, 186
Seal, 160
The Seeds, 15
Sevendust, 212
Sex Pistols, 94, 112, 210
Shakira, 138
Shakur, Tupac, 207
Shan, MC, 97
Shand, Remy, 126
Sharrock, Sonny, 37
Shaw, Greg, 17
Sheila E., 118, 119, 211, 212
Shernoff, Andy, 110
Shider, Gary, 71, 75, 77, 207
Shrapnel, 110
Shuggie Otis, 66, 211
Sick of It All, 98
Sigur Rós, 143
The Silhouettes, 155
Simmons, Russell, 178
Simon, Carly, 199
Simon, Paul, 126
Simpson, O. J., 23
Sinatra, Frank, 154
Sinatra, Nancy, 65
Sister Sledge, 211
68 (band), 205
Skatore, Rick, 214
Skillings, Muzz, 132, 209
Skin, 212
Skunk Anansie, 160, 212

Slash, 168, 195–202, 208, 212
Sly & the Family Stone, 39–51, 123,
    157, 160, 199, 206, 212
Smith, Bessie, 57, 150
Smith, Dante Beze. *See* Mos Def
Smith, Fred, 212
Smith, Fred "Sonic," 212
Smith, Larry, 178
Smith, Lonnie Liston, 92
Smith, Mamie, 150
Smith, V. Jeffrey, 123, 127, 206
Snakepit, 196, 212
S.O.A., 94
Sorum, Matt, 200
SOS Band, 118
Soul Babies, 121
Soul Stirrers, 3
Soul II Soul, 123
Sound Barrier, 204, 212
Soundgarden, 211
Southern, Eileen, 151
Sousa, John Philip, 150
Spacey-T, 212
Spearhead, 213
Spears, Britney, 138
Spector, Phil, 118
Spermicide, 98
The Spinners, 212
Springsteen, Bruce, 205
Stafford, Jo, 154
Star Kitty. *See* Gilliam-Gipp, Joi
Starr, Ringo, 208
Stax, 47, 48, 49, 156, 159, 166
Steely Dan, 63, 64, 70, 138, 176, 203
Stein, Chris, 211
Stein, Seymour, 105
Stew and the Negro Problem, 126
Stewart, Alpha, 41–43
Stewart, Freddie, 42, 43, 45, 47, 49
Stewart, Jermaine, 118
Stewart, KC, 41–43
Stewart, Loretta, 42
Stewart, Rose, 39, 42, 43, 45, 46
Stewart, Sylvester. *See* Stone, Sly
Stewart, Vaetta, 42
Stewart Four, 42

Stiffed, 213
Stilettos, 211
Stills, Stephen, 209
Sting, 126
Stokes, Odell, 5, 6
Stone, Charles, 143
Stone, Sly, 10, 39–52, 54, 57, 67, 72,
    75, 76, 91, 157, 205, 207, 208,
    211–213
Stoneground, 212
The Stoners, 46
Stooges, 106, 109, 203
Stowe, Harriet Beecher, 131
Stradlin, Izzy, 199
Strange, Billy, 18
Strange Boutique, 212
Stranglers, 113
Street, Craig, 142, 186
Streisand, Barbra, 63, 64, 70, 203
Strokes, 192, 194
Stuart, Michael, 20
Subject To Change, 213
Sugar Daddy, 152
The Sugarcubes, 180
Sugarfoot, 211
Suicidal Tendencies, 207
Summer, Cree, 213
Summer, Donna, 117
Sun Ra, 75, 6, 78, 80
The Sundays, 180
Supa Lover Cee and Casanova Rud, 97
Super 8, 204
The Supremes, 61, 166, 203
Suranovich, George, 20, 21
Swamp Dogg, 213
Sweet, Matthew, 208
Swizz Beatz, 180, 184
Sylvester, 116, 205

Taj Mahal, 12
Talking Heads, 214
Taylor, Mick, 211
The Teardrop Explodes, 20
Teenage Fanclub, 20
Teenage Jesus and the Jerks, 109
Templeaires, 60

Temptations, 91, 166, 212
Terrell, Tom, 54
Tharpe, Sister Rosetta, 3
Thin Lizzy, 204, 210
Thomas, Doug, 22, 23
Thomas, Jimmy, 6
Thompson, Chester, 212
Thompson, Skeeter, 213
Thornton, Willie Mae "Big Mamma,"
    43, 152
Three Dog Night, 14
Thunders, Johnny, 210
Timbaland, 119, 126, 179
Timberlake, Justin, 126
The Time, 118, 208, 213
Tobler, John, 16
Toomer, Jean, 25
Total Eclipse, 204
Toussaint, Allen, 66, 172, 209
Tower of Power, 57, 212
Trouble Funk, 210
Trullio Disgracious, 213
Tucker, Tanya, 66
Turner, Big Joe, 155
Turner, Ike, 5, 6, 60, 61, 154, 208,
    214
Turner, Tina, 5, 6, 57, 60, 61, 66, 68,
    118, 157, 203, 214
24–7 Spyz, 122, 212, 214
Tyler, Red, 2
Tympani Five, 86

U2, 208
Ugh Ugh Ugh, 214
United Sound, 206
The Untouchables, 214

Vai, Steve, 37, 210, 212
Valentinos, 12
Van Halen, Eddie, 200
Vanity, 118, 119, 211
Van Vlack, Gavin, 99
The Veldt, 193
Velvet Underground, 106
Velvets, 109
Venetta's Taxi, 64

Vicious, Sid, 104, 112, 209
Vienna Boy's Choir, 167
Vinx, 126
The V.I.P.s, 20
Viscaynes, 44
Voidoids, 106, 208
Voltage Guitar, 170
Volume 10, 179
Von, Donray, 192, 193, 204

Wade, Michael, 69
Walker, Albertina, 3
Walker, TBone, 152
Walsh, Joe, 66
War, 214
Ward, Clara, 3
Ward, Billy, 1
Wash, Martha, 126
Washburn, Donna, 209
Washington, Dinah, 213
Waters, Ethel, 150
Waters, Julia, 67, 203
Waters, Maxine, 67, 203
Waters, Muddy, 34, 152, 197, 199
Watrous, Peter, 123
Watson, Johnny "Guitar," 12
Watts, André, 139, 140
Weapon of Choice, 160, 213, 214
Weather Report, 143
Weatherford, W. D., 147
Weiss, Donna, 209
Wet Willie, 66
Wexler, Jerry, 152
White, Santi, 213
White Mandingos, 95
White Stripes, 118
Whiteman, Paul, 150
The Who, 14, 199
Wickham, Vicki, 54
Wild Child, 22
Williams, Andy, 155
Williams, Jerry, 213
Williams, Lamar, 203
Williams, Marion, 3
Williams, Marlon "Marley Marl," 97
Williams, Pharrell, 175–184

Williams, Saul, 180
Williamson, Sonny Boy, 1
Wilson, Brian, 10, 17, 19
Wilson, Cassandra, 186
Wilson, Devon, 205
Wimbish, Doug, 143, 181, 203
Winfrey, Oprah, 70
Witherspoon, Lajon, 212
Wolfman Jack, 152
Womack, Bobby, 12, 51, 107
Wonder, Stevie, 117, 160, 166, 212
Woods, Belita, 207
Woods, Clyde, 126
World Party, 212
Worrell, Bernie, 77, 131, 181, 203, 214

Wright, Edna, 62
Wright, Richard, 32, 33
Wynne, Phillippe, 207

X-Ray Spex, 211

Yeah Yeah Yeahs, 118
Yohimba Brothers, 129
Young, Neil, 10, 199

Zantees, 109
Zappa, Frank, 10, 213
Zeppelin. *See* Led Zeppelin
Zion I, 179
Zone, Paul, 210